Gary La Fontaine

Trout Flies
Proven Patterns

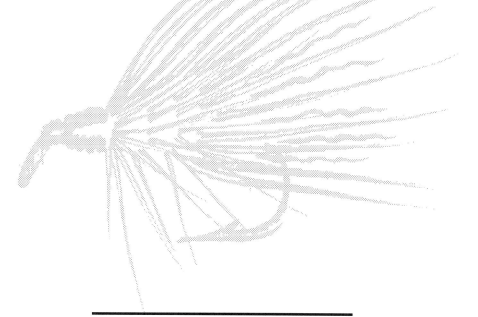

Trout Flies
Proven Patterns

by Gary LaFontaine

illustrations by Powell Swanser
photographs by Doug O'looney

Greycliff Publishing Co.
Helena, Montana

Trout Flies
Proven Patterns

Edited by Stan Bradshaw
Designed by Amy Budde of Q Communications Group, Inc.
Composed in Cheltenham and Eras on an Apple Macintosh by
Q Communications Group, Helena, Montana
Printed on Finch Opaque (acid-free) by
BookCrafters, Chelsea, Michigan

Printed in the United States of America

99 98 97 96 95 94 93   9 8 7 6 5 4 3 2 1

ISBN 0-9626663-1-9

Publisher's Cataloging in Publication
(Prepared by Quality Books, Inc.)

LaFontaine, Gary.
   Trout flies : proven patterns / Gary LaFontaine ;
illustrations by Powell Swanser ; photographs by Doug O'looney.
   p. cm.
   Includes index.
   ISBN 0-9626663-1-9

   1. Trout fishing. 2. Flies, Artificial. 3. Fly fishing.   I.
Title.

SH687.L34 1993   799.1'775
              QBI93-1075

To Jay Gaudreau

When I was ten years old my parents promised me a puppy. They brought me home a baby brother. He was so great that I didn't mind the switch (and he did learn tricks fast).

He always followed me. He always fished with me. He even came to Montana after his four-year term in the Navy to live near me.

He said to me last season, "When we were kids, you always had time to untangle my line."

Acknowledgements

My other books contain long lists of the people who share my unreasonable quest for truth and trout. These friends do much of the labor that leads to the new patterns. They are intelligent enough to know that none of this work is going to change the world—and wise enough to know that our obsession needs no justification. The fishing days with them are recorded in my log entries.

My fly fishing roots are traced in my other writings. Crediting precedents acknowledges the men who influenced my ideas. Sometimes it is through their books, but more frequently (especially with very practical tiers) it is simply with their own patterns. Innovators such as Jack Dennis, Randall Kaufmann, Gary Borger, Mike Lawson, Jack Gartside, Craig Mathews, and Al Troth influence me with flies that embody each man's philosophy of imitation and attraction on trout waters.

What concerns me are the casual encounters with fly fishermen and fly tiers. Most of those people have added to my theories about what makes a good fly. They have shared tying tips and fishing techniques on a stream, at a club meeting, or over a beer in a favorite bar. Their contributions are woven into the patterns in this book. Too often there is no record of their names in my notes.

None of my "original" flies are my own. All of the fly fishermen in my life share the credit for these patterns.

My appreciation goes to the companies that provided their fine equipment to my 1991 summer blitz of fishing. Being on the water every day made me more dependent on specific pieces of tackle, not less so. Every move became so ingrained that the shoot of a line, the flex of a rod, or the drag of a reel had to be exact for me to feel comfortable. In situations where the equipment was unfamiliar, as with borrowed tackle on trips to faraway places, my fishing enjoyment suffered significantly.

The new Simms Neoprene Waders with a seamless crotch are great for someone like me who moves as far and as fast as possible.

Heaven knows that pretty doesn't matter to me. My style of fishing beats most reels to death. Getting dunked in water, dragged through sand, and hammered on rocks kills most of my reels. The Abel models are still winding smoothly after all that and more.

There are at least forty rods in my closet. Most of them are casting levers, not fishing tools. The five that get used are on the water a lot. There is my basic nymph and dry fly Fenwick World Class, a wonderfully sweet, 9-foot rod for a #5 line. My main dry fly rod, and this is for all sizes of water, is a Sage 8-foot, 9-inch rod for a #3 line—it is part of the Sage light line series and it is to me the epitome of practical delicacy. For small streams my favorite is a Barry Kustin 7-foot bamboo for a #4 line. The one "power" rod in the set, for throwing big streamers and nymphs, is a Sage RPL 9-foot for a #7 line.

The full range of floating and sinking lines from Scientific Anglers and Cortland cast beautifully, of course, but just as important to me is that each model is tremendously consistent line after line (and this makes me more consistent).

The Cast Of Characters

There are people who fish with me all the time. They are the characters who appear in the log entries over and over. They have one trait in common (and except for that one trait they are incredibly diverse in their fly fishing propensities).

It struck me this spring. My brother Jay was with me on the Big Hole when the water was high and even discolored. The unusually wet spring had soured the trout on this normally consistent river, but there was Jay working a streamer with all the confidence . . . no, confidence is the wrong word. It wasn't because of confidence that he nailed a jumping fool of a brown trout at that moment.

What unites all of my fishing partners is that in the midst of their dog-crazy attack on the water, they never even stop to calculate the odds. Their attitude goes beyond confidence and strains the limits of good sense.

Here are very brief descriptions of my fishing partners.

In his own category:

■ Chester, the wonder dog, is no ordinary hound, going off to chase squirrels while the people flog the water. Chester stays beside me every moment, watching a dry fly drift downstream and woofing when a fish strikes.

His Indian name translates into "Dances With Trout."

In Montana:

■ Jay Gaudreau, my brother and the perfect outdoorsman, is always amazingly competent and clearheaded in any crisis.

■ Powell Swanser, nationally famous for his wildlife sculptures, is the big-trout specialist in the group; he doesn't even want to catch fish under 18 inches. He may be the only fly fisherman around who moves up a trout stream faster than me.

■ Tazun Swanser is Powell's wife, which in our group, buys her nothing. It would be sexist and silly to call her a great woman fly fisherman—she outfishes all of us too often for that.

■ Justin Baker started fly fishing and fly tying in the summer of 1991, frothing at the mouth from the first moment. That combined with a lifetime of experience in the outdoors and a natural athleticism made him a fast learner. Powell and I were his fishing partners and coaches, though perhaps not the best role models. In spite of us he managed to catch hundreds of trout, with more than ten over 20 inches, in his first season.

■ Heather LaFontaine, my daughter, is a great fly tier and national-class endurance athlete. She loves photography so much that she lugs a camera everywhere, but fishes long enough to catch trout. Her best last season was an 18-inch rainbow on Rock Creek.

Out of State:

■ Wayne Huft is the finest all-around fisherman in our group. It is almost unfair to the trout to unleash him on a stream, but he is the ideal person to test all of our flies in actual fishing situations.

■ Brester Zahm is a bass fisherman turned trout fisherman. He understands the predatory instincts of a big trout perfectly.

■ Tory Stosich, brilliant and mercurial, is a pure theorist.

■ Graham Marsh, the careful thinker, keeps Tory and me from jumping to half-formed conclusions. He is almost Socratic in his method of questioning.

■ Tom Poole is the painstaking observer who takes those extra seconds to watch a fly, an insect, or a trout. Perhaps this is why he defines a problem better than any of us.

■ Jennifer Koenig has been hard-core since the age of eleven (she's twenty-six now). She matches Tory for youthful enthusiasm, and is an even better fisherman than Wayne with small dry flies and skinny tippets.

Introduction

The idea for *Trout Flies* came to me full blown last spring. An angler asked me at Barry Serviente's Book Fair, "Do you remember your article about the Diving Water Boatman? That has been a great fly for me ever since then."

It was gratifying to know that someone remembered an article from more than twenty years ago. And it was also exciting to think that someone outside my own group of fishing friends had taken a fly and proven its worth to his satisfaction on different waters.

The questions from the other fishermen in the little cluster at Barry's fair led to a fly tying demonstration and lake fishing discussion that went far into the night. And it was all over a simple pattern that imitated a minor trout food, unique only in the way it tipped on the surface.

The elements of that get-together ended up being the structure for this book. The lead description addresses "What is the theory behind this fly?" The recipe answers "What is it tied with?" The tying steps respond to "How is it tied?" And the log relates experiences that answer "How has it worked for you?"

Most of the patterns in this book are mine. The ones that are not still belong in this book because of my strong connection to them. The Mohawk, for example, is not my creation. My daughter Heather fashioned this odd, effective hair fly. It came into existence with no help from me. So where is my claim? Any father will understand. And besides, who else has caught as many trout on it as me?

Fly fishermen ask me about the Gray Coughlin all of the time. The originator is unknown; it is listed along with a few thousand other patterns in J. Edson Leonard's classic Flies. My rave accounts about fishing with this drab searcher have made it better known. It will never be as popular as the dry fly it replaces in my angling, the Adams, but the Gray Coughlin deserves recognition as an effective pattern. It is included here because it, too, is linked with me.

Other than these two, the flies in *Trout Flies* all come from my whims or my ideas. They vary greatly in originality. All of these "new" creations can be divided into three rough categories: variations, adaptations, and innovations.

A variation features a minor change in the color or the form of an existing fly. It takes no great leap to make this kind of alteration. The only excuse for playing around with someone else's pattern this way is a strong need for the new color combination.

The Were Wulff, a variation, was concocted by Bill Blackburn and me specifically for the Brown Drake hatch *(Ephemera simulans)* on the Big Hole. None of the standard Wulff recipes possessed all the right parts for float fishing. The new creation needed the white wing for visibility, the mixed grizzly and brown hackle feathers for variegation, and the brown hare's ear body for color imitation. The fly worked not only during the Brown Drake hatch but throughout the season as a general searcher.

An adaptation is evolutionary. There is a significant change in the very makeup of the fly—so significant that if the change is bad the new creation does not survive and if it is good the new creation is recognized as clearly superior to the older styles. A fly fisherman looking at the pattern shouldn't be able to place it in any well-known family of flies.

The Air Head, a really odd adaptation, doesn't look like any other dry fly and, more important, it doesn't fish like any other dry fly. And yet none of the individual features are new. The head is made with closed, large-cell polyurethane foam, a common packing material that had been used on other patterns. The tying technique for that head, the bullet shape with flared edges, has been used on deer hair flies. But take a common material and a common tying technique and put them together for the first time and the result is a new fly. In the case of the Air Head the mutation creates a surprising attractor-imitation combination.

An innovation, a revolution in fly tying, is truly rare. The rich history of our sport means that creative tiers, experimenting with techniques and materials, have already played with most possibilities. Even rarer than a real innovation in pattern design is an innovation that is worth anything on or in the water.

A proud creator trumpets his latest killer in magazine articles or books, but when fly fishermen across the country test the pattern on their rivers or lakes it proves neither bad nor good. It ends up, like most new wonders, in that great middle ground of mediocrity. No amount of publicity can elevate it to the benchmark level of a "standard." It typically takes five to eight years for national opinion, the trial-and-error process, to pass judgment on a fly.

Any fly tier must make his claims of originality carefully. My reading is pretty thorough for both English and American fly fishing books; and, as far as these works codify major developments in fly design, my education is solid. But real historians dig much deeper, sifting through old fishing catalogs, early sport magazines, and even unpublished letters and journals to find important pieces of information. What they discover is that any modern writer is building his works on the heralded and unheralded experiments of the past.

What is my most original creation? On four points, the Emergent Sparkle Pupa. Some sharp historian might find precedents for three of the points, but the fourth one, the most important, can safely be called an innovation (for obvious reasons). The technique of dubbing the underbody, the Touch Method, creates a sparser, fuzzier covering than any other method of dubbing. The trick of a "loose" overbody is unusual even now. The Emergent, half in and half out of the water, is the first caddis pupa designed to mimic the hesitation of the escaping natural at the surface film.

These three claims would all require long, detailed defenses, but the fourth is easier to certify. No other fly ever used sparkle yarn, either DuPont's Antron (a nylon) or American Cyanamid's Creslan (an orlon), because these bright synthetics did not exist prior to this time.

Anyone is welcome to dispute the originality of any pattern in this book. The fact that honest debate is possible keeps me from putting my name on any fly. Some innovators get upset when historians question their claims. Not me. My work is too bound up with the teams of researchers who tie, fish, and scuba dive with me in rivers and lakes for me to expect full credit anyway.

My claim, not without its own conceit, is that every fly in this book is better in at least specific situations than any older pattern. Every year in the testing many interesting concepts of imitation and attraction are dumped simply because the new flies are *not* more effective than existing ones—and why clutter my boxes with more mediocre patterns? The creations that survive underwater testing, a process that lets trout accept or reject the flies, are proven in the purest sense.

The development of the Tear Drop Nymph, a deep-drifting mayfly imitation, culminated the series. The sixty-two pattern types in this volume fit nearly all major trout situations. The streamers, wet flies, nymphs, emergers, and dry flies all had a time and place where they were supposed to perform superbly.

The patterns may have been "proven" in the experimental phase, but no angler gains faith in a new fly until he catches fish on it. This includes me—just because I see one of my creations work underwater doesn't mean that I trust its effectiveness. These flies shock even my sensibilities sometimes. There is a difference between knowledge and faith.

All of my books upset certain anglers. After *Caddisflies* one older gentleman approached me at a Federation of Fly Fishermen Conclave and in a tremulous voice said, "You have to be wrong, sir. If you are not, then all of the great writers of the past are, and that is not acceptable to me."

The Emergent Sparkle Pupa was right and Antron was right; and every other piece of literature about hatching caddisflies was so damnably wrong that bad information doomed generations of anglers to failure in many important situations. But our belief in that truth didn't topple the old ways. It took eight years, from 1972 to 1980, for the new fly to make its way into commercial distribution and eight more years for the Antron revolution to really grip the fly fishing world. That happened only because some brave anglers tried the new concepts on their own waters; and their successes turned them into missionaries for the ideas.

The same process of acceptance is happening for *The Dry Fly* (apparently, considering the rush of letters, much faster). One of my favorite notes, because it has a wonderfully funny ending, is from James Carr of Cadillac, Michigan, who was fishing the Missouri River in Montana:

> . . . put a number 6 Royal Double Wing on and mentioned to my buddy, Scott, "Look at this crazy thing. It couldn't possibly do what LaFontaine says. It's supposed to bring a non-feeding brown up from the bottom."
>
> At the very moment I finished that sentence, a 24-inch, 7½-pound brown stuck his maw through the surface film, grabbed the fly and ran like hell. Thirty minutes later and two hundred yards down the river, I slipped the fly out of his mouth, held him for a few minutes and let him go.
>
> Oh, Great God of Trout Flies, I am now a believer.

Let's get something straight—none of my patterns come with a guarantee of a 7-pound brown. But even the skepticism that a fisherman has when he ties on something radically new is fun. The excitement of experimentation isn't limited to the creator of a fly. Every angler who uses one of the patterns shares the thrill of discovery.

My feeling with the new flies from *The Dry Fly* was that the Halo Emerger would get the most letters. It did, but not by a huge margin. The Halo, an imitation for a hatching mayfly, fit a common and popular fly fishing situation. Two attractors, the Air Head and the Double Wing, did not fall into the where and when of trout stream strategy so nicely. Anglers casting these patterns weren't just stretching the limits of credulity—they were risking ridicule. Maybe the shock when these flies worked, often spectacularly, drove people to write to me.

Not a single fisherman called or wrote with a story of failure. This doesn't mean that the flies never failed—of course they did somewhere or sometime. It just points out that fly fishermen are very nice people who will take the time to make a person happy but will not take the time to blame a pattern creator for blank moments.

The seasons of 1990 and 1991 were my chance to just fish these flies. The field work on *The Dry Fly* was done and the final summer of observations for my next book, *Bass,* wasn't scheduled until 1994. There were many patterns, especially among the new dry flies, that had satisfied the trout, and fishermen around the country had used them successfully, but flies such as the Air Head, Mess, and Halo Emerger hadn't become a regular part of my fishing yet.

That acceptance process turned out to be the same for me as it was for all those people who wrote letters—before the fishing there was skepticism; then, even when a fly fooled trout, there was disbelief; and finally, after a few successes, there was acceptance. Even the oddest patterns from the underwater, trial-and-error method of development proved themselves in this, a much more empirical, way. The days of casting even revealed things about fishing the flies that hadn't been clear in the underwater observations.

The entries from those 1990 and 1991 fishing logs are part of this book. They are not polished prose or fully thought-out theory; instead, they are hurried speculations that form questions for future research. An idea gets scribbled down, but then with a later reading my skeptical nature demands, "Can that be proven? And how?"

My goal, with hundreds of fishing days each year, was to find out when and where to use these new flies—not individually but as part of a comprehensive set—on my favorite waters. It would have been fun to scatter log entries from around the country into this account. The flies did do well for me in exotic places in 1991 (the Halo Emerger easily took the fussiest grayling rising on the Ferrogselva in Norway one morning). But the experiences on strange waters didn't teach me as much as my visits to the more familiar haunts of Montana.

In 1991 I fished more than any year since 1957, when I was twelve and my parents let me fish all the time because, in their words, "That's the only time he isn't getting into trouble." I fished hard, very hard. It wasn't like any of the past twenty years, when research and work would interrupt. I've always fished between 150 and 200 days a season, but often a "day" meant a few hours in the morning or evening. In 1991 I spent six to twelve hours nearly every day fishing for myself. Many times friends came with me, but if no one was available, my dog Chester and I went to any water that promised hot action.

The quest was for that feeling every angler wants but never gets in his fishing. Here I was with a full set of proven flies and enough time to work these flies on familiar waters. My goal was to wipe out doubt—the doubt that makes us stare stupidly into a box of imitations and attractors and mumble, "Eenie, meenie, miney, mo . . ."

My fishing car ended up with more than 30,000 new miles on it. The wear and tear of fishing destroyed a floating fly line roughly every four weeks. At the end of every day of dog-crazy flogging there was barely enough time to tie flies, knot leaders, and patch equipment. Telling any of this to friends inevitably made them hum screechy tunes and fiddle imaginary violins.

The log entries, recording successes on Montana rivers or lakes with all sixty-two of the patterns in the trout series, give a warped view of the fishing, however. Those experiences are culled from nearly four hundred days of fishing over two seasons. They are the moments when the answers to those trout mysteries seemed simple enough. The other days, the ones that are not here, the mindless flailing for the random fish or the endless casting for no fish at all, told the truth: The waters are not as great as they seem here; the flies are not as great as they seem here; I am not as great as I seem here—and there are no ultimate answers.

Trout Flies exists now not because of flies like the Emergent Sparkle Pupa, a major imitation which no longer needs my promotion, but because of flies like the Diving Water Boatman. The obscure Boatman is a minor imitation only because it works in a very specific situation—in the overall puzzle it is a small piece, indeed. There are a lot of minor imitations and attractors that fill niches, however, and without them there are big gaps in this fly fishing mosaic.

Is this the end of my innovations? No. Future observations will surely pinpoint more problems of imitation or attraction. Once recognized these problems become a challenge. New methods and new materials for fly tying will eventually provide solutions.

There is also an overlap with a series of bass flies. A crawfish imitation can be very useful for trout in lakes or streams, but that fly is indispensable in my smallmouth bass fishing. Many minnow imitations work as well for trout as for bass, but when studies show that a bait fish is more of a bass food, the matching fly goes into the warm-water series.

So, some of my flies that don't exist (but will in the future), and some of my flies that do exist, are not included in this book. The ones that are here cannot exist in a reader's mind. Ultimately, he must use them himself so that they become a page in his picture book of experiences.

Contents

Trout Flies
Proven Patterns

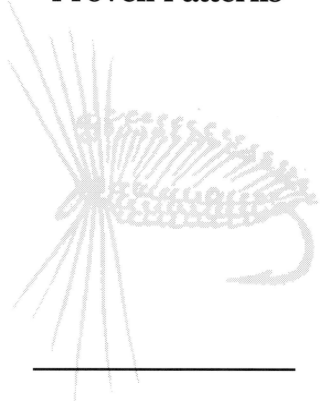

One

■

Streamers

My streamer fishing is in a rut. My way of thinking about these flies makes them disappear for most of the season. The box of steamers and bucktails comes out spring and fall, when various species of trout run in the rivers, but it stays in the vest all summer.

Over the seasons, underwater observations have provided plenty of insights into streamer fishing. For swimming patterns, either attractors or imitations, the indicators are strong, almost absolute—

- Trout exhibit a mixture of curiosity and caution at the first sign of the streamer entering the field of vision.
- Trout identify a bait fish as suitable prey by the vibrations the swimming minnow gives off; of course, they use visual clues at the same time.
- Trout strike the eye of a minnow or a streamer (whether the fly is an imitation or an attractor).
- Each species of trout reacts aggressively to display colors of its own species (yellow on brown trout streamers; red on brook trout streamers; silver, sometimes with a touch of electric blue, on rainbow trout streamers).
- Trout react positively to small amounts of fluorescent colors on streamers (colors that are unpredictable on dry flies).
- Trout respond more seriously (grasping instead of nipping) to flies that appear outside the holding area and swim into it rather than vice versa.
- Trout can catch and engulf the swiftest swimming streamer as long as the fly is moving in a steady, smooth line; erratic retrieves make them miss the fly.

A common method of fishing a streamer on our western rivers involves casting from a drift boat. The anger puts the fly very close to the shore (the holding area) and retrieves it in jerky spurts back towards the boat (the outside water).

Nothing could be worse for a swimming fly. The results are as pathetic as they are predictable—an occasional nice trout but many more unrequited swirls and taps. It only takes better methods and better flies

to increase the number of solid hookups with a streamer.

There are two other categories of minnow patterns. They are so different from the slimmer attractors and imitations that they require different methods of presentation. They are the bottom fly and the cripple fly.

The bottom fly imitates a feeble swimmer. Sculpins and suckers do not rise up into the water column or feed in the open current. They nose around the dead space among the rocks, moving slowly unless startled. When they are frightened, they respond with a quick burst, a one- or two-foot dash, and then they dive for cover. The matching fly has to act the same way. In shallow water the best presentation is an up- or up-and-across-stream cast and a gentle retrieve, sometimes at the same speed as the current and sometimes slightly faster, making the fly alternately drift dead and bob up feebly. In deep water, realism demands a weighted fly and a sinking line, a long upstream cast giving the imitation time to sink, and hard mends making the fly stutter and drift. Both techniques help the imitation to look like a bait fish hopelessly washing downstream.

The cripple fly mimics the death throes of an injured minnow. A hurt, floating bait fish struggles to the end, trying with every spasm to right himself and escape to the bottom. The performance attracts the attention of every predator—fish, bird, and mammal—in the vicinity.

An angler who lacks patience and imagination has no chance with a cripple fly. The fisherman has to project real pathos into the shivers he imparts to the pattern, making the moments of quiet exhaustion, when the imitation radiates the subtlest rings, as convincing as the moments of futile struggle.

There are so many possibilities with streamer patterns and techniques that these flies should not be restricted to any season. Nor should they be limited to any particular situation (for example, as patterns for larger trout). Streamer fishing should emphasize the versatility of these imitations and attractors.

The key to breaking out of a rut with streamers is faith. The angler who expects these flies to take numbers of trout and not just an occasional surprise will fish them carefully and intelligently.

Bread

Bread

There is a good reason why streamers seldom tally great numbers of trout. In any given population of fish only a small percentage will know how to prey on minnows. In the average river that percentage may be as low as 15 (and will be lower with rainbows than with browns).

Studies show that when trout reach eleven to twelve inches they begin including minnows in their diets. It isn't that simple, however—some trout stumble onto the technique for killing and eating bait fish but others apparently never learn the process. This division of feeding strategies seems to be a matter of luck for some strains of rainbows.

A particular trout rushes at a minnow, probably to drive the intruder out of his territory rather than with any intent to kill, and he stuns or cripples the prey. This happens frequently during spawning, already a period of heightened aggressiveness. The trout learns to recognize minnows as food and starts methodically hunting them.

Once, on an isolated, screened-off section of a Virginia spring creek, Graham Marsh hatched wild rainbow trout eggs from a Vibert box. The stream was totally devoid of any other type of fish, but there were plenty of insects in it and the trout grew quickly. After almost three years there were no fish smaller than fourteen inches and none bigger than twenty inches.

Graham dumped 20 thee-inch minnows into his stream, each of these fish marked with a highly visible, orange fluorescent dot. The rainbow trout chased those minnows the first day, but even in this confined stretch of water they only killed two (and neither of them was eaten). After a week the trout basically lost interest in the bait fish.

Underwater observations of trout showed us how a successful predator feeds on minnows. An inept fish nipped at the bait fish without delivering a crippling blow. The true hunter, however, slammed the minnow right on the side of the head, caught the helpless prey crossways, sometimes chomped him a time or two, and then turned and swallowed him.

The angler gets plenty of taps on his streamer from those inept but curious fish. Even though the fly is moving much slower and smoother than a real minnow, most of the trout don't know how to grasp it. They follow it and nibble at the tail instead. This fin-nipping habit is an agonistic, fighting behavior, not a killing maneuver.

To catch a lot of trout on a streamer, the bumblers as well as the true fish-eaters, give them a minnow that is already crippled. Presenting a helpless victim not only incites a killing instinct in natural predators but also makes the fly available to all of the trout large enough to attack it.

The Bread, imitating a crippled bait fish, is only tied on the Flex Hook. This hook is large for an insect imitation but small for a minnow imitation. The Bread doesn't scare off too many trout. Even 10-inch fish jump on it. At the same time, it wobbles so seductively, bending in the middle with every ripple, that this oddly balanced fly brings even large trout charging for the kill. The Bread can catch as many fish as any dry fly when the time is right for it.

Bread

TYING STEPS

ON REAR HOOK SECTION—

1. Tie in four to six short pieces of blue fluorescent monofilament for the tail (one quarter of the hook shank).

2. Tie in a piece of white sparkle yarn; let it dangle for the moment.

3. Tie in two or three wood beads along the top of the shank; fasten these by running a piece of monofilament through the hole in each bead and wrapping that down.

4. Tie in two or three clumps of white marabou, spaced along the hook shank as wings.

5. Wrap the body.

6. Tie in a throat of red marabou fibers.

7. Tie in a topping of four strands of peacock herl.

Whip finish the rear section of the hook.

ON FRONT HOOK SECTION—

8. Slit the bottom of the preformed foam head; slide it over the hook shank and seal it with Zap-a-Gap glue.

Hook:	8 (Flex Hook, TMC 80B)
Tail:	six pieces of four pound Stren blue fluorescent monofilament (short)
Back:	two or three wooden beads
Body:	white sparkle yarn (brushed out rough)
Wing:	two or three white marabou wings (at the rear, middle, and front of the shank)
Topping:	four long strands of peacock herl
Throat:	red marabou fibers

The head section for this pattern is a preformed, scoop-faced foam head.

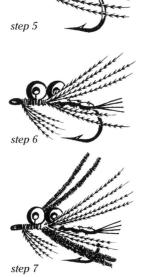

step 1

step 2

step 3

step 4

step 5

step 6

step 7

step 8

LOG ENTRY: AUGUST 15, 1990
BEAVERHEAD RIVER

Famous for its large trout, the Beaverhead located in southwestern Montana has been hurt by low winter flows the past few years. The population of very large trout has declined, but there are still plenty of rainbows and browns up to 22 inches in the river.

The problem for the first-time visitor to Montana is expectations. Will his or her trip be ruined without a 20-inch trout? It isn't particularly difficult to catch a 20-inch trout in our rivers. The pursuit of that big fish, however, must happen at the trout's convenience. Dawn and dusk are generally the two major feeding periods of any day. Minnow-eating trout have one reason for prowling, insect-eating trout have another. Some trout feed on nymphs and larvae drifting heavily in the currents at dawn and dusk. Other trout take advantage of the fact that their eyes adjust to changes in the light faster than the eyes of the bait fish and chase down their prey.

Somehow, probably in a case of wishful thinking, the myth has sprung up that an angler doesn't need to get out at dawn in Montana. It is true that there is plenty of excellent fishing during the middle hours of the day, but for consistently catching large trout in our rivers and lakes the early hours are by far the best.

Ralph Pelletti sat in the back of the raft as we nosed out into the Beaverhead. It was still dark and neither he nor Tory Stosich fished. Instead they just chatted and waited for dawn. My job as oarsman was to keep us out of the willows. At the chosen set of three pools, one for each of us, we pulled up onto a sandbar.

"I'll be happy if I can break the 18-inch barrier," Ralph said. "After five years coming out here, it's a bit embarrassing."

"It's a mind-set," Tory said. "One day you'll be fishing—it doesn't matter if it's dry or wet— and it won't look like you're doing anything different, but you've made a slight shift mentally and suddenly you are catching bigger trout."

> Somehow, probably in a case of wishful thinking, the myth has sprung up that an angler doesn't need to get out at dawn in Montana. It is true that there is plenty of excellent fishing during the middle hours of the day, but for consistently catching large trout in our rivers and lakes the early hours are by far the best.

Ralph watched us work the Bread as a cripple. Tory, even before the blackness broke, gave the fly enough slack line to slide it down the riffle and under a willow bank. The sound of the take let him know when to strike. He used the strength of his leader and pulled out a 20-inch trout.

The fishing got very fast for Tory and me when the light came. Ralph, on the bottom pool, didn't hook anything, but he had a few big swirls on the Bread. We took turns coaching Ralph, first Tory and then me repeating roughly the same instruction: "You're forcing the fly too much. It takes patience—no, make that faith—that almost nothing is enough. Don't pull it across the current."

Finally, with the morning feeding binge nearly over, Ralph slowed his nervous flogging. No longer fearing failure now that he was facing it, he began floating the Bread with the proper degree of nonchalance. He let the fly wobble feebly right onto the main bowl of the pool. When his 21-inch brown trout sucked the Bread down, he lifted the rod ever so smoothly.

He released the fish. "The hard part is that no matter how badly I want to catch big trout, I'm going to have to relax and just let it happen."

Tory said, "That's the mind-set. And it's always the hard part."

Bristle Leech

Sometimes it's not the way the animal looks that betrays it to the trout; sometimes it's what it does that draws attention. In that case it is the job of the imitation to re-create that telltale action.

Leeches, common in lakes throughout the West, burrow in the silt. Wherever they are found, these invertebrates are a favorite food for trout. The fish cruise the shallows, hunting for leeches caught in the open, but usually the prey stays well hidden.

The large trout in my mountain lakes ignored precise imitations. The few fish caught with these patterns were taken only when the fly accurately intercepted the path of a moving trout, a rare happening with these erratic cruisers if the angler was casting blind.

One day I gave up on fishing entirely and just watched the fish that were covering the shallows. Even when I saw the rainbows suddenly change direction to root a leech from the bottom, I couldn't spot whatever attracted the attack. Then, as I followed one particular fish, I noticed a small puff of silt just before the trout darted into the ooze. Once I started searching for those clouds of mud stirred up by the leeches, I recognized the cause-and-effect link.

It was difficult, even after discovering that the mud disturbance was the important characteristic, to devise a pattern that would stir up the bottom like a leech. There were limitations to how much the fly could be weighted and still be a fly rather than a leadhead jig.

The Bristle Leech, instead of having more weight, has stiff bristles poking off the bottom of a keel hook. These spines are slanted forward so that the pattern, settled on the lake bed, digs up mud with every sudden strip of the line. With a floating line in shallow water or a sinking line in deep water, this fly mimics the first kick of a fleeing leech.

Bristle Leech

TYING STEPS

1. Bend the hook, forming a "keel"; wrap the lead wire on the "keel" of the hook.

2. Tie in the two pieces of stiff monofilament at the bottom of the neck of the hook; angle them forward and down in a V-shape.

3. Wrap the rabbit fur for the body.

4. Tie in two whole marabou feathers flat over the body.

Whip finish.

Hook:	4–8 (Keel Hook)
Weight:	lead wire
Spines:	two short pieces of stiff, heavy monofilament
Body:	gray rabbit fur (still on the skin)
Wing:	two whole, gray marabou feathers

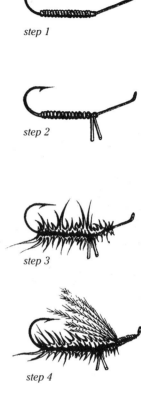

step 1

step 2

step 3

step 4

LOG ENTRY: AUGUST 7, 1991
RAINBOW LAKE

Rainbow is an extremely rich mountain lake up the Gold Creek drainage in western Montana.

Rainbow Lake was the spot where this fly was born. I never mentioned the name of this wonderful fishery in my writings, not even in the first article about the Bristle Leech (in the May 1978 issue of *Sports Afield*). It was a lake with very large trout, but it was too easily reached by a short walk off a dirt logging road.

The problem was poachers. At that time every lake and river in the area was fair game— and not just for people with fishing rods. There were a lot of big fish killed that never saw a hook.

These people used blasting caps (known as Montana Spinners) on Rainbow Lake. They rowed along predetermined lines and killed the trout in a series of explosions. Then they picked up the stunned or dead fish, many of them rainbows in the 20- to 30-inch range.

One day a friend of mine caught two people dynamiting the lake. He drew a .357 Magnum, and my first fear was that he was going to shoot at the men in the boat, but he walked back out to the road to their vehicle. He emptied the gun into the first number on the license plate, the county

Bristle Leech Log

designation, and in the process he destroyed the bumper, grill, and possibly the engine of the truck.

The rumor is that Rainbow Lake is coming back. The fish aren't monsters yet, but there are supposed to be good numbers of trout up to 20 inches. The fact that there is more fishing pressure on the lake now than there was in the late seventies means more legal kill, but the presence of anglers there helps scare off the poachers, too.

I went there alone today, my first trip to the lake in almost fifteen years, as much to visit a personal shrine as to fish. I went first to my perch near the inlet, the spot where I would watch trout cruise the patchwork bottom of sand and weeds.

> The nice part about fishing all the time is that an angler can spare moments for just sitting and watching the water. These spells don't even have to have a purpose, but it is hard not to discover some secrets during such interludes. The fisherman without a schedule doesn't need to rush about, casting furiously in a hunt for every possible trout. For this reason, he usually catches more of them.

For more than an hour I never even made a cast. I tracked fish—one 16-incher covered an oval that came very close to shore and another 16-incher swam a crooked line that traced the inside weed bed. Then, far out, at the limit of my sight, a huge shape passed briefly over a sandy patch. For a long time he was impossible to spot, but finally he drifted over this clear piece of bottom again.

I wanted to catch that trout more than any other fish I've seen this year. It wasn't going to be easy, however. He moved too quickly through the only area where I could see him. The Bristle Leech had to be the pattern. What else was going to excite such a big fish? And yet the perfect moment to make the puff of silt was when he was still three to ten feet away, not when he was on top of the fly.

The thing about cruisers in rich lakes is that they're wonderfully consistent. They turn at precisely the same spots, the beginning and end of their feeding territory. They move over the same path, as if there was a line etched on the bottom. They swim at the same rate of speed each trip.

I used my watch to time the interval between his appearances at the patch—four times it was close to 7 minutes and 45 seconds. I threw out the Bristle Leech and, although I couldn't see it in the deep water, I had to hope that it was resting on the sand. A few seconds before he was supposed to reach the target area I gave the sharp pull and the dirt puffed up in the clear water. I kept retrieving steadily, the Leech coming out into the open, and a moment later the hurtling rainbow rushed up behind the fly and engulfed it.

The fight was short enough. He pulled free on the first long run. He must have been twelve pounds.

Creature

The Creature is one of the simplest flies in intent. It imitates a small mammal of some kind. Most anglers have either seen or can picture an animal swimming in a trout stream. The fly is fished the same way.

Anyone who cannot imagine a swimming creature, a little frantic, trying to reach land, should borrow a Pekinese puppy. He can take that bit of fluff out in a boat to the middle of a river and toss the puppy into various types of water—a slow pool, a choppy riffle, a white-capped rapid—all the time studying how the animal reacts to these currents. It is best to choose a river without pike, bass, or unusually large trout for this training exercise.

The Creature doesn't have to be tied on large hooks. It is a less intimidating fly, even for big trout, in baby sizes. The pattern, a puff of fur, has worked well on size 14, long-shank streamer hooks. Still, it takes a predator to grab the Creature, and in my experience it is a waste of time casting it on streams that lack good populations of one-pound browns or two-pound rainbows.

My favorite rivers for the Creature are winding, brushy flows, every out sweep a deep undercut. On that kind of smooth, dark water the fly cuts a clear arc on the surface. The trout do not attack the Creature like a streamer. On the tiny sizes they frequently just suck it down. On the bigger sizes the fish often burst up under the fly instead of chasing it, and then the angler has to wait for the jumping trout to turn downwards before setting the hook.

My best fish on a Creature was caught many years ago, in the Bob Marshall Wilderness on the South Fork of the Flathead, in the huge pool where the Danaher comes in. A bull trout drifted up slowly from the bottom and rolled on a size 8 Brown Creature sitting dead on the surface. That fish weighed twelve pounds.

Creature

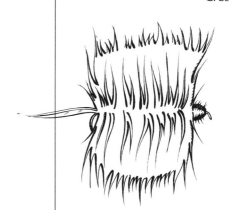

Creature

step 1

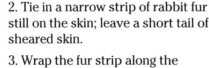

step 2

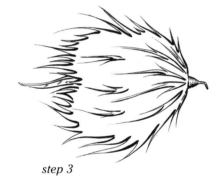

step 3

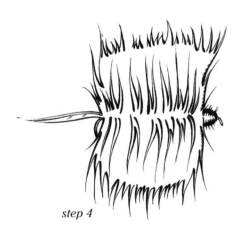

step 4

TYING STEPS

1. Wrap the hook with yarn and spread head cement; slit a cylinder of foam or balsa and fit it over the hook shank; close the slit with Zap-a-Gap glue.

2. Tie in a narrow strip of rabbit fur still on the skin; leave a short tail of sheared skin.

3. Wrap the fur strip along the shank, forming the shaggy body of the fly.

4. Dub a very thick head of fur.

Whip finish.

Hook:	2–8 (up-eyed Atlantic salmon dry fly, TMC 7989)
Foundation:	yarn (wrapped and soaked with glue)
Flotation:	balsa or foam
Skin:	rabbit fur still on the skin
Head:	dubbed fur

**LOG ENTRY: AUGUST 16, 1991
THE SETTLING PONDS**

The Settling Ponds, in a certain sense, are my waters. It isn't just that they are close to my home, only fourteen miles from Deer Lodge, or that my fishing days on them over the years number in the hundreds. The memories make them special to me, but they do not give me the right to be jealous of these waters.

The Ponds are now famous. On any summer day there might be cars in the parking lot from a half dozen states. At first glance this popularity seems very odd. The Ponds sit in a true wasteland. The ground around them consists of the tailings from a hundred years of upriver mining. Bare patches, called slickens, spread over acres—nothing can grow in the iridescent glimmer of copper sulfate leachings. Where the old river bed shifted, dead, gray forests stand like spindly barriers. And the Ponds themselves are not beautiful. They are shallow potholes, surrounded by man-made dikes.

So why would anyone fish there? The main flow of the river from Butte is diverted into the pond system and the water is treated with lime to precipitate out the heavy metals. This makes the potholes extremely alkaline. The bottoms, carpeted with billows of weed, produce the insects and crustaceans that grow large trout. There are browns up to sixteen pounds, rainbows up to eleven pounds, and even an occasional cutthroat, washed in from Brown's Gulch during the flood of a high-water year, up to two pounds. These overfed slobs cruise in clear view.

My reason for being jealous? I was the first person to fish these waters with a fly rod (and the second person ever). For years no one even suspected that there might be trout surviving in these ponds. Bob Newell, who worked in Denver for ARCO, the mining company that owned the complex, wrote me a cryptic note, "The man at the on-site trailer isn't a fisherman, but he saw fish rolling and went out with a spinning rod and caught an eight-pound brown."

Bob is not only a fisherman, a scientist, and one of the main people who helped me research *Caddisflies,* but a friend. I went up to the Ponds, wondering if the report was a hoax, and sat for three hours without casting. Near evening the trout started rolling.

There were far fewer fish in the Ponds then, and they were all browns, but they were much larger. For three months that summer I was, as far as I know, the only one to fish the area. The first week gave me a fourteen-pound brown and an eleven-pound brown. My greatest day was twelve fish over five pounds. The secret of the Ponds never slipped from me, but somehow word spread and by fall other anglers started showing up.

The state Fish & Game, to their credit, acted quickly and put the entire complex under special regulations. They also stocked the Ponds with rainbows. These fish not only flourished but they proved much easier to catch than the brown trout.

For the past two years the Ponds have been closed most of the time while ARCO works on this Environmental Protection Agency Superfund site. The huge earth movers cleaning the Mill Creek-Willow Creek bypass make the area unsafe for the public.

My plan was to wait until 1992 and the general reopening, but the frustration of the two-year absence from the Ponds boiled over today. Mike Lontis wanted to fish them, too. If we could be there at dawn it might be possible to work the Hog Hole for an hour before the commotion drove us out.

It was just getting light when we crossed the newly expanded dike and walked down to the Hog Hole, the middle pond in the complex. There wasn't a whiff of wind. That is how we saw the mouse, or maybe it was a shrew, leave one of the islands and swim for the shore. On the flat surface he left a long V-wake behind him.

It was only twenty yards to land for the mouse, but he had to cross a deep channel where fish always cruised. Something bumped him, lifting him up on a hump of water. Then two or three trout, large ones, churned the surface with swirls. The mouse disappeared in one of those attacks.

Mike and I stood at opposite ends of the channel and cast to the island. I was going to let the Creature sit on the water until the ripples dissipated, but a rainbow bolted into the shallows and ravaged the fly. Before I landed that fish, Mike hooked a brown on a Creature.

The activity was steady, a trout here and a trout there, as we moved from one holding pocket to another in the pond. We caught fish right up until the moment the sun hit the water, seven trout for the two of us (the smallest eighteen inches and fat). Once it got bright everything stopped on the surface. Oddly, for this valley, there was still no wind.

It was the first time I ever used a Creature on a pond or lake.

Hair Sucker

Trout and suckers go together. It might seem strange for a fly fisherman to spend so much time observing and studying suckers, but at some point—just like aquatic insects— they become fascinating for themselves. It is a crime to waste them; it is shameful to throw them up on the bank to die. Both as scavengers and as forage they are an integral part of the energy flow in a healthy trout stream.

The Hair Sucker is a bottom imitation (and not just because it is heavily weighted). It wobbles with the current, struggling like a real sucker caught in the open. It mimics an injured fish; and since every predator attacks suckers it is not unusual to see a small one hurt or stunned in the drift.

The "stutter-drift" technique makes the fly appear vulnerable. A fast-sinking shooting head is cast above and beyond the prime slot. Just as drag develops and starts to roll the Hair Sucker off the bottom, the angler mends the floating shooting line vigorously downstream. The force of the mend tugs the fly (the stutter), but the new slack lets it flutter back with the current (the drift).

Bill Seeples, the master of this technique, can work a fly with at least seven mends, letting out more line with each roll and running the imitation along the bottom for thirty or forty feet.

"Don't get lazy," he yells. "It takes too much work to get the fly down there not to fight for every inch of drift once it's at the prime level."

Hair Sucker

TYING STEPS

1. Tie strips of lead onto the sides of the hook shank.

2. Tie in pheasant fibers for the tail.

3. Tie in the oval gold tinsel; let it dangle for the moment.

4. Tie in and wrap the body of eggshell-white yarn.

5. Wind the tinsel rib.

6. Tie in the underwing of dark olive hen feathers flat on top of the shank (the full length of the hook).

7. Tie in the overwing of dark gray marabou flat on top of the shank (half the length of the hook).

8. Spin a deer hair collar of red deer hair; trim the stubs right down the shank.

9. Spin a collar and full head of gray deer hair; trim the head into a triangle shape.

Whip finish.

Hook:	8–2/0 (up-eyed Atlantic salmon hook, TMC 7999)
Weight:	lead wire
Tail:	six to eight fibers of a pheasant tail feather
Rib:	oval gold tinsel
Body:	eggshell-white yarn
Underwing:	two dark olive hen feathers (tied flat on top of the shank, tips to the bend of the hook, eventually lashed Matuka-fashion to the hook)
Overwing:	a whole gray marabou feather (tied flat on top of the shank, tips only halfway down the hook.
Head:	two bands of deer hair—red and dark gray (the deer hair tips overlap in a prismatic collar)

The colors of the marabou fibers are changed to match the species.

step 9

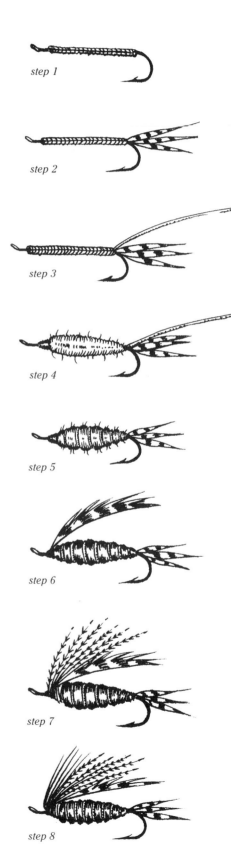

step 1

step 2

step 3

step 4

step 5

step 6

step 7

step 8

LOG ENTRY: APRIL 24, 1990
MISSOURI RIVER BELOW CANYON FERRY RESERVOIR

This spot is my secret haunt for both spring and fall fishing. It is a short section of the Missouri River, so short that the maps don't even picture it. The water is shown tumbling out of Canyon Ferry Dam right into Hauser Lake, but there is a river channel between these projects. In all my visits to this place there have rarely been any fly fishermen working this section.

It is impossible to reach the channel from shore with a fly rod during a normal water year because of the wide, shallow flats. The mud bottoms

Hair Sucker Log

are too soft to wade in many places; and trout seldom cruise over these areas. The channel itself is mediocre fishing during the summer, but each spring and fall trout migrate into it.

The rainbows and browns move from the lake into the channel for two reasons. They come either to spawn or to feed. The browns spawn in the fall, the run peaking from late October through late November. The rainbows, depending on the strain, spawn spring or fall (most rainbows spawn in the spring, but the run of Arlee-strain hatchery trout peaks from early October through early November).

The in-and-out waves of feeding fish are less predictable than the spawning movements, but it is worth waiting for one of these migrations. It is worth flogging away for five days, ten hours at a time, catching very few trout and nothing big at that—which is what happened to me one spring. My mistake was trying so hard to understand the trout.

> The in-and-out waves of feeding fish are less predictable than the spawning movements, but it is worth waiting for one of these migrations.

Paul Cheuse checks out the worm fishermen for me. He strolls along the bank, chatting with people watching propped-up bait rods. He calls me when the anglers hit a spree of suckers. "Better hurry. You never heard so much cussing, 'Damn suckers. Where are the trout?' They're throwing so many suckers up on the shore to die that by nightfall the whole area stinks."

Most of the dead fish had been cleaned up by scavengers during the night, but the carcasses left were mostly white suckers *(Catostomus commersoni).* That meant that the main rush of the spawning run was on—and this abundant species of sucker certainly attracts the trout. The browns and rainbows from the lake had to be right behind them.

I put a half dozen Hair Suckers into a jar of water to soak and paddled out in my float tube towards the center of the river. Even though it was spring the water over the flats was warm; the current of the river caught me as soon as I hit the colder water of the channel. I backed up ten feet and started casting a 1/0 Hair Sucker on a fast sinking line.

It was a tedious search up and down that channel. After an hour a fish hit, nothing huge—just a very fat 18-inch rainbow. A few casts later another rainbow about the same size took the fly. And then my best stutter-and-drift passes caught nothing. The pod of trout was gone, chasing the back-and-forth shifts of the main sucker run.

Periodically throughout the day I'd find the trout, but after one or two fish, at most, I would lose contact with them. This didn't bother me. There were enough spurts of action, always with those same two- or three-year-old rainbows, to make it interesting. And the casting and the kicking were great exercise in the warm sun.

I have to admit it. I started daydreaming (this seems to happen more in the spring). I'd think about other times, when the white suckers were farther along in their spawning and more likely to concentrate in one place; and those were the times when the trout, especially the large browns, would stay there too and gorge on both the bait fish and freely drifting eggs. Those were the days with sprees of three- to six-pound fish.

Plain Jane

There is nothing special about this fly. That is its strength—not its weakness. This is a hard concept for anglers to grasp. Not every pattern should present a strong visual package. When trout are already feeding generally and aggressively, it is better to let them find the fly instead of trying to pull them to it. The same rule applies to an effective searching dry fly, such as the Adams, or to an effective searching nymph, such as a Hare's Ear.

Plain Jane

The Plain Jane features a diminution of every objectionable trait on a Muddler Minnow. The characteristics on a Muddler that can repel as well as attract, the very traits that make it a powerful fly, are replaced with simple drabness. The head is reduced greatly, creating not only a smaller silhouette but also diminishing vibrations sent out on the retrieve. The stiff turkey feather and hair wing, as well as the turkey feather tail, are replaced with marabou fibers that slim down and wave softly in the water. The garish gold tinsel body, the major flaw when trout prefer subtlety, is changed to a wrapped body of regular eggshell-white yarn.

Plain Jane

step 1

step 2

step 3

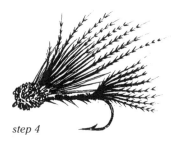

step 4

TYING STEPS

1. Tie a fairly thick bunch of marabou in as a tail; clip this bunch into a short stub.

2. Wrap a body of regular eggshell-white yarn (no taper, no unusual thickness).

3. Tie in a sparse marabou wing.

4. Spin a deer hair head; clip it rough but small.

Whip finish.

Hook:	10–12 (3X long streamer hook, TMC 5263)
Tail:	marabou (clipped in a stub)
Body:	eggshell-white yarn (wrapped)
Wind:	marabou fibers (extending to the end of the tail)
Head:	natural gray deer hair

The tail and the wing are always the same color; the standard variations are green, black, brown, and natural gray.

LOG ENTRY: OCTOBER 20, 1991
RACETRACK CREEK

This is one of the small tributaries of the upper Clark Fork River.

The seasonal cycle is even more exaggerated on small streams than on big rivers in the mountains. The high flush of opening day (late May) makes a rocky creek extremely difficult to fish. There is no sloping edge, so instead of sliding into the shallows to escape the current the trout hug the bottom. The only technique that works for me then is a weighted nymph and a leader draped with lead wire (the Outrigger Method).

On a small stream the prime period, the magic two- or three-week transition as the runoff fades, produces the only easy fly fishing of the year. The trout spread out because the water is high enough to provide protection for the fish. A searching technique with almost any pattern takes these opportunistic feeders.

But then the summer, and normal low water, hits the streams. The riffles get too shallow, too exposed, for the wild, skittish trout. The fish drop back to the deeper pools and runs. They still rush out after an active wet fly or crash up for an attractor dry fly, but there is nervousness in every decision.

There had not been any significant fall rains or early snowstorms to freshen up Racetrack Creek. This didn't stop me; it did slow me down, of course. Every pool was a special problem. It would take me a few minutes of sitting and studying the water. Even after puzzling out the best way to slide or swim a fly through the prime pocket of each pool, it took time to make a creeping, quiet approach.

It wasn't an afternoon of incredible trout numbers. At first the fishing was frustrating. The cutthroats flashed and nipped at a size 14 Royal Trude, but except for a few lip-hooked fish that quickly pulled free, none of them grabbed it. These weren't big trout, of course—the size range for Racetrack fish, mostly richly colored, firm-bodied cutthroats, is eight to twelve inches.

That water was cold. I was wading wet, seldom entering the stream. When I had to cross the creek, it was never over calf deep. But, after a few seconds standing in this liquid ice, my legs would start to ache. And here I thought that I would look foolish dressed in full neoprenes on such a piddling stream.

If the dry fly wasn't going to work, then maybe a drab wet fly would be more acceptable. It was. A sparse, size 16 Quill Gordon, fished with a single split shot on the leader, started hooking the cutthroats, brooks, and occasional rainbows in every pool except the best looking ones.

The "empty" pools, however, were the reason that I was on Racetrack this afternoon. The best water wasn't holding smaller trout because of a predator.

The small fish were fun. I never downplay this type of fishing. The "empty" pools, however, were the reason that I was on Racetrack this afternoon. The best water wasn't holding smaller trout because of a predator. On Racetrack the lord of the domain might be either a brown trout on a spawning run up from the Clark Fork or a resident bull trout. There are some surprises even on a piddling creek like Racetrack.

The first big pool established the angling pattern for the day. The wet fly, worked with hangs, swings, and retrieves a half dozen times through the dark, brushy cuts, did nothing. It was replaced with a weighted, size 6 Yellow Marabou Muddler, a gaudy version with a tinsel chenille body. The Marabou Muddler was the finder—not the catcher. A big shape rushed out after the streamer on the third swim. The fish, already stirred up, was looking for something, and on his first chance to hit a size 10, green Plain Jane he chased the minnow fly right to my feet.

The Plain Jane became the "finisher" on every prime pool. It was so ordinary that those trout had no doubt that it was safe to eat. If they missed it on the first pass, they still came just as confidently the second or even the third time.

The tally for the day was not huge—the fishing was a game where the rules changed for each pool. There were two bull trout, best of eighteen inches, and three brown trout, best of sixteen inches, and enough smaller fish on the wet fly to make it a full day.

Silver Bi-Color

Silver minnows contain cells of pigment (iridocytes) that reflect the light entering the water. These cells are very sensitive to changes in brightness, coloring the minnow gray if the sky is overcast or silver if the sky is clear. The pigment shifts quickly to match variations in light intensity.

When these small fish pack tightly into a school, their coloration is protective because a predator sees only a single sheet of reflection. Actually, attacking fish seldom kill anything in a charge through the school, a tactic designed simply to scatter and disorient the bait fish. The minnows separated from the pack are much more likely to be victims than those in the bunch.

It is easy for the scuba diver to see that certain fish are always excluded from the school. Sometimes there are obvious reasons why fish are on the fringe. Maybe they have crippled swimming motions or bleeding wounds. But usually the reason isn't so clear—it takes a close look for the diver to see why certain fish are segregated and exposed.

The trait that singles out the sacrificial victims, outcasts from the protection of the school, is the inability to change color to conform to shifts in the light. Because of a malfunction of the iridocytes, due to either a genetic deformity or a wound, some minnows cannot assume the coloration of the rest of the bait fish. These individuals tagging along on the fringes of the pack are the main targets for marauding bass and trout.

The Silver Bi-Color streamer, with split wings of gray and white, imitates a sick minnow unable to completely alter color. Either the gray or white stripe stands out, depending on the light of the sky. In proper size, this fly consistently fools more predators than a streamer that imitates the healthy bait fish.

Silver Bi-Color

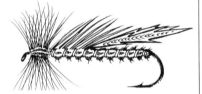

TYING STEPS

1. Tie in a piece of silver wire; let it dangle for the moment.

2. Tie in a piece of white sparkle yarn; wrap it as a body.

3. Color the top halves of four white hackles gray with a permanent marker; match the four hackles and tie them in; snip the tips of the two inside hackles off.

4. Wrap the silver wire, binding down the front half of the wing Matuka-style.

5. Wrap a collar hackle.

Whip finish.

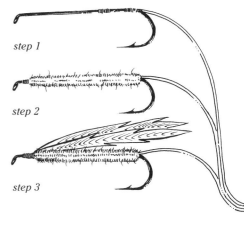

step 1

step 2

step 3

step 4

step 5

Hook:	4–10 (3X long streamer hook, TMC 5263)
Tail:	matched tips of two hackle feathers (colored gray; these are the same feathers that form the wing
Rib:	silver wire
Body:	white sparkle yarn (wrapped)
Wing:	four white saddle hackles (but the top halves of the hackles are colored gray with a permanent marker)
Hackle:	grizzly hackle (collar)

Silver Bi-Color

LOG ENTRY: OCTOBER 8, 1990
CANYON FERRY LAKE

This major reservoir on the Missouri River near Helena, Montana, is one of the most popular fishing waters in the state.

This is my favorite time of year to use the Silver Bi-Color. The winter is coming; the first frosts have chilled the lakes in Montana. It is *culling* time for the minnows. Some biologic mechanism triggers a die-off among the old and unhealthy individuals in the bait fish population. These fish turn gray as they sicken and weaken.

There was no doubt about it. What we were doing in Canyon Ferry when we found the trout was trolling with float tubes. Four of us—Tom Poole, W. J. Witts, Chris Kincheloe, and me—were trailing streamers with sinking lines. We were kicking across the bay at its mouth when we hit the pod of rainbows.

Tom caught the first fish on a Silver Bi-Color (a pattern he worked on extensively with me during its development). No one else had one of these flies, not even me, but Tom shared his supply generously. W. J. and I both put one on, but Chris, always the skeptic, stayed with a brown-and-yellow, feather-wing pattern.

The rainbows were concentrated off a shelf at the mouth of the bay. They were school fish, all amazingly similar at a fat sixteen inches (probably second-year holdovers). There must have been hundreds of them down there, staging for a sweep into the bay.

What an incredibly strong instance of selectivity this was. Those trout wanted gray—other gray streamers, such as a Gray Ghost, caught trout. White streamers hooked a few fish, but not nearly as many. Meanwhile, Chris, with his brown-and-yellow fly, didn't get a tap during the entire spree.

The scuba diving in lakes taught us how selective predators can be when they are hunting minnows. Size, color, and style (a filmy, feather wing producing much better than a hair wing fly in still waters and vice versa in running waters) are all critical.

> They were school fish, all amazingly similar at a fat sixteen inches (probably second-year holdovers). There must have been hundreds of them down there, staging for a sweep into the bay.

Stub Wing Bucktail

It takes better methods and better fly designs to increase the number of solid hookups with a streamer. The better fly is an odd looking pattern that violates representation. The pattern perfectly suits the trout's disjointed perspective of what's right or wrong.

This imitation breaks a formidable barrier. There is always the notion that somehow any pattern meant to mimic a life form has to be put together in a natural sequence. Tails at the back on mayfly nymphs, wings on the top on caddisfly dries, eyes at the front on minnow streamers. Why? That is nature's plan.

But sometimes nature is a practical joker. There are minnows that have exaggerated false eyes on their tails. A predator, conditioned to strike the eye of a bait fish, slams into the tail, missing all vital organs, and the fortunate minnow dashes away.

Couldn't the predator see that the false eye wasn't at the head?

The answer is one of the secrets for developing imitations for all food forms (dry or wet). A fish, with its rudimentary mind, focuses on individual parts of whatever he is feeding on and ignores the entire picture. The predator does not try to kill a small fish—he tries to kill an eye.

It doesn't matter where the eye is on the hook of an imitation, either. It can be at the front—and this is sort of the fly tier's version of nature's practical joke. The predator bangs the end of the fly that has nothing to grab him, and then the streamer swims away unharmed. Or the eye can be at the back, where any strike puts the predator's mouth around the hook point.

Maybe it is just their poor sense of humor, but my friends want a trout's mouth around the hook point. They want that large, exaggerated eye on the Stub Wing Bucktail at the bend because in underwater observations this change alone increased the number of solid hookups by roughly 30 percent.

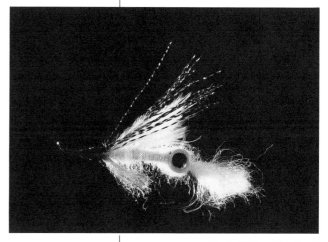

Stub Wing Bucktail

step 1

step 2

step 3

step 4

step 5

step 6

step 7

Stub Wing Bucktail

TYING STEPS

1. Tie in a piece of white sparkle yarn; comb it out.

2. Wrap a knob of black thread; paint a prominent eye on the knob or glue on a doll eye.

3. Tie in a piece of white sparkle yarn; wrap it halfway up the shank as a body.

4. Tie in a short clump of marabou for the rear wing (tips extending to the bend of the hook).

5. Wrap the sparkle yarn near the eye of the hook to complete the body.

6. Tie in a short clump of marabou for the front wing (tips extending halfway down the hook shank).

7. Tie in a topping of green flashabou.

8. Tie in a piece of red yarn; wrap enough for a joint and let a short piece dangle under the hook as a trailer.

Whip finish.

Hook:	8–2/0 (up-eyed Atlantic salmon hook, TMC 7999)
Tail:	white sparkle yarn (combed out and clipped)
Eye:	painted-on built-up, black tying thread, or a glued doll's eye
Body:	white sparkle yarn (wrapped; brushed out or picked out to make it fuzzy)
Joint/Trailer:	red wool yarn (the trailer is a combed-out piece of yarn on the underside of the hook; the joint is a wrap of the same red wool)
Rear Wing:	marabou (short, stub wing)
Front Wing:	marabou (short, stub wing)
Topping:	strands of green flashabou

The colors of the rear and front wing vary to match the predominate bait fish—white, gray, green, blue, and brown are important colors.

step 8

LOG ENTRY: AUGUST 31, 1991
TONGUE RIVER

This river has fascinated me ever since the original Streamside Angler opened in Missoula; Frank Johnson had a pair of mounted brown trout of eleven and seven pounds that he caught on the same day in the Tongue.

The Stub Wing Bucktail has worked so well for trout all year that it is natural to wonder how it will do for bass. That is the target, smallmouth bass, not trout, but there are giant browns in the river, too. The Tongue is famous for those trout. They are the obsession in my state and as a result the great smallmouth fishing is ignored (but not by me).

Pete Hanzel goes too far the other way. "We don't want any of those mushy, slimy trout in my boat."

I made him launch near the dam anyway. Brester Zahm and I cast Stub Wings from the moving raft, firing flies into the bank and retrieving out. We weren't using a normal retrieve, though. It was the Streak. We started catching trout, no bass, and at first that wasn't unusual, but as we drifted further down river and we kept getting trout, including some respectable fish, and no bass, we decided that it must be because of the method.

The Streak isn't normal. An angler usually casts into the bank and works the fly out in erratic twitches. With the Streak the oarsman doesn't even back row to slow the progress of the boat. He turns that raft around and pulls downstream as fast as possible. The caster throws down and across, and as soon as the fly touches he puts the rod between his knees and strips line with both hands. He not only moves the streamer very smoothly this way, but when the speed of the retrieve is added to the speed of the boat, the fly cuts incredibly fast nearly straight across the river.

The Streak Method doesn't catch many bank fish. The fly usually gets slammed halfway between the shore and the boat. Even though it is moving so swiftly that the angler has to wonder how anything can catch it, trout rarely miss the fly. The rate of solid hookups is incredible, 80 percent day in and day out with the Stub Wing.

How many strikes does it get compared to other methods? That depends apparently on how aggressive the trout are at any given time. Some days it draws very few hits; on other days it brings fish flying from all sides. The best day with the Streak, the rowing split among Jennifer Koenig, Tom Poole, and me, was ninety-eight trout for the three of us in eleven miles of the South Fork of the Snake in Idaho.

Today we were definitely below the trout water. It was farther down than I had ever seen a brown. All three of us were worn out from rowing for the Streak and we pulled in to wade for smallmouths.

The wade fishing technique was still different from the usual across stream presentation. The angler stood on the bank or in the shallows and threw the Stub Wing almost straight downstream. This was much more like an Atlantic salmon cast than a trout cast. The fly didn't swing, pulled across the river by the bellying line. It landed about fifteen feet out from the shore and sidled into the deep curl.

I caught bass. Brester caught bass. What does Pete hook? A twenty-four-inch brown trout.

STREAMERS ADDENDUM

■

The angler needs two other streamer methods for slim swimming patterns:

1. Especially when trout are rising to insects, a streamer thrown straight upstream and brought back downstream just slightly faster than the current gets hit hard.

2. Casting across stream is fine, but once it lands the fly shouldn't be pulled away from that initial drift. The line is mended again and again to keep the fly dropping down broadside in the flow.

The one method the trout fisherman doesn't need, in my opinion, is the most common. The act of throwing the fly across stream and jerking it erratically back is the poorest hooking method of all.

Two

■

Wet Flies

Cataclysm never leaves the realm unchanged. An event can encompass the earth; or it can strike one arcane little endeavor, as precise as the phenomenon that nearly drove fly fishing to extinction. A radically different world always blooms after the collapse of the old structure.

The winged wet fly was a major method of fly fishing up until the mid-1940s. It was a complete approach, encompassing both imitation (with patterns such as the Grannom and Deer Fly) and attraction (with patterns such as the Harlequin and Jennie Lind). There were effective techniques for drifting, swimming, and dancing these flies.

Certainly, the dry fly was already replacing the wet fly as the dominant method, and both the nymph and the streamer were actually designed to take over specific wet fly functions, but if fly fishing had evolved smoothly maybe the winged wet fly wouldn't have vanished so completely. The example of older masters, so deadly with one or two wet flies, would have inspired new anglers to practice the techniques on our streams and lakes. But history doesn't always move in an unbroken line.

Tom Nixon told me, "In the early 1940s, even in my state, Louisiana, 80 percent of the fishermen used fly rods. A few years after World War II, the number of fishermen who even carried fly rods on a trip dropped to 3 percent."

The cataclysm that swept the angling world was the introduction of the spinning rod. Fly fishing, already mired in the confusion of an indecipherable system of letters for choosing line weights, was suddenly relegated to small groups of fanatics. The ordinary fisherman, who had carried a fly rod and a bait casting rod, gladly chucked both outfits for the ease of spinning. The popularity of fly fishing dropped to dismal lows in the following ten years, and in this span the wet fly, the common man's method of choice, also faded into oblivion.

When fly fishing boomed again, beginning in the 1960s, with a revolution of practical, inexpensive glass rods, plastic lines, and nylon leaders, it was a vibrant, exciting rebirth. All ideas seemed new to the influx of raw beginners. Those methods, such as the classic winged wet fly, that were lost in the cataclysm did not seem important in the scientifically oriented approach of the sixties and seventies. When the old masters started pass-

ing away, the art of the wet fly virtually died with them.

The demise of the winged wet fly has left gaps in imitation and attraction that no other method will ever fill. Modern anglers still need the old flies. Just as important, they need the techniques—single fly, dropper rig, and dead drift presentations—that make the classic winged pattern so deadly.

My scuba divers rabidly defend the wet fly because of what they see underwater. They watch how concentrations of swimming adult insects, unique in both appearance and behavior, lock trout into rigid selective feeding. They notice how the constant drift of drowned adult insects pulls trout from the holding spots into feeding lanes (even when those fish are letting the occasional nymph go past).

Attraction with multiple wet flies, even more than imitation, fascinates me. It is always more difficult to make judgments about what prompts trout to attack an odd fly, but those instinctual responses of curiosity and competitiveness definitely play a role when patterns are fished with two-fly techniques.

There are plenty of adult insects that do not survive their time in or on the water. Egg-layers frequently drown after reaching the bottom, never returning to the surface. Hatching mayflies, even after successfully shedding the nymphal shuck, often get sucked under by undertows. Terrestrials fall on the stream and, if not eaten there, eventually sink. All of these drab, dead insects wash along with the current,

The method for mimicking drab, drowned insects can be a bottom bouncing technique, but usually a "wash" presentation serves up the fly more realistically. The fly, unweighted, is cast upstream and fished dead drift, and it is deadly if it hangs only an inch or so, no more, under the surface.

The live insects require a different approach. Adults survive below the surface by carrying their own air supply, tucking a bubble under and around the wings (a process known as plastron respiration). Egg-laying caddisflies are not the only insects that glimmer with this silver package of air as they swim to the bottom. Species of mayflies, damselflies, two-winged flies, and aquatic moths do the same thing.

The best technique for simulating the active adult, with either one fly (for tight-casting waters) or two flies (for open waters) is a "draw" presentation. The pattern is cast across stream and slack is controlled by lifting or lowering the rod, creating just enough tension to keep the winged wet fly dropping down broadside to the current.

Trout feed heavily on both drowned and swimming insects. The complete imitation demands wings. The drowned fly needs soft materials that move with every wisp of flow. The swimming fly needs the natural brightness of sparkle yarn (Antron or Creslan).

The winged wet fly is also unique when it comes to attraction. The fact that it can swim, dance, dip, dangle, and drift adds the aspect of motion to the picture. Any movement enhances the mystery.

The flat expanse of the wet fly wing is the tier's billboard. The message is painted in colors, either solid or broken, with different levels of intensity. Red, pink, orange, chartreuse, or blue? Nature is still the starting point, every fly needing some points of realism, but the absurdity of certain colors clearly excites trout.

Here is the key with the wet fly (the one fact that slapped us hard in the underwater observations)—with the classic method of two-fly presentations it is wrong to think either-or for imitation and attraction. Not only is there no need to choose between the two philosophies; it is wrong to choose. The attractor wet fly enhances the imitation, and vice versa.

That bit of information started a fevered search for an even wilder attractor. The wing was the billboard. Why not fluorescence? A new fly was developed not only as the supreme attention-grabber (pulling fish to the drab fly), but as a surprisingly effective trout-catcher itself. Two opposite patterns, one for imitation and one for attraction, did better than two odd flies or two realistic flies on the same leader.

The major element in the two-fly pairing, even if it isn't the pattern drawing strikes, is the attractor. The realistic fly flits and darts on and below the surface, always apparently escaping the garish pursuer. The fake chase tantalizes trout. In tandem the two-fly rig provides stronger attraction than a nymph and subtler imitation than a streamer.

Modern anglers demand reasons for using any type of fly. The winged wet fly is still extremely effective for three situations—the drab imitation of the drowned aquatic or terrestrial adult insect; the bright imitation of the live, swimming adult insect; and the strong attraction of movement and color combined (making the fly either an enhancer or a primary target). When these wet flies, and the appropriate strategies, are missing from the angler's bag of tricks, there is a block of fishing time, between 10 percent and 15 percent, that is lost on the normal trout stream.

Black June

The standard wet fly dressing, with black crow for the wing, was never anything special for me. A simple substitution was born on a messy fly tying table. The feather wing was replaced with glossy, black monga ringtail hair. This changed not only the look but the intent of the pattern.

Leaving the hair wing free, instead of binding it over the back, also made this a more effective fly—during our underwater observations divers saw a more vibrant form. There was little doubt, even if the tied-down variation was not a traditional representation, that the Black June was imitating a beetle.

Black June

30

TYING STEPS

1. Wrap in silver tinsel, winding slightly down the bend of the hook.

2. Tie in the silver tinsel rib.

3. Tie in strands of peacock herl; wrap the body.

4. Wind the rib.

5. Tie in the hair wing, spreading it flat over the top.

6. Wrap a collar hackle of black hen.

Whip finish.

step 1

step 2

step 3

step 4

step 5

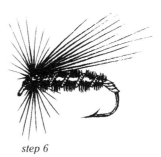

step 6

Hook:	10–18 (1X heavy wire)
Tag:	flat silver tinsel
Rib:	oval silver tinsel
Body:	peacock herl (wrapped full)
Wing:	black monga ringtail hair (tied flat over the back)
Hackle:	black hen (collar)

LOG ENTRY: JULY 24, 1991
BIG SPRING CREEK

One of Montana's premier spring creeks, Big Spring Creek runs through Lewistown, far from all of the other famous waters in the state, and it doesn't draw big crowds.

The Black June is one of my fishing secrets (just like a Joe's Hopper drifted wet). On all types of water, no matter what the season, a trout will probably have beetles in his stomach. A lot of these, considering the swimming ability of the average beetle, have to be taken subsurface.

Four different people asked me what I was using today; and after I'd say, "Just this little wet fly," they would wade out to peek at it. Not one of them, though, asked me *how* to fish it.

The stream was in wonderful shape. The water below town [Lewistown] still held the bigger fish and with some of the weed washed out earlier in the runoff those trout were easier to find. They were congregating around rocks and logs instead of hiding in what was left of the weed bunkers.

Three big trout snatched the Black June. Two browns broke me off, one by tearing under a deadfall. It was just bad planning—or rather, no planning—on my part. The third trout, 19 inches, tried the same trick with the sticks. By comparison, the rest of the fish fought hard but seemed predictable. Most of the browns and rainbows ran and dug instead of jumping.

The flow was heavy enough so that it took two wraps of lead wire about 18 inches up the leader to get the fly down. Usually, since the Black June itself isn't weighted, it washes just under the surface—not my normal nymphing method, but my favorite way of probing the weed lanes in spring creeks. Today the trout wanted the fly scraping the bottom.

Diving Caddis

The reason caddisflies will always be a bit of a mystery is that they are phantoms. An angler learns to study the water for signs of life when trout are visibly feeding. But what happens with caddisflies? The fish are rolling and jumping, obviously taking something at, if not on, the surface, but the angler can stare himself cross-eyed and never spot an insect. The caddisflies, either emerging or egg-laying, hesitate in the rubbery meniscus, not on it, and they are invisible to the casual observer.

Caddisflies demand faith. When a fish feeds on them he typically follows a swimming insect to the top and sucks it in when it hits the surface film—and *then* the trout's momentum carries him out of the water in a roll or a jump. The angler, even when he cannot see a caddisfly, has to trust the rise forms, believe in phantoms, and show the trout an imitation of either an emerging pupa or an egg-laying adult.

Fly choice, at least, is easy. Both the Emergent Sparkle Pupa (for the pupa) and the Diving Caddis (for the adult) are crossover patterns. The brightness of the Antron on these flies matches the brightness of the air carried by the insect. That brightness is the overwhelming characteristic, diminishing the importance of size, shape, or color. So the Diving Caddis works fairly well when trout are taking the natural pupae and the Emergent Sparkle Pupa works fairly well when trout are taking the natural adult. These patterns are such great all-around exciters that even when the trout are not slurping some stage of caddisflies, instead making fools of themselves over some other active insect, one of these imitations will probably fool a Judas fish.

Once one of these flies catches a trout, the angler has a chance to gently pump the fish and carefully examine the most recent food items in the gullet. With a sample of the natural in his hand the angler chooses an imitation perfectly matching the secondary characteristics. He takes off the fly that performed fairly, puts on the great imitator, and wreaks havoc among those trout.

Diving Caddis

Hook: 8–20 (standard wet fly hook, TMC 9300)

Rib: stripped hackle quill (optional, listed for some of the color variations)

Body: half sparkle yarn and half fur (blended for color, dubbed)

Underwing: soft hackle fibers

Overwing: clear Antron fibers

Hackle: rooster hackle (low quality)

The four main color schemes, covering 90 percent of the situations an angler will encounter, are:

- brown-and-yellow (brown soft hackle wing, rusty yellow body, and brown hackle)

- brown-and-bright green (brown soft hackle wing, bright green body, and brown hackle)

- dark gray (dark gray soft hackle wing, gray body, and dun hackle)

- ginger (lemon soft hackle wing, cream body, and ginger hackle).

TYING STEPS

1. Dub a body of sparkle yarn and fur.

2. Tie in an underwing of soft hackle fibers.

3. Tie in an overwing of clear Antron filaments.

4. Wind a rooster hackle one turn at the head; force these fibers into a backward slant with wraps of tying thread.

Whip finish.

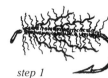

step 1

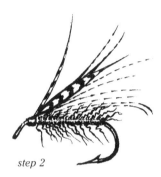

step 2

step 3

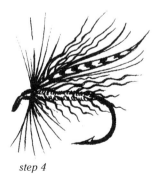

step 4

Diving Caddis

LOG ENTRY: JULY 9, 1990
UPPER CLARK FORK

This is my home river—my days on it, from the Settling Ponds at Warm Springs to the town of Deer Lodge—total seventy-five or more a season; the number would not be nearly this high, even with proximity, if the river did not have one of the highest populations of catchable-size trout, most browns, per acre foot of water in Montana.

The upper Clark Fork is so overwhelmingly a caddisfly river, and mostly of one family, that entomologists describe it as monotypic. There are enough *Baetis* mayflies, *Tipula* craneflies, and midges to occasionally attract the attention of the fish, but day in and day out the trout feed on various stages of caddisflies (which explains why for me there was little choice except to research and write *Caddisflies*—rivers shape the anglers who fish them).

The caddisfly family is Hydropsychidae. These are net-spinners. Genera such as *Hydropsyche* (Spotted Sedge) and *Cheumatopsyche* (Little Sister Sedge) are tremendously abundant because the river is very rich, with a pH over 9, and produces a lot of algae. The bottom of the Clark Fork is cemented by a hundred years of mining discharge, the sediment destroying the spaces between the rocks, the interstitial habitat, where most aquatic insects live, but the net-spinners colonize the sides and tops of the rocks and filter food from the drift.

The hatches are so heavy that at their peak in June the insects overwhelm the trout. There stands the poor angler, knee deep in the river, so many adult caddisflies flying at dusk that his buddy fifty feet away is lost in a haze, and he cannot decide which slurping fish to cast at. His fly not only has to be right, but in the wicked competition with a blizzard of naturals, it has to appear in front of the trout's nose at exactly the right moment.

I've been rebuilding my stock of Diving Caddis, tying them in various sizes and colors. If the trend of the past week continues on the river, I am going to need a supply of them for me and my friends. Why don't they carry the fly? They all fish the Emergent religiously, but there's something about a "wet fly," even a modern imitation, that makes them ignore an obvious need.

Tom Owlsley brought along a couple of great fellows from Michigan— at least they seemed great after a long night of drinking beer and talking fishing. Bob Dentner and Duane Vickrey are fanatics with opinions, but they have done some real studying on their own trout streams.

Bob, the one with the questions, represents a group that drives me a bit batty sometimes—there are anglers who believe so strongly in the Emergent that they embrace it as a universal pattern for caddis situations. "Why should we need the wet fly tonight?"

"The browns will show a preference."

We arrived on the special regulation water, the five miles of river below Warm Springs, at 5:00 p.m. That was a little early, but a few fish were already rolling under the brushy banks. Unfortunately, Bob made two casts with a size 16 Brown and Yellow Emergent Sparkle Pupa and caught one of those trout, a 14-inch brown, and even if he didn't say anything, he looked rather smug about the whole thing.

The egg-laying blitz started for real, fish started rolling, and the laws of selectivity started tipping the odds. Bob was situated close enough to me to notice the difference in the way trout were responding. He wasn't doing badly with the Emergent, but he was getting some obvious refusals, too. The Sparkle Pupa was fooling one in three or one in four fish; the size 16 Brown and Yellow Diving Caddis, drifting and swimming a few inches under the surface, was ripping every one.

I picked out one trout by the hearty glug-glug of his rises. I put the fly upstream, into an open notch in the willows, and let it slide out of sight. When the line tip twitched, I set the hook and had the fish solid. He came out grudgingly, ripped into the air magnificently, and ran downstream to Bob's pool.

Bob helped me release the fish. "As long as you're here, let's try that wet fly."

He wanted to hook one particularly snooty trout, so I explained the single fly technique, "Make it splash a few feet above him. Lift the rod slowly to take out slack, instead of pulling in line, but don't destroy the drift of the fly. Lower the rod and give back line as the fly drops downstream."

"Is this a dead drift?"

"Not really. There's the slightest bit of tension, enough to make the imitation struggle without cutting across current lanes."

He was on his own from then until dark. With the heart of a true skeptic, he experimented for the next few hours, changing back and forth, often over the same fish, from the Diving Caddis to the Emergent Sparkle Pupa. He discovered that preference the trout had for the wet fly, too.

Bob said afterwards, "I don't need anything except the Emergent on the Muskegon. I can almost always get twenty or more trout an evening. But I have to admit, here it's different."

"I'd bet that there are a lot of times on the Muskegon when the Diving Caddis would have the edge, too. Maybe because there aren't really anything except caddisflies here, and only a few types of them, the results are clearer, but the difference between the two patterns, and the shifts in preference from one to the other, have to be universal."

The caddisfly hatches had peaked a few weeks earlier on the upper Clark Fork. During the heaviest emergence times in June the Emergent Sparkle Pupa had been the better pattern (though there was an overlap of emerging insects and egg-laying insects on the water even then). By tonight the number of new insects hatching was sporadic at best, some popping all summer, but the adults from the earlier peak abundance were still around—as with many species of caddisflies they would live for many weeks. The females were still splashing on the stream and, carrying air bubbles as portable breathing units, swimming to the bottom to lay their eggs. The trout were seeing so many more adults than pupa that they chose the brighter and slimmer Diving Caddis wet fly.

> There are pockets of fishermen around the country who are strongly devoted to the Diving Caddis (and the wet fly strategy), but many of us are convinced that the only reason it isn't even more popular is because the times and places for using it overlap with the times and places for using the Emergent Sparkle Pupa.

Firecracker

For dry flies and emergers the negative and positive effects of fluorescent colors are linked to light intensity—in low light fluorescence attracts fish and in bright light it repels them. And this seems to happen no matter what the "color" is (remembering that the trout eye sees fluorescent colors differently than the human eye).

But what effect does fluorescence have on a sunken pattern? Once a fly is more than a foot deep, fluorescent colors provide a strong positive attraction throughout the day. The deeper the fly goes, the more important fluorescence becomes in determining success or failure (making these colors essential for sinking line techniques on lakes and ponds).

The purpose of my work was to find out *how much* fluorescence a fly needed to attract trout. There were patterns with blended colors—this might mean a fluorescent material chopped up and added to the dubbing, or a fluorescent hackle wound with a regular hackle. Either way the negative effects of fluorescence on trout were minimized (critical with dry flies or emergers). Other flies had solid fluorescent sections, but the "hot" portions constituted less than one third of the fly. This much fluorescence didn't repel fish on deep drifting nymphs. On the brightest flies, the fluorescent parts, solid blocks, might total nearly half of the visual package, but such gaudy displays were only practical on patterns fished with motion, the wet flies and streamers.

The key for the Firecracker—as it is with many bright flies—is the right amount of contrasting drabness. The strip of gray duck quill along the top edge of the wing defines the fluorescent center. The pattern is more effective with the gray section than without it, both on a fresh fly with wings married or on a bedraggled fly with the wings frayed.

Firecracker

TYING STEPS

1. Dub a fur body in a neat taper.

2. Marry the quill wings; seat the wings on the top of the hook shank.

3. Wrap a hen hackle.

Whip finish.

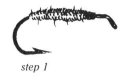

step 1

step 2

step 3

Hook: 10–16 (standard wet fly hook, TMC 9300)

Body: fur (dubbed in a neat taper)

Wing: married quill wing, one third gray duck on top and two thirds fluorescent duck on bottom

Hackle: hen (wrapped as a collar)

The main color variations for this pattern are the Orange Firecracker (cream body/gray and orange wing/brown hackle), Blue Firecracker (olive body/gray and light blue wing/dun hackle), Pink Firecracker (brown body/gray and pink wing/ginger hackle), and Chartreuse Firecracker (pale yellow body/gray and chartreuse wing/olive hackle).

Firecracker

LOG ENTRY: SEPTEMBER 28, 1990
MADISON RIVER

The Madison, like the Yellowstone, Jefferson, Big Hole, Smith, Missouri, Clark Fork, and Beaverhead, is mine in a very special way—fishing it for four years wouldn't have taught me as much as guiding on it for four years did. Someone who fishes a river uses his own bag of tricks over and over, but someone who guides on it learns from every client because every new person, even if he is following directions, brings himself to the day with his own flies, techniques, and strategies—and every smart guide is as much a student as a teacher.

My goal, on a heavily fished water such as the Madison, is always separation. Certain sections of a river can get stale during the rush hours. Those periods of heavy use are always the same, however, and it is possible to break away from the crowd. As a matter of fact, for really great fishing on the Madison, it is absolutely necessary to be different than the masses.

On the floating stretches the commercial boats all put in at one spot at a specified time and take out at another spot at a specified time. Naturally, like a bulge moving slowly down a snake, the guides and their clients are all pounding a particular section of the river at any given moment.

Whenever possible I would avoid the 9 o'clock put in and 5 o'clock take out by starting at 12:00 noon. Even giving the trout a three-hour rest, especially in areas seldom reached by wading anglers, made the fishing much more productive. Sometimes my clients couldn't stay on the water late, however, and I had no choice but to join the flotilla.

There was another way to separate. Every other boat drifted parallel to one bank or the other, the anglers pounding the shore with dry flies. The floaters ignored the middle of the stream because the trout out there were scattered. The chances of hooking a fish in the center, even with the lack of pressure, were less than at the banks.

The exception was a "slot." All an angler had to do to find a slot was kneel down and peer upstream. What looked like a giant riffle at first glance was really a series of benches and slides. These gradient changes, so obvious from a low angle, told something about trout populations in the middle of the river—the slides held very few decent fish and the benches, typically a hundred yards of perceptibly slower flow, held a lot of good fish, but they were still scattered over most of the area. The one place that had a concentration of trout was the slot at the base of every slide, a deeper trench going all the way across the river. It had everything, but most important, it had depth (and even an extra foot of it was critical in a shallow stream).

The first thing Larry Mostad said, after the introductions, was, "I hate this river."

Gene Mize said to me, "I told you that he must want to fish with us real bad if he agreed to come to the Madison."

Larry shrugged, "I'm sorry. It's just that it intimidates me."

"Nothing like this in Kansas?"

We were floating but not casting. Only wade fishing was allowed and the boat was just a way to hop from spot to spot. We pulled in a half mile below the access, a little further than most people are willing to walk, and started working attractor dry flies.

I made Larry get close to the water and look upstream. I started explaining about the slots, but he was getting excited on his own, "It's so easy to see the changes. I always thought it was all one speed."

It was still chilly, the last of the morning mist burning off the river. Larry worked half way across the slot with a Royal Wulff before he got his first strike. He seemed happy enough, going to shore to finally land his 17-inch brown.

"This is one of my best slots." I tied on a team of a size 14 Brown and Yellow Diving Caddis at the stretcher and a size 14 Orange Firecracker on the dropper, "It should fish better."

"That's all right. This is my biggest trout ever from the Madison."

The Madison couldn't have been designed more perfectly for the wet fly. There was plenty of room for casting, a steady current to swim the winged patterns, and a very few snags to hang the sweeping flies on. My line landed every time halfway up the slide, and with a few mends to keep the presentation dropping downstream, the flies swam into the slot showing their sides to any trout.

The wet flies easily out-fished the dry attractors from 9:00 a.m. until 11:00 a.m. It didn't matter who was using them because the three of us kept taking turns with my softer, slower rod. The wet flies fooled five trout to every one fooled by a dry fly—the Firecracker caught nine trout (the best a 16-inch rainbow) and the Diving Caddis caught five trout (the best a 19-inch brown). The tally would have been higher, but naturally it took Larry a few times to master the drift-and-swim technique.

At 11:00 a.m. everything switched around, of course. The dry flies started getting more strikes as soon as the first insects popped from the river. The Firecracker stopped catching anything, but the Diving Caddis still took the occasional fish.

The results of my summer/autumn wet fly experiments would have been more valid with a few more anglers flogging the water, but three of the best dropper-rig fishermen in my group couldn't make it to Montana in 1990. This left Gene Mize, superb at the technique, and me to work with the fluorescent wet flies. Here are the rough conclusions:

Early morning—

Best combination: Diving Caddis stretcher and Firecracker dropper (the wet flies out-fished dries and held their own against nymphs—the two wet flies together made the ultimate attractor, but the Firecracker usually out-fished the Diving Caddis).

Mood of the trout: The fish fed heavily at dawn (fishing was great with nymph patterns), but after that the drift rates of naturals was low and there was not much on the surface. The trout were actively looking but not feeding much.

Midday—

Best combination: Winged Hare's Ear stretcher and Diving Caddis dropper (no wet flies outperformed dry flies; feeding fish shied away from garish attractors).

Mood of the trout: The trout were feeding generally.

Late afternoon—

Best combination: Firecracker stretcher and Diving Caddis dropper (the Diving Caddis, imitating the actual egg-layers, always outfished any color Firecracker, but if anything came clear this autumn it was that a Firecracker and Diving Caddis combination did better than two Diving Caddis flies).

Mood of the trout: The trout fed more and more selectively as the evening caddis activity started.

Three

■

Nymphs

Are trout more selective or less selective to nymphs than to dry flies? Dry flies float in a world of light. That light, and the way it affects color, size, shape, and brightness, gives a trout a precise view at times of items on the surface. When there is more than one of any particular item—for example, when an important insect species hatches on a stream—the fish, from his specific vantage point, sees the same image over and over again. In the right conditions, mainly slow and clear water, he develops a search sequence, looking for various characteristics to appear in a certain order, and he rigidly selects a specific food form (or a matching fly).

Nymphs also depend on light to define color, size, shape, and brightness. But there is a major difference—a trout does not see nymphs in direct light. A trout feeds on insects drifting near the bottom by lining up at eye level with them. Most of the light striking those insects comes from the sides, the view of the fish, and is made up of scattered, reflected rays even in clear water. The strength of this diffused light depends partly on how deep nymphs are drifting. In shallow water, one or two feet, objects are bathed in light; in deep water, beyond two feet, the light gets progressively weaker.

The sequence of selecting or rejecting an item remains the same with a nymph or a dry fly. The trout looks forward for sunken food or up for floating food, but in either situation he searches for the first trait that tells him that this item is the one he is feeding on at the moment. This triggering characteristic (it triggers recognition) is the one he can see further away than any other. It is something unique to the food item. On a floating object that trigger (and this applies only to an object on top of the meniscus, not an emerger half out and half in it) is the first one to appear in the circular window of vision. On the sunken object that trigger is usually size—and the deeper the insect or the fly the more certain that that will be so. In weak light any item drifting in the current loses a lot of detail, the silhouette itself blurred by movement, but size remains a constant. When the insect or fly gets close to the fish, secondary characteristics such as color and shape become more important.

Once on the Green River in Utah a fish snubbed all my nymphs (including the fly that hooked every trout Emmett Heath sighted for me the

previous day). Emmett and Steve Horton stood high on the rocks watching the movements of this fussy gourmet. Jack Dennis, my ghillie for the moment, stood next to me in the current, making suggestions and handing me imitations. The patterns kept getting smaller and smaller, and the leader tippets kept getting thinner and thinner. After more than seventy drifts, with all of us reading his intentions each time, the trout made a serious move at the ninth fly, a size 22 olive mayfly match. He broke off from the pass at the last moment when the nymph slipped into a faster current to his side. He sipped the fly on the next drift as if he had been waiting for it.

Maybe this 23-inch brown was wise from a few catch-and-release moments. Or maybe he was simply involved in a period of very heavy feeding. No trout before or since in my fishing ever worked that selectively on bottom-drifting nymphs, but there was no doubt in my mind that size was the characteristic he locked onto in accepting or rejecting my flies.

At times trout feed as selectively on nymphs as they do on dry flies. In conditions with high visibility—shallow, clear, and slow water—they want impressionistic imitations ("perfect" being much different than "exact") of the drifting naturals. It is not possible to fish tough rivers effectively with just a few general nymphs—it is no fun trying to cover even easy waters without a good selection of subsurface flies.

Blackfly Larva

The trick of tying a piece of white thread or white horse hair onto the leader as a tippet is one of those ancient techniques proven successful by years of trial-and-error fishing. There is a wonderful little deception still practiced for brook trout in the small streams of Maine—wet fly fishermen snip the wings on a Black Gnat and tie on the white sewing thread.

Why does this trick work, though? If anyone ever knew the answer, it was lost back in those early wet fly days. The white thread obviously served as a triggering characteristic, but it was a mystery why it should have any effect on the success of an imitation.

I traveled through the brook trout regions of upper New England, asking questions to ferret out the history of the technique. I even found and talked to fly fishermen who still used the white thread tippet. Mostly, however, I studied those streams where the trick was especially effective.

On one brook in Vermont, where the white thread almost guaranteed good fishing, I put on a snorkel and pushed my face into the riffle. When my eyes adjusted to the light, I recognized strands of white silk billowing in the current. I yanked up a rock that was a squirming mass of blackfly larvae.

This insect, so abundant in streams in the spring, pastes a safety line to a rock. If it is swept away in the flow, the white silken excretion unfurls until the larva hangs taut. Then the insect draws in line to regain the hold.

The white thread on a fly advertised that vulnerability of the blackfly larva. With a new pattern that better imitated the secondary characteristics of the natural, and with knowledge based on an understanding of the insect, this "old" trick became a deadly deceit for fooling trout.

Blackfly Larva

TYING STEPS

1. Wind lead on the front half of the hook shank and lacquer it.

2. Wrap a piece of dark olive floss over the rear half of the hook; make a smooth taper (bowling pin shape).

step 1

3. Dub dark gray muskrat fur over the front half of the shank.

4. Wind a head of black ostrich herl or black marabou fibers.

Whip finish.

Hook:	16–20 (standard, 2X heavy nymph hook, TMC 3761)
Weight:	fine lead wire
Rear Body:	dark olive floss (wrap it over the back half of the hook)
Front Body:	dark gray (dubbed over the upper half of the hook shank)
Head:	black ostrich herl or black marabou

step 2

step 3

step 4

**LOG ENTRY: APRIL 9, 1990
MADISON RIVER**

The Madison fishes wonderfully during the early spring months; this is still winter fishing some years, but the river, benefiting from the controlled releases out of Hebgen Lake, is usually low and clear no matter what the weather.

There are parts of the Madison that have heavy populations of blackfly larvae *(Simulium tuberosum,* the common Buffalo Gnat). Why some patches do and other patches don't is a mystery to me, but the distribution of these insects might be connected to seepage into the river.

My discovery of one of those sections, right below a high bank of weeping springs, was not due to any wonderful speculation. The trout were just fussy enough to make me curious. They snubbed most of my best flies, occasionally grabbing whatever happened to be on my line at the moment out of charity. It was a trout here and a trout there all morning, most fairly small, but finally one rainbow was large enough to safely stomach pump.

My samplings over the years have turned up plenty of blackfly larvae in fish, but except in small brooks, no trout has ever been crammed exclusively with them. This rainbow today was full of insects, the larvae taken from high in the gullet still alive and seemingly very grateful for release back into the water.

Blackfly Larva Log

A size 18 Blackfly Larva, and a leader with the last 12 inches whitened with a Mean Streak marker, changed my day around those springs. The small fly didn't take a lot of monster fish, but it took the numbers. As usual with the white tippet, the trout hit the nymph harder than normal, too.

Downstream, away from the springs, the Blackfly Larva wasn't nearly so spectacular, but it still fooled trout and whitefish as well as any other nymph. Two 17-inch rainbows hanging along a bank, one after another, snatched the fly (but it would be wrong to characterize this in any way as a day for big fish—it seemed as if the 9- to 13-inch trout were feeling friskier in the chilly water).

In a few weeks, when the bigger fish start to prowl, it might be wise to hit the Madison again. They will still want small flies, and the Blackfly Larva *should* be a good trick for finding feeding trout (it has always worked well on rainbows).

It is possible to use an 18-inch length of strong sewing thread for a tippet, but it is difficult to tie this to modern monofilament. It is easier to just rub a Mean Streak marker (made by the Stanford Corporation) along the last section of leader.

Actually, this "revelation" about the effectiveness of the small blackfly imitation and the white leader tippet disturbs me. There are at least a dozen other entries in my logs over the years with a note something like, "Isn't it time to start using the 'white tippet' more, with either a blackfly larva pattern or a caddisfly larva pattern, as a general searching technique?"

The real question is, "Does it ever hurt to use the white tippet with a nymph?" I don't have the answer.

Cased Caddis Larva

Why are the case-making caddisfly larvae so seldom imitated by anglers? The facts from entomologists and fish biologists indicate that this is the one food form that fly fishermen *must* be ready to match. Case-makers, with houses of stone or vegetable matter, live in all types of trout water. Fish feed on them selectively at particular times and in particular habitats. Even without professional studies showing when and where trout concentrate on these larvae, an angler has to wonder about those sticks and stones that end up in the stomachs of fish.

Cased Caddis Larva

In still waters the larvae inhabit weed beds. Early in the spring certain species, when they migrate from deeper water into the shallows, get air bubbles trapped inside their cases and float to the surface. Even on the bottom this trip is perilous for the larvae, exposing them to predators. In many cold-water lakes the case-makers rank as the most important food item—more important than midges, damselflies, scuds, or leeches—for a full month of the early season (see the 1971 study by M. J. Winterbourn, "The Life Histories and Trophic Relationships of the Trichoptera of Marion Lake, British Columbia," *Canadian Journal of Zoology*, 49 (5): 637-45).

In streams the larvae drift with the currents, case and all. Like most aquatic insects they have fluctuations in daily drift rates—sometimes there are a lot of them available to the trout and at other times there are very few. This phenomenon, behavioral drift, controls which nymphs fish eat more than any other factor. Trout grub the bottom very inefficiently, so when insects are not drifting free in the currents hungry trout look to the surface for food.

There are two kinds of drift—catastrophic and behavioral. Catastrophic drift is as unpredictable as the name suggests. A catastrophe, as localized as a wading angler or as widespread as a flood, disrupts the bottom and flushes insects into the current. Behavioral drift, in contrast, is very predictable. As the

Cased Caddis Larva

nymphal or larval population of a species matures, the prime microhabitat for that species gets crowded. The excess individuals in that population disperse to new areas by drifting downstream with the current.

Most insects drift in higher numbers during the night, rates peaking after dusk and before dawn. This group includes mayfly nymphs, stonefly nymphs, and free-living caddisfly larvae (oddly enough, these night-active nymphs and larvae are the ones strongly represented in the angler's fly box). These imitations are important at specific times, especially when a particular species nears emergence, but as a daily food source the case-making larvae make a more sensible model for the nymph fisherman. These larvae, many of them sizable insects, drift at their highest rates during the day. That is when trout see them; and that is when the overwhelming majority of anglers dead drift nymph patterns.

The fly fisherman's box of imitations should contain rows of cased caddis larva patterns. There should be a range of sizes from at least 2 to 18, a variety of shapes and trims from square and smooth to round and ragged, and an assortment of case colors from light to dark. No matter what the shape or color of the case on the fly, there has to be a hint of body color, a band of pale yellow, pale pink, or pale olive just behind the head. These flies should be the main choice, not an oddity, for nymphing streams.

There is another important phenomenon with cased caddis larvae. At least two major genera, the Little Tan Short-Horn Sedge (*Glossosoma* sp.) and the Giant Orange Sedge (*Dicosmoecus* sp.), abandon their cases in mass and drift naked in the current. This happens during the daytime, too. It is not a rare event, but it is not as predictable as the normal, daily drift. When it occurs, the trout gorge on the pale olive, pale pink, or pale yellow caddis larvae flooding the currents.

Special flies for these uncased insects resemble the regular free-living larval imitations, just a bit stubbier in appearance, but the colors are much more striking on these patterns. The olive, pink, and yellow variations match the fresh brightness of a rare food item—one with no protective coloration whatsoever.

TYING STEPS

1. Wrap lead wire on the rear two-thirds of the hook shank; lacquer the wire.

2. Tie in soft hackle feathers (partridge, grouse, etc.); wrap them; trim them to desired shape.

3. Dub a section of fur.

4. Tie in soft hackle fibers as a beard hackle.

Whip finish.

step 1

step 2

step 3

step 4

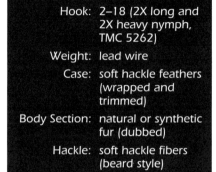

Hook:	2–18 (2X long and 2X heavy nymph, TMC 5262)
Weight:	lead wire
Case:	soft hackle feathers (wrapped and trimmed)
Body Section:	natural or synthetic fur (dubbed)
Hackle:	soft hackle fibers (beard style)

LOG ENTRY: AUGUST 23, 1990
GALLATIN RIVER

My favorite stretch is outside of Bozeman, below the confluence of the East Fork and the West Fork. This is a river that meanders, cutting deep into the banks—and, of course, it hides a lot of brown trout.

Lump me with the great majority of fly fishermen who settle into a comfortable rut on most days. It is so easy to wade or float along a stream, slapping a particular pattern on every piece of water. Some spots are right for a fly and some spots are wrong for it, but it is just too much trouble to change setups for even the best looking places.

Today was different. Ambition ruled—somehow it usually does on my trips to the Gallatin. I get so few chances to fish this river; and yet the water thrills me, even though it isn't the bouncing pool and riffle configuration that most anglers consider the ideal trout stream. The darker, deeper cuts of this river, the gradient less in the valley flood plain, make anticipation a part of every cast.

My fishing logs from past years record spectacular days on the stream (and, oddly, not a single poor one): Aug. 1973 with Ken and Steve Parkany—a 25 fish day; Oct. 1976 with Marlon Strick on a night fishing trip—a brown trout over eight pounds on a White Deer Hair Moth; Sept. 1984 with Marc Brannon and Peter Ingraldi—not only a lot of trout, but most of the fish were between 15 and 20 inches. Such an unbroken string of great days has been due more to luck than skill.

I used a Flex Hopper on the open flows, letting the jointed hook waggle with the dead drift (as usual browns found this especially tantalizing). But on the overgrown banks I switched to a more aerodynamic Henry's Fork Hopper, bouncing this fly with a skip cast as far back as possible into the wood tangles.

Cased Caddis Larva Log

It's unusual for me to change patterns that much during an afternoon, continually snipping off one for another, occasionally repairing a leader tippet. The fishing was so fast for nice trout that on any other river it would have put me into a grinning, mindless stupor. But this was the Gallatin.

Even Graham Marsh, who knows my routine as well as anyone, said, "You're possessed. This river owns you. You fish one way on Big Spring Creek, another way on the Big Hole. On Rock Creek you're always very relaxed. Here you try to squeeze out everything the river can give you."

I did something that I never do on a fishing day. At every big back eddy I switched tackle completely, clipping off whichever hopper happened to be on the leader, winding up the floating line, and changing reel spools to one with a sinking line. Then I tied on a weighted, roughly trimmed, size 6 Cased Caddis Larva.

Out of curiosity I timed this changeover. Without rushing the process at all it took a bit more than two minutes. Two minutes is small cost for the chance to work a piece of water properly. The fact that dry flies drew no strikes out of these large eddies forced me to make an either-or decision—either rig tackle for slow water or skip the deep backwaters entirely.

Our main spot for scuba diving in the Big Hole, the Bridge Abutment Pool, taught us that trout act more like lake fish than river fish in the large eddies. There the current roars down a chute, dividing the hole, but on either side of the flume the water spins off into reverse flows. The eddies swirl slowly on top, but the force nearly disappears near the bottom. Trout in the backwater cruise like lake fish, nose into whatever slight current there is, circling and feeding a few inches off the leaf-and-stick litter of the bed.

On the Gallatin the Cased Caddis Larva pattern served as a slow water imitation. The sinking line carried everything below the spinning surface flow. Then it was my job to count down until the fly was skimming the bottom debris. An excruciatingly slow retrieve moved the fly along almost like the natural crawler.

All of the trout struck hard, and this surprised me so much that the first two fish broke off the fly. I wasn't going to wait for my nerves to settle, so I tied an 18-inch piece of shock gum rubber into the leader. The timing was perfect because the next trout, a 24½-inch brown, slammed the Cased Caddis hard, too.

All of the backwater trout were big. On the four eddies where I changed tackle the counts were: (1) two browns (best of 24½ inches), (2) no fish, but a big one pulled free after a long run, (3) five browns and two rainbows, (4) two browns and one rainbow.

No other technique, neither dry fly nor streamer, worked on these fish. A Cased Caddis Larva, with as slow a retrieve as possible, excited the trout. In slack water, where case-making larvae congregate, fish recognized a moving house of sticks, natural or artificial, as a chunk of food and ate the case and all.

Cat's Ear

There are a lot of cats in my house. Some I know well; others are only vaguely familiar. They show up at the back gate and spot the two watch dogs, a lab-shepherd cross and a Doberman-shepherd cross, and somehow they know that these canines have been slapped around by cats ever since they were puppies. The strays strut up to the porch and take their place at the feeding dish. The dogs watch them faithfully.

My favorite cat is an eight-year-old, twelve-pound neutered male that has been in the family since he was a kitten. He is a common, "gray tiger" color. His hair is fascinating, each strand a barred whited, black, and gray pattern. No one remembers his original name—everyone calls him Patches.

The gray variegation on the Cat's Ear Nymph works as wonderfully as the brown variegation on the Hare's Ear Nymph. The broken up pattern of colors, especially when the main one is drab, lulls any doubts a feeding trout might have about the fly. There is nothing unusual about these patterns, nothing that would attract or distract a fish that is actively picking the drift line. The Cat's Ear and the Hare's Ear are both tremendously consistent underwater searching flies.

Cat's Ear

Cat's Ear

step 1

step 2

step 3

step 4

step 5

TYING STEPS

1. Tie in a short tail of guard hairs.

2. Dub a thin abdomen of cat's fur.

3. Tie a section of mallard feather; let it dangle for the moment.

4. Dub a rough thorax of cat's fur (pick it out).

5. Pull the section of mallard feather forward and tie it down as a wing case (leave the stubs exposed).

Whip finish.

Hook:	6–20 (standard nymph hook, TMC 3761)
Tail:	the longer guard hairs from a "gray tiger" cat
Abdomen:	dubbing from a "gray tiger" cat
Wing Case:	section of mallard feather
Thorax:	dubbing from a "gray tiger" cat (pick out for a long and rough appearance)

**LOG ENTRY: JULY 10, 1972
LOLO CREEK**

In 1972, while my wife attended graduate school at the University of Montana, our home was a trailer court a hundred yards from this stream. Lolo was my everyday stream—my log that season records seventy-two fishing days on this Bitterroot River tributary.

Why trout will take a gray nymph and not a brown nymph, or vice versa, is beyond me. It seems that in rich environments steadily feeding fish can get very choosy about the secondary characteristics of sunken patterns. Sometimes a particular insect species is drifting in heavy numbers, a common occurrence a few days before an abundant mayfly emergence, but at other times samplings show a hodgepodge bouncing along in the current and trout can still show a strong preference for one color or the other.

Lolo Creek is a rich environment. It receives a lot of its flow from springs, both cold and hot, but unlike a 100 percent spring creek it has a diverse insect community. There are good populations of caddisflies, mayflies, stoneflies, and two-winged flies. On any July evening various species of these insects hatch in one pleasant grab bag for the trout. But during the middle of the day in July the fish choose a gray nymph over any other color (just as a month earlier, in June, they chose a brown nymph over any other color). Fishing Lolo Creek so much for two seasons tells me this.

My day started at the first pool, the big one right above the highway bridge. It is the only hole large enough to hold a school of whitefish. Many fly fishermen don't even fish this spot, figuring that it is dominated by the whitefish and suckers. My largest trout have always come from here, though.

The whitefish are the secret. When they stack up in the riffle at the head grubbing nymphs, their bodies flashing silver as they nose and twist among the rocks, a catch of three or four nice brown trout is a sure thing. The trick is to cast and drift the fly over the school without catching a whitefish.

I threw a size 14 Cat's Ear too far upstream, giving the nymph time to sink to the feeding level of the school, and caught a strong, 16-inch whitefish. I released him carefully and tried again, making the nymph plop right behind the school. On the fifth cast the fly slid into the slower, deeper pool, the line tip twitched, and with the set of the hook a trout burst upstream and scattered the pack of whitefish.

I was supposed to stop him, of course, keeping him down in the lower water. It was a rainbow, not a brown, though, and that surprised me. Instead of starting with a strong sweep sideways, he jumped and ran up into the riffle. I landed him and forgave him for ruining the pool because, at 18 inches, he was my biggest rainbow ever from Lolo Creek.

I've caught hundreds of browns by working a nymph behind grubbing schools of whitefish, and on occasion, with a big stonefly nymph, even bull trout, but this was the first rainbow.

For those of us who need to speculate there may be an entomological reason for the trout's preference for a gray nymph during July on Lolo. There is a good population of Gray Drakes *(Siphlonurus occidentalis)* in the slower, bottom portion of the stream. The nymphs, which have a strong, grayish cast, are especially active in the month before they hatch.

This pattern is not a part of a commerical series. It is an example of what the tyer can—and should—do with materials available in his own house. The secret is the ability to recognize which materials are special.

VARIATIONS:

Metal, with its unnatural glitter, isn't my favorite material for nymphs. Even the famous Gold Ribbed Hare's Ear gets refusals by critical trout.

A blend of half gray sparkle yarn and half gray tiger cat hair makes a Sparkling Cat's Ear. A blend of half brown sparkle yarn and half mottled brown hare's mask hair, likewise, makes a Sparkling Hare's Ear. These brighter variations work well in deep, rough water or in slightly tinged water, anywhere that visibility is a bonus.

> The whitefish are the secret. When they stack up in the riffle at the head grubbing nymphs, their bodies flashing silver as they nose and twist among the rocks, a catch of three or four nice brown trout is a sure thing. The trick is to cast and drift the fly over the school without catching a whitefish.

Cranefly Larva

The major trout stream craneflies (family Tipulidae) are not really aquatic insects. With few exceptions they are semi-aquatic, burrowing in the decaying leaf packs and the muck of stream banks. They breathe atmospheric oxygen. During the larval stage they rarely wash out into the currents. They are worthless to fly fishermen as models for general imitation.

The feeding study in *Caddisflies,* with stomach samplings from more than 2,000 fish, proved how seldom trout see cranefly larvae. The Missouri, the research site, while not a spectacular cranefly river like the upper Clark Fork, the Beaverhead, or the Lewis (in Yellowstone National Park), still provided a good habitat for the insect. An entire summer of sampling found only a few immature craneflies in all those stomachs.

It takes a catastrophe to dump a number of those fat larvae into the flow. Almost any disaster that wipes out the banks of a stream also ruins the fishing, but it doesn't really take the destruction of the river bank to free the cranefly larvae. Any sudden rise in the water level pushes the current against fresh earth and dislodges the loose detritus.

All the feeding studies on normal days mean nothing for spate conditions. During high water trout gorge on many strange invertebrates, food they never see otherwise, but in certain rivers the cranefly larvae enter the drift in such great numbers that fish focus strictly on them.

Cranefly Larva

TYING STEPS

1. Wrap the lead wire over the front half of the shank and lacquer it.

2. Tie in a piece of green floss; let it dangle for the moment.

3. Dub a rough body of green craft fur (tapered to a thicker front).

4. Wrap the green floss as a rib.

5. Chop up white marabou, twist it in a dubbing loop, and dub the fibers; trim them.

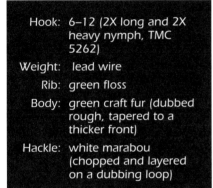

Hook:	6–12 (2X long and 2X heavy nymph, TMC 5262)
Weight:	lead wire
Rib:	green floss
Body:	green craft fur (dubbed rough, tapered to a thicker front)
Hackle:	white marabou (chopped and layered on a dubbing loop)

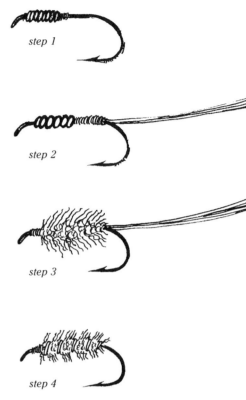

step 1

step 2

step 3

step 4

step 5

LOG ENTRY: APRIL 18, 1991
UPPER CLARK FORK RIVER

The river bottom itself supports mostly caddisfly larvae in this upper water, but the soft earth banks hold huge numbers of cranefly larvae. Most of the time these insects are unavailable to the trout, but occasionally they get washed out of the muck and into the open currents.

It is worth mentioning the adult cranefly on this river. At dawn during August the water looks like it has an orange haze as insects swarm for mating and egg-laying. Trout feed boisterously on the adults, often jumping into the air for them, and an Orange Skating Spider bounced on the surface catches fish in grand, exciting fashion.

There is one catastrophe for aquatic nymphs that is very predictable. The local newspaper gives anglers a few days warning in its weather report. During most years in Montana a false spring, an unseasonably warm spell, pops during March or April. The high temperatures, in the sixties or seventies, even reach the mountain valleys and a pulse of snowmelt raises the level of the river. In the best years the higher water is not enough to muddy the river, just tinge it a bit, and trout feed heavily on a sudden flush of free-drifting food.

One spring Galen Wilkins and I stretched out a kick net to see what was in the Clark Fork. Galen moved upstream to stir up the bottom, but before he even got into position the face of the net was dark with writhing life.

Cranefly Larva Log

We hauled it out onto the bank and checked the organisms. In less than a minute twenty-six cranefly larvae and seventeen aquatic worms, plus a few midge larvae and net-making caddisfly larvae, had collected in a 2-foot wide and 1½-foot long mesh.

I have missed this spring flush the last two years on my home rivers. With all my traveling this season for speaking and shows I thought for certain that I would miss it again, but the wind died, the sky cleared, the sun shone, and the air warmed—the classic high pressure system needed for a flush—and I knew that if the weather held for a few days the river would freshen up.

Even last night was warm, never dropping below 45 degrees F., and by 10:00 a.m. the river level was up eight inches on the government gauge in town. The Clark Fork, largely spring fed, was tinged only slightly, but the water washed against the undercuts.

I was grumbling to myself about having to fish alone when the telephone rang. It was Warren Lumbley, who comes out every season from Tennessee, and he was at the Butte airport on a one day layover. "I was hoping that we could tie some flies together," he said.

"No. We're going fishing, Warren."

"I don't have any tackle. I didn't expect to fish. After all, it's only April."

"I'll have everything you'll need."

We started fishing at 1:00 p.m. The river by now was a soupier brown, and Warren stood in one of the last snow banks, looking at the water, not understanding at all my excitement for this day. He shivered a bit, "The only thing I don't miss about summer right now is the crowds."

I strung a cork indicator up his leader and pinned it with a piece of toothpick. "Trust me. Run this cranefly nymph from the riffles into the heads of the pools and down the slots against the banks."

I left Warren, having full faith in his fishing abilities, and staked out my own stretch of the river. The section we were on was right above Deer Lodge, where spring seeps enter the Clark Fork every quarter mile or so, and although the river isn't known for holding huge fish, just incredible numbers, this was an area with the occasional brute brown trout.

The action started immediately for me, with a lot of 12-inch to 16-inch fish. My best spurt with larger trout came at the slot just below the big spring coming in at Renfield's place, the old junkyard, with two 16-inch fish, one 17-inch fish, and a 19-inch fish. They were all browns, of course— from Warm Springs all the way to the mouth of Gold Creek there is virtually nothing except browns. They all took a size 8 Cranefly Larva.

Warren worked his way downstream to me, not walking the bank but wading and fishing, grinning like a fool with every hookup. "I couldn't catch this many fish in a hatchery. I've been getting about twenty an hour. How many days does this cranefly flush last?"

"Three or four at most. Something will happen. Either a real thaw will flood the river, or a hard freeze will clear it and drop the level."

"Do you mind if I stay a few days?"

"That's one more person praying. Here's what we want—cool nights, just below freezing, to delay the runoff early in the day, and then gradually warming mornings that start the river inching up."

We came home and tied nymphs, one person wrapping and lacquering lead on the hooks, the other winding a thick, rough dubbing. With this production line we popped off a few dozen size 8 Cranefly Larva flies each for tomorrow's fishing.

We hauled the kick net out onto the bank and checked the organisms. In less than a minute twenty-six cranefly larvae and seventeen aquatic worms, plus a few midge larvae and net-making caddisfly larvae, had collected in a 2-foot wide and 1½-foot long mesh.

Diving Water Boatman

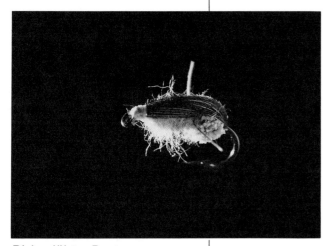

Diving Water Boatman

During the 1976 spring thaw the drive over the dirt roads to check the pond became a ritual, a performance necessary every five days or so to ease the tensions of a fishless winter. By late April, the snow had melted, puddles were collecting on the ice, and small wedges of open water were forming in the shallows. Finally a warm wind arrived in the hollow, breaking up the cracked shell ice and mixing the waters of the pond.

At the Dredge Ponds I trudged over the soggy meadow, bypassing the lower basin. After circling the hulks of gold-dredging machinery, I climbed a waste pile of gravel and sat there to watch the welcome spectacle of 20-inch fish cruising the shallow cove below. Eventually, satisfied that the feeding binge was in progress this year, I snuck down to the edge.

Some stones rattled off the hill on the opposite bank, where a man and woman were walking along the crest. They stopped and stared at me, clinging to their spinning rods and cans of bait. My thoughts were a bit selfish, triggered by a fear that they would come down and scare everything back to deeper water.

They sat on the rocks, watching me until I landed the third brown trout on the new water boatman imitation. "I've been fishing this spot for three days," the man said loudly to the woman. He stood up and more stones clattered down the slope, popping along the edge of the water and scattering the trout. "The son-of-a-bitch comes here and makes it look easy."

"Easy?" I yelled as they started to walk away, wanting to run up there and tell him about the four fishless years here, the long days of frustration when these same trout snubbed every fly, the experimental patterns and techniques that had failed.

"I never caught anything," he shouted at me as he left.

At various times during the year, a common aquatic true-bug—the water boatman (family Corixidae in the order Hemiptera)—becomes the prevalent food form for trout in numerous ponds and lakes around the country. The insect goes through a developmental cycle that includes an egg, five nymphal stages, and the adult. The adult over winters—not in the pond itself if it freezes over, but in headwater, spring-fed streams—and mates in early spring.

All our studies of trout feeding preferences in ponds revealed an amazing summertime gap—the fish were eating water boatmen in the spring and fall, but during the summer one or two might show up in a sampling of a dozen trout. During mid-season the insects stayed in the weedy shallows, exposed only to smaller fish (and not a single water boatman ever turned up in a trout smaller than 10 inches, and only trout larger than 15 inches ever ate a lot of them).

The incredible feeding binges occur in the spring. The adult water boatmen return to the newly thawed ponds, flying as far as ten miles. They hit the surface with a splat, buzz in circles to break through the surface tension, and swim for the bottom. The insects usually choose shallow coves or edges, seldom open water, for a landing area. The trout come from all over the lake and crowd into a cove, rushing the insects just as they crash onto the surface film.

The fall feeding is more general. Any insect sampling late in the season, especially after the *Callibaetis* hatch, turns up few large nymphs, but each sweep of the net scoops up hundreds of active water boatmen. When the weed beds start dying back with shorter, colder days, all of those insects are suddenly exposed.

Water boatmen do not have the nasty reputation of other true bugs, the back swimmers (Notonectidae) and giant water bugs (Belostomatidae). Those insects are also piercer/carnivores, feeding by inserting a stinger into a victim and dissolving its insides to liquid—the sting of a giant water bug, especially, can bring tears to the eyes of a strong man. The water boatmen cannot penetrate the skin of a hand so easily.

Graham Marsh found out why small trout do not feed on water boatmen. As he swept up a handful of them off our collection net to lift them into the aquarium, he squeezed them in the creases of his palm. Maybe this gave the insects enough push to puncture the skin. Graham opened his hand with a yelp and a curse. The welts on his palm showed that water boatmen, pressed inside the tender folds of a throat, might present a problem for a fish.

In the aquarium we watched the nymphs and adults (exactly alike in appearance) chug along the surface, replenish their air supply by sticking their back ends upwards, and then dash in slanting dives back to the weeds.

Diving Water Boatman

We listed the visible characteristics of the insect that might control trout selectively—the shimmer of enveloping air globules, size, shape, and color. But there was more—the most important recognition factor for trout, advertising a vulnerable moment, was the peculiar tip up and swim down display by a water boatman at the surface.

Graham Marsh and I sat down at the fly tying bench, putting together prototypes and dropping them into the water. Finally, we constructed an imitation that tipped head first and sank—a pattern that would "dive" with the proper rod manipulation.

TYING STEPS

1. Wrap the lead wire over the front half of the hook shank; lacquer it.

2. Tie in pheasant tail fibers; let them dangle for the moment.

3. Spin a rear body of deer hair; trim into a ball.

4. Pull two pheasant tail fibers forward, one on each side of the hook, and tie them down and back as legs.

5. Dub the sparkle yarn front body shaggily.

6. Pull the remaining pheasant tail fibers forward and tie them down as a back.

Whip finish.

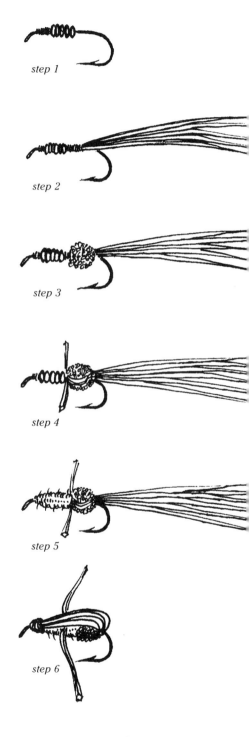

step 1

step 2

step 3

step 4

step 5

step 6

Hook:	14–18 (1X fine wire hook, TMC 5210)
Weight:	fine lead wire wrapped over the front half of the hook shank
Back:	pheasant tail fibers
Rear Body:	spun deer hair (back third)
Front Body:	gold sparkle yarn (front two thirds, dubbed shaggy)
Legs:	two pheasant tail fibers (one on each side)

LOG ENTRY: MAY 1, 1991
GOLD CREEK DREDGE PONDS

These are not natural ponds. Just as the name states, they were created in a gold dredging operation that peaked in the 1930s—the Gold Creek drainage was the site of the first gold strike in Montana in 1852.

This fly has taken trout for me on still waters from one coast to the other, but nothing makes me happier than coming back with it to the Dredge Ponds. The appearance of the natural water boatmen, arriving in massive flights each spring, triggers the only predictable spree of fast and easy fishing on these ponds all year.

There are two ponds. The upper one has mostly cutthroat trout and the lower one has mostly brown trout. Each of them, surrounded by huge mounds of rock rubble, has areas over thirty feet deep—and these are not large ponds. The configuration is the result of the gold dredging; and it makes both of these spots extremely fickle. They are rich enough, over the years the lower pond giving up an eighteen-pound brown and the up-

Diving Water Boatman Log

per pond giving up an eleven-pound cutthroat to fishermen, but when the trout disappear into an abyss no method works particularly well on these waters.

One late summer evening I was out on the lower pond in a float tube, working the edge of the drop-off with a damsel nymph, hoping for one or two nice fish, when a fall of flying ants covered the surface. Within minutes the entire pond was boiling with rising trout. I switched to a floating line and a matching fly and started catching one brown after another, the fish a hodgepodge of sizes from 10 inches to 22 inches.

That was the last time I ever doubted the incredible trout populations in these fisheries (no matter how rudely they treated me on most of my visits).

I have been on a roll here, coming out three times this week. Each afternoon the water boatmen have flown in, groups of them returning from the winter sanctuary, and trout have moved into the shallow back cove of the lower pond to feed on the insects. The Diving Water Boatman has been fooling on the average a half-dozen browns over 15 inches per trip.

> The Diving Water Boatman took three cut-throats, the best being seventeen inches, and slipped off the lips of a few others. Maybe those fish were nipping not only the fly but the naturals on purpose, a cautious taste of a stinging insect—it was unusual for me to lose that many trout in a lake.

So why didn't I just go back to the lower pond? There was the question of challenge. There was nothing more for me to learn about that spot. But the upper pond? It was still a mystery. I had to find out if the water boatmen were landing there, also.

On the upper pond there is a shallow, weedy cove next to the road, but out of sight, at the end of a twisting, narrow neck, there is a steep-sided, seemingly bottomless bowl. This deep area supposedly hides a few, very large cutthroats.

I was sitting out in the deep water, paddling around the bowl in my tube, when the first insects splatted along the edges and up into the neck. The water boatmen crashed, buzzed, and dove pretty much unmolested around me, but one fish took an occasional bug far up in the channel. I kicked in until my feet were actually dragging in the weeds. I had to start retrieving immediately after the cast, instead of letting the fly tip and sink on its own, but a 16-inch cutthroat took the imitation trustingly enough.

I was just slipping that first fish back when something chugged behind me. Sitting so low in the water, one of the disadvantages of a float tube, I couldn't spot any trout cruising the drop-off, but in a moment a fish rolled at the edge of the weeds.

The sink-tip line hit and started to drift downwards. The fly, well wetted by now, broke through the surface film and tipped head first. Two strips into the retrieve a large fish hit the diving fly—it wasn't a monster trout, but with him going one direction and the swimming imitation the other, the hook pulled through some soft skin and popped free.

At the mouth of the channel, where there were a number of nice fish rolling, the Diving Water Boatman took three cutthroats, the best being seventeen inches, and slipped off the lips of a few others. Maybe those fish were nipping not only the fly but the naturals on purpose, a cautious taste of a stinging insect—it was unusual for me to lose that many trout in a lake.

Then something much bigger rolled on the fly. This one went towards the middle of the bowl, going deeper every second—he must have been near the bottom because he was well into the backing. I maneuvered the float tube almost directly over him and began lifting him up, but he kept swimming around and around the tube. When he came close enough to see me kicking in the water, he pulled line out on another plunge.

These Dredge Pond cutthroats have always been strong fighters, but when I netted the trout I was a little disappointed. Maybe my dreams were too full of 11-pound monsters; this one was a prize, weighing 4 pounds 11 ounces in the net, but he had battled hard enough to make any brown or rainbow of similar size proud.

I gave myself a slap for being ungrateful. He was, after all, almost 2 pounds heavier than my previous best fish from the upper pond. More important, he gave me hope for the future by proving that a few big ones still exist in that pit.

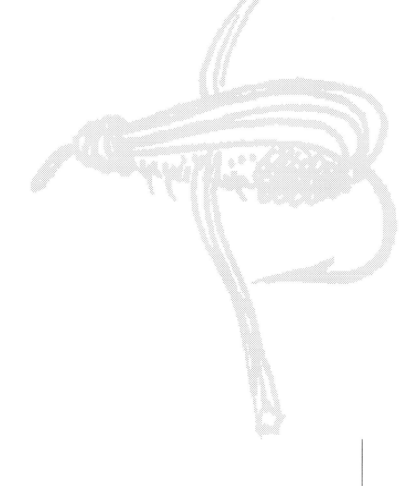

Floating Caddis Larva

There are patterns that are never going to be used a lot—the Flying Ant, the Foam Inch Worm, the Spruce Moth. They are designed for specific situations during a season. The need may pop up once or twice at most. But how can anyone who is on the water all the time risk not having such a fly? The insects that these patterns match are not random, not bugs that end up on or in the water occasionally, one here and one there throughout the season. These insects appear for brief periods of time in such numbers that trout gorge on them selectively for as long as they are available.

Floating Caddis Larva

The Floating Caddis Larva, although it comes from the water and not the land, belongs with those more recognized forms. The fly matches the larva of a case-making caddisfly, the Great Late-Summer Sedge (*Onocosmoecus* sp.), an insect widespread and abundant in still waters throughout the Northwest.

In late spring, soon after ice-out, the *Onocosmoecus* larvae migrate into the shallows. They get air bubbles trapped inside their cases and float to the surface in such numbers that clumps of a hundred or more individuals drift on the lake. These larvae are so vulnerable that trout feed on almost nothing else for days at a time.

The angler faces a simple equation with any of these sporadic food sources: No fly equals few fish (and incredible frustration as trout rise all around).

TYING STEPS

1. Spin the case of the insect with deer hair; trim the hair rough and shaggy.

2. Wrap or dub a short section of dubbing or chenille just in front of the deer hair (this section is on the bent part of the hook).

3. Tie in a beard hackle of grouse feather fibers.

Whip finish.

step 1

step 2

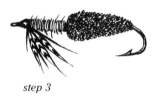

step 3

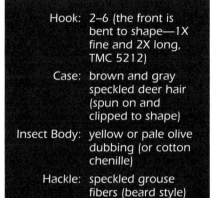

Hook:	2–6 (the front is bent to shape—1X fine and 2X long, TMC 5212)
Case:	brown and gray speckled deer hair (spun on and clipped to shape)
Insect Body:	yellow or pale olive dubbing (or cotton chenille)
Hackle:	speckled grouse fibers (beard style)

LOG ENTRY: MAY 20, 1991
GEORGETOWN LAKE

In the late 1940s this lake was nationally famous—and why not? The rainbow trout averaged almost five pounds. Then the Fish & Game, in their infinite wisdom, slowly turned this naturally rich lake into a put-and-take fishery for bait fishermen. The trout by the mid-1980s averaged eleven inches.

There is nothing wrong with having a place where a family can go and catch hatchery trout. Turn a sterile lake into a put-and-take fishery. Why destroy Georgetown, one of the greatest natural trout producers in the state?

Finally, a very fine biologist was transferred to this area. Wayne Hadley changed the regulations and the stocking practices on Georgetown. The result was an immediate increase in the size of the fish—the Kamloop rainbows especially flourished, some of them growing to ten pounds in three years. The lake was on its way back to glory.

There is a quote from a professional study, "The Life Histories and Trophic Relationships of the Trichoptera of Marion Lake, British Columbia," by Michael Winterbourn, that should be tattooed on every lake fisherman's chest: "The May stomach samples [of Kamloop rainbows] were dominated by *Onocosmoecus* cased larvae."

Floating Caddis Larva Log

Why do I say this? No one knows this study (and its observations of larvae on the surface) better than me, but who was caught out on Georgetown yesterday without the right fly? The only pattern that caught trout was a rough, heavily greased Hare's Ear nymph.

The nice part about fly fishing is that a man can look like an idiot one day and a genius the next. A poor outing is not failure—it is preparation. Tie flies, adapt tackle, plot strategies. Then go back and wreak havoc on those uppity trout.

The fish were not spread randomly across the lake. This close to spawning, the Arlee rainbows (a hatchery strain that produces eggs in the fall) were drawing close to the tributaries, around places such as Stuart Mill Bay and the Pump House, but they were also stacked up feeding in the slop lines within these general areas.

> The slop lines are easy enough to spot on a windy day. They are not only flat but also scummy. The currents draw all kinds of surface matter into the lane—debris, foam, and drifting insects. The greatest part of any lake is devoid of fish, but the one feature that always attracts trout is a slop line.

A slop line, or wind lane, is always the secret with floating cased larvae. The lane, a ribbon of flat water mysteriously persevering amidst the waves, collects drifting food (and the food attracts trout). This is a physical phenomenon, and it is predictable. The water in the lane flattens out because there are vertical convection currents in a lake, looping from bottom to top. When these currents hit the surface, they drive back downwards, pulling the waves right off the water and creating a slop line.

The slop lines are easy enough to spot on a windy day. They are not only flat but also scummy. The currents draw all kinds of surface matter into the lane—debris, foam, and drifting insects. The greatest part of any lake is devoid of fish, but the one feature that always attracts trout is a slop line.

Wendell Arnett brought his boat up again to the lake. We moved to the windward side, watching all the time for surface activity. Even when we found a great wind lane and set up twenty-five feet away, we couldn't see any obvious slopping in the scum. Finally, with binoculars, Wendell picked up some gentle rises at the upper end.

It was my first choice for the fishing. Wendell maneuvered the boat to the top and just feathered the electric motor to maintain distance. The point was to let the boat drift downwind parallel to the lane. There was no doubt about the fly after the previous day's stomach samplings. The pattern was a size 8 Floating Caddis Larva, fished with a long leader and a cork strike indicator.

The trout may not have been showing, but they were there. The first drift with the boat, over 150 yards, produced four rainbows for me (best of eighteen inches). They were fat, Arlee-strain fish. Only one jumped, but they all ran strong. This early in the year there wasn't the weed growth they love to dig into during a fight.

Wendell just used my rod, with the same set up, when it was his turn. He had a handicap—my boat handling. This lake drift technique was new to me, and it was hard for me to keep the perfect distance and speed. He was incredibly patient, whispering suggestions as the boat careened down the lane.

Thank God he hooked a Kamloop. That alleviated my guilt. As strong as those Arlee-strain fish fought, they were wimps compared to that Kamloop. It was not just size. His trout, nearly six pounds, simply had a nastier disposition. When it was too tired to run, it just kept circling the boat. He finally brought it close enough for netting.

"You fish," Wendell insisted. "I don't want to tarnish that memory by casting again today."

Each slop lane gave up at least a few trout. The best lanes weren't necessarily the longest. Some held more scum than others and these were generally the most productive. There were none of the big brook trout in the day's catch, and none of my rainbows were distinctly Kamloops. A few of the fish, out of a total of eighteen, weighted over three pounds.

"I want a brook trout, Wendell."

"I've never been able to really pinpoint the brook trout. Some people can on this lake."

"They know where the springs are."

"What's the biggest brook trout you ever caught out of here?"

"I never caught one big enough to be called the biggest. If we hit a pod of big brook trout, I'll start fishing again."

What a difference from one day to the next. The previous day the trout were even more active, or at least more visible, but Woolly Worms, Prince Nymphs, Carey Specials, greased Muddlers, and Little Rainbow Trout streamers all failed on the slop feeders. Except for the smallest fish, the recently stocked dummies, the rainbows apparently were working selectively on the floating larvae (even though the insects were petering out).

My problem on Georgetown is that there is such an incredible damselfly population, with a blitz emergence in June, that it's easy to forget about any other insects. For a few days each spring at least the caddis larvae are abundant, vulnerable, and unique enough to dominate this fishery.

Maybe if this lesson keeps hitting me often enough, it will stick someday.

Floating Damselfly Nymph

On the outside the Floating Damselfly Nymph looks ordinary enough. The difference, hidden underneath the dubbing, is a cylinder of foam or balsa. The buoyancy of either of these materials makes the imitation float to the surface.

Real damselfly nymphs, of course, stay on the bottom. Even during emergence they swim to the shallows and climb out into the air. They cannot be imitated effectively by the floating fly alone.

This pattern is designed for an incredibly efficient method of still water fishing. No other damselfly nymph can get down to the prime depth, whether it is one foot or twenty feet, and stay there as long as this one can with the diving technique.

The angler fishes the Floating Damselfly Nymph with a high-density, fast-sinking line and a short, two- or three-foot leader no matter what the depth. When he casts, the line plummets downwards, taking the fly with it. Once the line hits the bottom, with the fly floating a foot or so above any weeds, he starts retrieving. Every time he tugs on the line the Floating Damselfly Nymph undulates in a snaky up-and-down swimming motion, following the contours of the bottom all the way.

Consider the alternative method: The angler casts a weighted fly and through a time-consuming process determines how high he has to count to give his imitation time to sink just above the weed tips; on his retrieve he must pull in line at precisely the right speed to keep the fly at the exact depth, but when he is fishing blind like this his imitation does not dive into depressions—it does, however, snag on any high spots.

There is a special situation for the Floating Damselfly Nymph in the spring seeps around Deer Lodge. These seeps are short, shallow, and very slow flowing channels, but they hold brown trout up to eight pounds (and almost none under four). The problem is that any cast near one of these cruising fish flushes

Floating Damselfly Nymph

him. It is impossible to let an ordinary nymph sink to the bottom because of the weeds.

The trick with the Floating Damselfly Nymph is to pinch some split shot on the leader. The weight settles on the bottom and the fly floats just above the vegetation. The Floating Damselfly Nymph can stay there forever, ready to start swimming when one of the brown trout approaches the spot.

There is another special situation for this fly. Anglers on the Missouri working the great Trico spinner falls stalk sipping trout in the coves, but they wonder about those random explosive rises out in the main current. Every summer day on the weedy water below Holter Dam there are migrations of emerging damsels, the insects swimming to the shallows. A Floating Damselfly Nymph, cast from the bank and retrieved with spurts, draws the same type of violent takes as the naturals.

Floating Damselfly Nymph

step 1

step 2

step 3

step 4

step 5

TYING STEPS

1. Lash the foam or balsa cylinder to the hook shank.

2. Blend olive marabou and clear Antron fibers and tie this mixture in as a tail.

3. Dub an abdomen of olive fur and olive sparkle yarn mix; form a loop of thread and twist a shaggy rope for wrapping.

4. Dub a thorax of olive fur and olive sparkle yarn mix.

5. Wrap a scraggly, swept-back collar of grouse.

Whip finish.

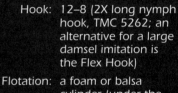

Hook:	12–8 (2X long nymph hook, TMC 5262; an alternative for a large damsel imitation is the Flex Hook)
Flotation:	a foam or balsa cylinder (under the thorax)
Tail:	olive marabou and clear Antron fibers (combed together)
Abdomen:	olive fur and olive sparkle yarn mixed (dubbed)
Thorax:	olive fur and olive sparkle yarn mixed (dubbed; the commercial blend, Haretron is fine for this fly)
Hackle:	grouse fibers (swept back in a long, scraggly collar)

LOG ENTRY: JULY 24, 1990
MITTEN LAKE

This is one of the best lakes on the Blackfeet Indian Reservation—and that makes it one of the finest anywhere. There are Kamloop-strain rainbows over twenty pounds in Mitten, but more important for anyone fishing with insect imitations there are also plenty of trout over three pounds.

My strangest day ever on Mitten happened about eight years ago during a trip with John Gierach. Neither John nor I was ambitious enough to believe in early fishing, which put us on the lake about ten o'clock. The water was glass smooth, the usual wind not just calm but totally dead, and there were so many *Callibaetis* duns on the surface that the lake shimmered with millions of pairs of insect wings. In this whole silver carpet not a single fish rose. At our feet the remnants of the morning's damselfly hatch, hoards of struggling nymphs, swam in the weeds, but no trout cruised the shallows, either.

The moral of the story? A fly fisherman should get his butt out of bed and hit a lake at first light. That is when the gorging takes place. For the rest of the day, until dusk, the fishing is usually a hunt for the occasional stray feeder. In rich lakes this early and late regimen, barring the appearance en masse of some odd food source, is much stronger than in streams.

This was an invasion, not a fishing group. There were nine of us—Graham Marsh, Tory Stosich, Tom Poole, Winfield DeLorme, Jennifer Koenig, Brester Zahm, Bill Redmann, Hal Patman, and me (for these people, all workers on *The Dry Fly*, this was a sort of wrap-up party).

There was no camping allowed on Mission, but the three trucks, a string hooked together by headlights, bounced over the dirt road to the lake in the dark. By the time the horizon turned pink all of us were in float tubes paddling towards predetermined positions.

Our experiment, born in a bar the previous evening, was designed to answer Jennifer's question, "Which works best for the damsel hatch? Bringing the fly from the lake back into the bank, from the bank out into the lake, or parallel to the shore?"

Most of us, including Jennifer, had observed underwater the incredible migration of damselfly nymphs towards the land. It was not a crisscrossing of swimming insects. The damselflies, wiggling along like miniature minnows, moved straight into the shallows.

Common sense dictated that the fly travel the same direction as the naturals. Wasn't it a shame that none of us trusted anything common, and that as skeptics in our own fly fishing realm we had seen the obvious proven wrong and the absurd proven effective too many times?

Three of us retrieved the fly back into the bank; three of us retrieved the fly out into the lake; and three of us retrieved the fly parallel to the shore. All of us used fast-sinking lines, two-foot leaders, and Floating Damselfly Nymphs.

Floating Damselfly Nymph Log

The group casting towards the shore and retrieving the fly out into the lake did the poorest (one trout in three hours). Their failure wasn't totally attributable to the fact that the imitation was swimming in the wrong direction. Still, their catch was less than expected.

Moving a fly from shallow water into deep water is always inefficient—the fly, even with a slow retrieve and a sinking line, swims off the bottom within a few yards. The fly catches fewer trout because for most of the retrieve it is far over the heads of the fish.

The group casting out into the lake and retrieving the fly back towards the shore did better (four trout in three hours). This was not bad fishing—the trout averaged six pounds and no one expected furious action with these large rainbows.

It wouldn't be fair to declare the group casting parallel to the shore the best. The three anglers lined up so that each of them was swimming the fly at a different depth. Tory and Bill caught one fish each during the three hours, but Jennifer, working in roughly six feet of water, caught seven fish all by herself.

The trout didn't care what direction the fly was swimming. They were concentrated in a band along the break between shallow and deep water. They were cruising and, as always when cruising, they were not changing depths (which is why bottom-feeding trout move roughly parallel to the shore).

Jennifer was on that break line. Her retrieve worked best because it was the most efficient, not pulling the fly through the prime zone in one direction or the other, but keeping it where there were feeding trout.

The Floating Crayfish utilizes the same concept. In various sizes, with a sinking line and short leader, it is attractive to bass, perch, pickerel, and trout in lakes and ponds.

Free-Living Caddis Larva

There are two distinct types of trout streams that have large populations of free-living caddisfly larvae. In one kind of water, the cold, tumbling brook or river, a heavily oxygenated environment, the most primitive caddisflies, free-crawling hunters and scavengers, thrive. In another kind of water, the rich river, a flow with good production of algae, net-making filter-feeders flourish.

The critical characteristics for a matching pattern are color and shape. Especially for those free-living, bright larvae, the Green Sedge *(Rhyacophila* sp.), the brilliant coloration must be imitated on the fly. Even for the drabber net-makers, the contrast between the lighter abdomen and the darker thorax is a key trait.

When these insects break away from the bottom and wash in the current they curl up into a protective hunch. This shape is matched with a curved caddis larva hook. Any weight on the fly has to be carefully positioned, more of it on the bottom of the shank than on the top, to prevent the finished pattern from flipping over on the drift.

Free-Living Caddis Larva

Free-Living Caddis Larva

step 1

TYING STEPS
(FOR BRIGHT GREEN
CADDIS LARVA)

1. Tie in a stripped brown hackle quill; let it dangle for the moment.

2. Dub an abdomen of half olive fur and half bright green acrylic Craft Fur over the rear two thirds of the hook shank.

Hook:	8–16 (curved, caddis larva hook, TMC 205BL)
Weight:	lead wire (optional)
Rib:	light brown hackle quill (stripped)
Abdomen:	half olive fur and half olive acrylic Craft Fur (mixed and dubbed)
Thorax:	dark olive-brown fur
Hackle:	dark speckled grouse fibers (beard style)

Other variations match olive brown, yellow, pale green, and pink larvae.

step 2

3. Wrap the stripped quill as a rib; dub a thicker thorax of dark olive brown fur.

4. Tie in a beard hackle of speckled grouse fibers.

step 3

step 4

**LOG ENTRY: JUNE 26, 1991
RUBY RIVER**

My favorite story on the horrors of agricultural dewatering involves the Ruby. It also illustrates a way of thinking. One rancher, after the river was emptied, could not understand the public outcry, explaining, "It was only dry for two days."

The Ruby, like many rivers below dams, has a huge population of net-making caddis larvae, thousands per square foot. The reason for this fecundity of Spotted Sedge (Hydropsyche sp.) and Little Sister Sedge (Cheumatopsyche sp.) is the lake above the dam, its vast surface area absorbing solar radiation and providing space for algal growth. These one-celled forms, running out through the dam, feed the caddisfly larvae in the river.

It always surprises me how attuned trout get to the shape of caddisfly larvae in rivers like the Ruby. The fish develop such a general preference for these insects that the normal mayfly and stonefly patterns do poorly as searching nymphs. Those flies just don't look like caddisflies.

Clip Hathorn stopped in Deer Lodge this morning, "I hope that you weren't kidding when you said to just call."

"Anyone can come fishing with me, Clip."

Actually, I wasn't going to go to the Ruby today. I had planned on going to Storm Lake, but when Clip showed me his fly boxes crammed with caddis patterns—larval, pupal, and adult—I wanted to give him a caddis stream to try them on.

There was a spurt of action with diving egg-layers in the morning. The Little Sister Sedges, already changing from the darker shades of spring to the lighter shades of summer, came in a surprisingly concentrated flight. A Diving Caddis in matching size and color (size 16 Ginger) took trout for us.

The interesting part of the day came with the afternoon doldrums. The large brown trout in particular disappeared, and there was no doubt where they went to on a river as overgrown with trees as the Ruby. For the rainbows in the riffles a size 16 Olive Brown Caddis Larva did better than other nymphs.

This is the situation that I have been waiting for ever since early spring. That was when I fished a Slinky Rig for steelhead. What is a Slinky? Someone more qualified than me can decide if the method is even fly fishing.

None of the bottom-bouncing nymph methods, which incorporate so much weight that normal casting is impossible, satisfy the pure definition of fly fishing. Separating what is and what isn't fly fishing, however, is a task beyond my meager expertise as defender of the sport. Each angler can decide for himself the place for the Slinky Rig. It does put a pair of flies efficiently on the bottom, getting the nymphs deep, as deep as five or six feet, in a pool or run.

With the Slinky there is no fly line (and this is the philosophical evil for many). The 13-foot or longer leader is tied directly to a fluorescent orange Dai-Riki Shooting Line (to quote the package, "a combination of Dai-Riki monofilament and Scientific Angler Slime-Line coating"). The actual weight, a few pieces of split shot, is put into a length of hollow parachute cord. This nylon tube, heat-sealed at both ends, hangs from a snap swivel on the leader, one and a half times the depth of the water. There are two flies—the angler ties in an 18-inch piece of monofilament right to the eye of the first pattern and knots on a second one.

This rig, because of the fine diameter of the monofilament as much as the weight, cuts through a flow. The Slinky itself, smooth nylon cord, slides over rocks and sticks without hanging up in them. There is no bulky, sinking line to billow in the current—the bright Slime Green running line, acting as a strike indicator, points directly down to the fly.

What were the possibilities for a Slinky Rig presentation?

On a winding, brushy river like the Ruby, where trout hid back in the undercuts of every outside bend, it could drift a nymph right past these

Jim Johnson, of Johnson's Pere Marquette Lodge, guided me for spring steelhead on the Pere Marquette. He showed me the Slinky set-up, tied on a couple of Glo Bugs, and spotted and named every steelhead in the river for me. With help like this, and the incredibly efficient bottom-bouncing method, it was impossible not to have a spectacular day on seven- to fifteen-pound fish.

Where there is an entire group of trout, like the undercut browns of the Ruby, that cannot be touched by ordinary fly fishing methods, they become an exciting challenge. A deep presentation technique, such as the Slinky, might never become a regular method on resident trout for me, but every once in a while it feels good to stir up these usually untouchable fish.

Free-Living Caddis Larva Log

fish. This method might break the midday doldrums with brown trout on this kind of water.

After changing tackle and stringing the proper amount of weight on the leader, I started working the darker water with two flies, both size 14 Olive Brown Caddis Larva imitations. At first I missed the hits, possibly because these brown trout struck differently than steelhead, but with the Slinky and the almost taut connection between the hooks and the bright green running line, it wasn't hard to detect pick-ups.

The deep presentation broke the doldrums. The brown trout, hidden under the banks, slid out and grabbed the nymphs passing at eye level. Most of them took the upper fly rather than the end pattern. With the set of the hook they always tried to rush back into the undercut, and since some wonderfully big fish were snatching the small imitations, the first moments of any battle were often conclusive. Some broke free; some didn't.

The surprise was definitely the size of the trout in the undercuts. Clip caught as many or more fish out of the riffles, with a best of 18 inches. All of my trout were browns, none under 14 inches, with three over 20 inches. The only reason for the difference in average size was location—the Slinky Rig showed the flies to an entirely different segment of the trout population.

Marabou Single Egg

My friends who fish for spawn-eaters offer different insights into egg patterns. Mark Alspaugh insists that most egg flies are too big, preferring a smaller imitation, no matter what the other features, over a larger one for sea-run brook trout in eastern Canada. Mike Lawson believes that the rainbows in Alaska that trail the waves of Pacific salmon up a river become very selective to color. And John Cobbe, who haunts the spawners out of the reservoirs on Colorado's South Platte, wants more than anything else a fly that pulsates, changing shape, as it drifts dead with the current.

My opinions about egg patterns were formed over the years by observing the effect these imitations had on trout. The flies never needed a great deal of magic themselves—the food item they were matching had a wonderful hold on the fish at certain times all by itself.

That power encompasses much more than imitation. Just as no artificial can ever be a "miracle fly" without being both imitation and attractor at the same time; no food item can be special without exciting more than one instinctive feeling at the same time. The real egg triggers both the need to eat (hunger) and the urge to attack (aggression).

One afternoon last spring Steve Gayken and I watched a pair of spawning rainbows hovering over a patch of gravel at the shallow inlet of a pond. We kibitzed while Justin Baker, who couldn't see the fish from his position, presented various flies. Justin showed these trout the reliable standbys, a Hare's Ear, a Pheasant Tail, and a Woolly Worm, and although these nymphs passed within inches, the fish never even glanced at them. Justin changed to an egg pattern and on the first cast the male rainbow, nervous the moment the bright fly plopped into the water, dashed forward and grabbed the fly. In the face of such indifference a moment before, this enthusiasm by the trout was magical enough for us.

Marabou Single Egg

Marabou Single Egg

The Marabou Single Egg, always tied on a lightly weighted, size 16 hook, is a tricolor fly. The marabou, humped in a semicircle over the back, varies—pink, purple, white, red, chartreuse, and burnt orange are popular with my group—but the pink sparkle yarn body and the red hackle stay the same. The marabou itself, tied down front and rear so that it never collapses, breathes with every tug of the water.

These characteristics were part of the fly from the start—and it was odd that all of the features that experienced anglers wanted on an egg imitation were equally obvious during the underwater testing. The Marabou Single Egg worked during all seasons, not just spring and fall, but there were different levels of aggression—in the summer, when an egg would be just a memory, a trout tentatively sucked it from the drift; when a fish was feeding on real eggs, but not spawning himself, he worked in an efficient , side-to-side search, grabbing every passing egg and taking the fly like just one more piece of food; and during spawning, all species of trout snatched the pattern, often with a surge forward and a shake of the head. The major aspects of the Marabou Single Egg together made this an effective fly, but each feature seemed to be especially critical during specific times—the size had to be right in the summer for generally nymphing trout; the color had to be perfect for fish actually feeding on eggs; and the lump had to pulse for spawners.

TYING STEPS

1. Wrap in a strip of lead on the bottom of the hook shank; lacquer it.

2. Tie in a bunch of marabou fibers; let them dangle for the moment.

3. Tie in a piece of pink sparkle yarn; wrap it as a body.

4. Bring the bunch of marabou fibers forward and tie them down.

5. Wrap the scarlet hackle one turn; slant the fibers slightly back with turns of the thread.

Whip finish.

Hook: 16 (standard, 2X heavy wet fly, TMC 3769)
Weight: a piece of lead wire
Egg: marabou
Body: pink sparkle yarn (wrapped)
Hackle: scarlet rooster

Only the color of the marabou "egg" changes; popular colors are pink, purple, white, red, chartreuse, and burnt orange.

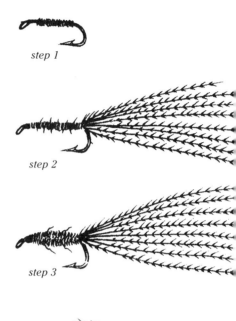

step 1

step 2

step 3

step 4

step 5

LOG ENTRY: OCTOBER 19, 1991
GIBBON RIVER

The Gibbon, which joins with the Firehole to form the Madison in Yellowstone National Park, is fun to fish throughout the year—there are some great grasshopper meadows in the upper reaches. During the fall, when not only spawning browns, but hatchery rainbows manipulated over generations for autumn egg-laying, run up out of Hebgen Lake, this little river gets jammed with large trout.

There is a network in Montana, overlapping into Idaho, Wyoming, and even southern Alberta, that no faraway angler can really tap into for fly fishing information. News spreads from friend to friend, telephone lines burning; the talk may be about a stream coming into its post-snowmelt prime, a hatch of insects bursting out on a lake, or a run of trout moving into a river. This network isn't about secret places—everyone knows the waters—it is about being on a river or lake at precisely the right moment. The period of great fishing is usually so brief that any one of us, hearing about it, drops everything and rushes to the promised killing. It isn't unusual for me to drive a few hundred miles on the word of a reliable friend a half dozen times during the summer.

Hitting a river or lake at the perfect moment makes every other aspect of successful fly fishing trivial. When trout are giddy, aggressive, or hungry, to the point of being suicidal, almost any pattern or any presentation

Marabou Single Egg Log

fools enough of them. It seems greedy to search for the ideal fly in the midst of such hot fishing.

Spawning trout running up from lakes are just like spawning steelhead or sea-run browns moving up from the ocean. There are stale fish and there are fresh fish. The fresh ones hit a fly much more eagerly.

Wayne Huft called me from West Yellowstone, "Right now the fishing is so fast on the Gibbon that a man works up a sweat real quick."

The trout on the Gibbon, from the description, were pushing into the river in waves. The bigger fish were undoubtedly coming all the way from Hebgen Lake, migrating up the Madison and turning into the Gibbon at the Junction. Many of them were going as far as possible, to the falls, and gathering in the large spill holes.

I drove down that night and by daybreak the next morning we were spread out on the pool at Gibbon Falls. Within minutes Wayne hooked a trout, a 19-inch, football-shaped rainbow up from the lake. My first two trout, both rainbows, measured a little over 19 inches, too.

We split the pool into sections, drifting Marabou Single Egg variations at different depths and down different slots, searching the water because we were not satisfied with just the 16-inch to 19-inch rainbows, all of these fish the same year class of Arlee-strain hatchery stock. When Wayne found the brown trout he called me over and we worked together at refining the terminal tackle for a better combination of fly, lead weight, and leader.

Wayne's setup for slow, deep, deaddrift nymphing consisted of only one strike indicator, a section of fluorescent orange monofilament. With this rig he still missed a number of strikes, seeing the movement of the hot butt but reacting too late to it.

This was so frustrating that we started fooling around with different kinds of indicators. The fishing was fast enough, with a hit every few drifts, that we should have been happy enough hooking one out of four trout. But, of course, we were not at all happy. This quest for a better method had nothing to do with greed.

My setup evolved over the day into a rig with two strike indicators, not just one. My leader was 18 feet long, with lead wire wrapped around the bottom two blood knots. I slid a cork up and down the monofilament until I discovered the right depth for the lightly weighted Marabou Single Egg. Then, after a hit or two, I cut out the regular leader section just below the cork and tied in a length of hot orange monofilament.

The take on a nymph in deep, slow water was usually so subtle that either the cork or the hot butt hesitated too late for a good set on the strike. But the floating cork marked the start of the hot orange section—and if I stared down into the water, following the fluorescent piece of monofilament *below* the surface, I gained a critical split second in detecting the take.

Wayne hated to admit to using any egg pattern, but his regular assortment of nymphs never did as well as the bright fly on spawning trout. He grumbled about the Marabou Single Egg, refusing to try it as a searcher during mid-season, and even today when late coming anglers asked him what we were catching our trout on he said with all seriousness, "A Rainbow Emerger."

A man on the bank nodded his head, "I've heard that that's a good fly. I'll have to pick some up in West Yellowstone if that's what they're rising to."

There is no denying it. Fishing that hard when the fishing was so easy was a bit excessive. Such wonderful moments are better medicine in small amounts, not seven-hour stints. Even after finding a few larger-than-average rainbows (with that nice average being 18 inches or so) and a wide range of browns, from 13 inches to 23 inches, our enthusiasm never slacked off. The only excuse was that it was late fall, and it felt like late summer with the warm day, and our worry about winter drove us to catch a lot of trout.

In the last few weeks, before winter came to the region, the Double Indictor system became my regular way of fishing a nymph. It gave me—and other anglers who tried it—instant grasp of that wonderful "sixth sense" that fanatic nymph fishermen develop only after weeks of watching a drifting fly. The added time to strike, as well as the certainty that the movement really meant a strike, boosted the percentage of hookups.

It is going to be fun next summer to go underwater and see the system at work—one angler will use a single indicator and another will use the double indicator (the "below the surface" marker). Our studies already show that even a great nymph fisherman like Wayne Huft only sets solidly on 60 percent of the takes. Can the research provide a concrete number; for example, would the Double Indicator method increase hookups by a third for the average nymph fisherman?

Marabou Spawn Sac

Marabou Spawn Sac

The nymph is no different than any other type of fly—presentation is still more important than pattern choice. The nymph, for optimum effect, has to drift at the eye level of the trout. When fish are feeding on items near the bottom, a drift a few inches over their heads makes the best looking fly mediocre and a drift a foot over their heads makes the best looking fly worthless.

It is easy to imagine insects, scuds, worms, and eggs in the currents, filling the water column top to bottom. In reality objects caught in the flow concentrate in a narrow mixing zone. Entomologists estimate that 70 to 80 percent of free-drifting life forms move at any given moment in an interface between the dead water of the rocks and the unobstructed water of the open flow. This turbulent band, with its circling eddies, tenaciously holds organisms until they reach an area where the flows are slow enough for them to settle to the bottom.

The nymph fisherman, whether he realizes it or not, searches for the best way to keep his fly in this mixing zone. He chooses a method of weighting, wrapping lead on the fly, applying lead to the leader, or using a sinking line.

My weighting technique for the Marabou Spawn Sac is different than my normal nymphing strategy. Why? Fish eggs drift differently than insects. The eggs are dense, sinking rapidly—they have to, or else they would wash downstream and not settle into the gravel for incubation.

My favorite approach with most of my other flies is to put the lead on the leader (Outrigger Method)—wire is wrapped at the first blood knot, 18 inches up from the fly; at the second blood knot, 30 inches up from the fly; and if necessary at the third blood knot, 42 inches up from the fly. This rig drags the leader down to the bottom in a riffle, the wire tapping the rocks, but it allows the unweighted or lightly weighted fly to ride freely in the mixing zone.

My goal with the Marabou Spawn Sac is to make it, not the leader, bounce the bottom. The fly is heavily weighted so that it drops through the mixing zone—the countering effect with any weighted fly is the unweighted leader, the monofilament pulled and tugged so much by the upper, faster currents that it tends to lift the heavy pattern back up into the interface. This nymphing technique mimics the natural drift of the real fish eggs better than the Outrigger Method.

Marabou Spawn Sac

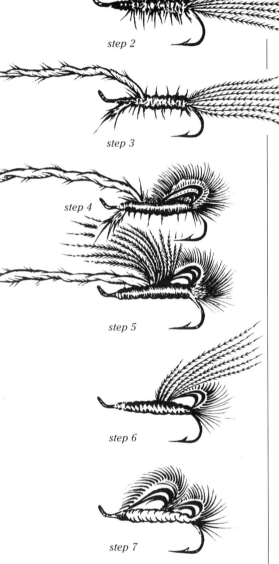

step 1

step 2

step 3

step 4

step 5

step 6

step 7

TYING STEPS

1. Wrap lead wire along the hook shank; lacquer it.

2. Tie in a clump of marabou fibers; let them dangle for the moment.

3. Wrap a piece of pink sparkle yarn a third of the way up the hook shank; tie it off, but do not cut the excess.

4. Pull the clump of marabou forward and tie it down.

5. Tie in a second clump of marabou; let it dangle for the moment.

6. Wrap the piece of pink sparkle yarn two thirds of the way up the hook shank.

7. Pull the second clump of marabou forward and tie it down.

8. Wrap a scarlet hackle one turn; slant the hackle fibers backwards with turns of the thread.

Whip finish.

Hook:	8 (up-eye, Atlantic salmon, TMC 7989)
Weight:	lead wire
Egg Sacs:	marabou fibers
Body:	pink sparkle yarn
Hackle:	scarlet rooster

As with the Marabou Single Egg, only the color of the egg sac changes; pink, purple, white, red, chartreuse, and burnt orange are effective variations.

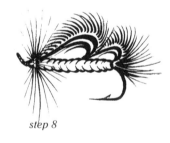

step 8

LOG ENTRY: OCTOBER 25, 1990
GOLD CREEK

Gold Creek still has plenty of scars from mining a hundred years later, but its cold and clear water invigorates the Clark Fork. Around the mouth of the stream cutthroats push out into the main river, joining the predominant brown trout.

There wasn't much excitement for the first few hours. Most of that time was spent walking and searching for trout in Gold Creek itself, starting two miles upstream and moving down towards the mouth. My total catch was one small cutthroat.

Actually, I was starting to think that I should have gone to Lost Creek , my favorite place for hunting spawners, but I had to keep looking for, in Kevin Vause's words, ". . . there's one big brown trout, maybe 28 inches."

Then I started spotting groups of spawning fish up from the Clark Fork in the final half mile of the stream. None of these brown trout was Kevin's monster, but I did get three over 15 inches on a Marabou Spawn Sac. All of the fish rushed the fly hard.

I had gone upstream two miles because I thought that the trout might have moved from where Kevin saw him yesterday. When I spotted him he was against a steep bank, at the end of a fallen log, and it might well have been the exact water that Kevin had described to me.

He had the place right, which wasn't bad for a beginner flustered by a huge trout. Kevin's estimate on the size of the fish looked off to me, though, the trout maybe going 23 inches. The kype showed clearly on the male, a richly spotted, dark fish.

On the first drift the trout ran up to meet the drifting Burnt Orange Marabou Spawn Sac, stopped within an inch of it, and finally dropped back downstream with the pattern (a type of inspection common with dry flies but rare with a nymph). On my next few casts he ignored the fly.

Unlike egg-eaters, spawners would take an egg pattern the first time or not at all, disregarding it with a bit of disdain on every subsequent drift. Once they knew it was a fraud, the fly couldn't stir up any more aggression in them.

This brown trout passed up a series of Marabou Single Eggs and Glo Bugs in a variety of colors, looking at only the yellow one. I was going to change to a streamer, some type of yellow aggravator, when I sighted the larger female under the log for the first time.

All I could think was that she was getting excited over my artificial hatch of egg imitations. I put a bright Yellow Marabou Spawn Sac on and cast further upstream than usual, aiming the drift for the top fish instead of the bottom one. So what did the male do? He bolted up, flashing in front of the female as she neared the fly, and sucked in the Spawn Sac.

I didn't want him any longer, not at the risk of spooking the female. I let him mouth the fly, never setting the hook, and after carrying it down-

> This battle of wills between us was now approaching nearly an hour, and it was starting to get personal (and it didn't help that he was winning). My only alternative, if he didn't get tired of this game of dare, was to catch him and carry him in a bucket to a place, maybe another watershed, far, far away. Then maybe it would be possible for me to come back and hook the huge female.

83

Marabou Spawn Sac Log

stream for a moment he spit it out. I tried to draw the Spawn Sac aside, but he grabbed it again.

Finally he let it go and I picked it up as gently as possible, plopping it upstream for a repeat of the last drift.

Again he rushed up, and again he bullied the female off from the Spawn Sac, but this time he didn't eat the fly himself. He repeated this routine, facing off the more passive female twice without touching the Spawn Sac.

This battle of wills between us was now approaching nearly an hour, and it was starting to get personal (and it didn't help that he was winning). My only alternative, if he didn't get tired of this game of dare, was to catch him and carry him in a bucket to a place, maybe another watershed, far, far away. Then maybe it would be possible for me to come back and hook the huge female.

On a hunch, I took off the Yellow Marabou Spawn Sac and put on the Burnt Orange Marabou Spawn Sac again. The darker color didn't excite the male as much and he let it pass along the log. On the third drift the female positioned herself in front of the oncoming fly and sipped it in gently.

She burst out of the run, going straight downstream through two smaller pools, never trying to bury into cover. The male even started to follow her, but when he saw me in the channel he flushed into deeper water. The female, fighting spectacularly but not particularly intelligently in the confines of the creek, was still fresh when she almost landed herself on a gravel bar. She wasn't 28 inches, but with a bit of stretching on her tail she touched 25 inches on the tape. She swam away strongly on the release.

Those two brown trout were so different. The male was motivated by aggression when he took the fly—the female simply craved a caviar snack. The male actively tried to control the situation—the female passively accepted the possibilities.

Marabou Worm

My original patterns go into two separate boxes. In one box sit all the dainty insect imitations, dry and wet, and these are the ones shown to anyone who wants to see my creations. In the other box lie the rest of the innovations, the ones born seemingly in the nightmares of a madman—the Marabou Spawn Sac, the Creature, the Bristle Leech, and this aberration, the Marabou Worm.

If these innovations range from the ridiculous to the sublime, it is because years of stomach samplings have shown clearly that what trout eat also ranges from the ridiculous to the sublime. Much of what trout eat is not being imitated properly by fly fishermen; some of its food is not being imitated at all.

The diet of a trout can roughly be split into two categories. There is the staple fare—caddisflies, mayflies, stoneflies, two-winged flies, some terrestrial insects, and *Gammarus* scuds—that dominates the menu in most habitats. The second type of food is neither as predictable nor as consistently important. As a matter of fact, part of my fascination with these oddball foods is that, most of the time, imitations are not needed at all. The reason for carrying these patterns, however, is that when they are needed they are usually indispensable.

The supply of real worms comes from two sources—not one. This is the key to fishing the imitation successfully. The naturals are ever present, both along the stream and in the stream itself. The matching fly works best when one of those two types of worms is abundant in the drift.

There are aquatic worms, of the same class *(Oligochaeta)* and frequently of the same appearance as their terrestrial cousins, that spend their entire life cycle underwater. Streams and rivers with some silty areas, but with clear, oxygen-saturated water, provide prime habitat for these aquatic worms. Most spring creeks and tailwater rivers, and many freestone waters, fit into this category.

Marabou Worm

Marabou Worm

Aquatic worms burrow through and strain the stream silt. They commonly concentrate along slower current areas, the pool bottoms, weed beds, and bank edges, where dirt and decaying leaves accumulate into the deepest piles. At night, they come out of their holes to mate and feed, crawling around on the bottom. They drift naturally at dusk and dawn but can be washed away if any force, whether a wading cow or a sudden change in the current, stirs up the silt bed.

These aquatic worms are common enough so that trout are exposed to them continuously. Based on the best available information on drift rates, a trout holding below a silty area in a river with a good population of aquatic worms sees roughly five to ten of them during a summer day. This is not a lot—certainly not enough for a fish to feed on worms exclusively. But aquatic worms look so unlike most other drifting food that ten of them a day, passing by all summer, can make a strong impression on a trout. It is evident from the numbers found during stomach samplings that trout show a general preference, if not a selective one, for aquatic worms.

Terrestrial worms, both the night crawler and the common red worm, are the bonanza for predators on the land and in the water. When a steady rain saturates the ground, the earthworms escape to the surface and crawl blindly about. This begins an amazing carnage, evident from the dried carcasses on sidewalks and roads the next day. The same natural phenomenon dumps incredible numbers of worms into rivers.

But an angler cannot take advantage of the resultant feeding binge by the trout unless he arrives at a productive spot at the right time. Not all waters receive the influx of worms. Streams bordered by rocky or sandy soil too infertile to support earthworms might get some food washed into them by the runoff, but such streams are not great rainy-day fisheries. The best waters, cutting through grassy meadows, have overhanging banks of rich soil. Frequently, one section of the river might be poor for worms, but a different section proves ideal. So often, successful worm fishing becomes simply a matter of picking the proper stretch of water.

Drop a live worm in water, and it contorts into seemingly impossible shapes. It wriggles so well because it has two types of muscles—one set runs the length of the body and the other set circles the body. And if the water is well aerated, even a terrestrial worm does not drown because it can breathe by absorbing gasses through its skin. In laboratories, worms have lived for as long as six months submerged in water.

There is no doubt that the sinuous, twisting movement of the real worm is the primary visual clue for the trout. It isn't too hard for most fishermen to recall the main rule of their early, bait-fishing beginnings: A live, wriggling worm always catches more fish than a dead one. The same principle applies to the fly used to match such an animated organism.

Soft materials are generally used as long, trailing extensions only on flies designed for active retrieval. On a streamer, for example, the marabou fibers straighten out and wave enticingly when the fly is pulled through the water. This pattern fishes best when brought back with long, continuous strips; too many pronounced pauses during the retrieve hurt the effectiveness of such a fly. The problem with marabou fibers is that there has to be something pulling on both ends before they can appear sinuous and alive. During a retrieve, the force of the water flowing around the fibers achieves this effect for the marabou streamer. But during a true dead-drift presentation, this pull from both directions cannot happen without a bit of help.

On the Marabou Worm, a buoyant piece of foam, split and cemented near the end of the long tail, provides the counter-pull. The foam floats up and the weighted fly body sinks down; and in between, the soft marabou flexes easily against these weak, contrasting forces. As the fly tumbles downstream with the current, the tail section mimics the weaving dance of the natural worm.

Marabou Worm

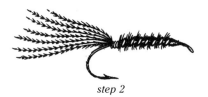

step 1

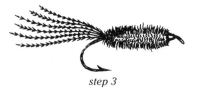

step 2

step 3

step 4

TYING STEPS

1. Wrap the lead wire onto the hook shank; lacquer the wire.

2. Fasten a clump of marabou fibers twice as long as the hook shank at the bend of the hook.

3. Tie in a clump of long marabou fibers and wrap them along the hook shank (forming the body).

Whip finish.

4. Slit the foam cylinder, slide it around the marabou fibers (placing it near the tip of the tail), and cement the cylinder shut with Zap-a-Gap glue.

Hook:	8–18 (2X long)
Weight:	lead wire, wrapped and lacquered
Tail:	free-hanging marabou fibers
Tail Float:	a thin orange or white cylinder of high density foam
Body:	marabou fibers

The main colors for matching aquatic and terrestrial worms are black, off-white, orange, and natural gray.

LOG ENTRY: AUGUST 27, 1991
JEFFERSON RIVER

This isn't the best river in the state for catching numbers of fish; the population studies show only 1,000 trout per mile in the best stretches, but those trout are almost all browns, well-conditioned, and frequently very large.

There is a meteorological phenomenon in Montana known as the August Singularity. It refers specifically to August 21st. For sixteen out of the last twenty years that day has been rainy and cool. This wet weather typically breaks the summer doldrums.

A sudden change in conditions on any single day for sixteen out of twenty years can't just be luck (not in our near-desert climate)—and it isn't. A high pressure system sits over Montana during the summer months, deflecting the jet stream north over Alberta. In August the jet stream, flush with moisture and cooler air from the Gulf of Alaska, gets stronger, and around the third week it breaks through the high pressure barrier in the first of a series of autumn pulses.

This year, with its strange weather, had to be the exception. August 21st came and went without a menacing cloud in the whole sky. My fishing stayed in that warm weather pattern, but as hard as it was for me to wish for a break in shirtsleeve days there was a reason to pray for that first hard, soaking rain.

The plan was actually born right after the Federation of Fly Fishermen Conclave. Justin Baker and I were driving from West Yellowstone to Deer Lodge on Sunday morning and we stopped to fish the Jefferson at the Cardwell access.

After the dry summer, the river was pretty low and warm. We popped a few small browns from the first riffle, but nothing real exciting happened under the midday sun. Then, just upstream from us, a big brown jumped into the air and splashed back on the surface. A few minutes later another brown trout, this one clearly 22 or 23 inches, leapt high just downstream from us.

I moved up to a slack-water edge off the main current. One trout came out three times, twice half rolling and once clearing. It was very random feeding and never in exactly the same spot. I had no idea what he was taking. Maybe it was a caddis rise but neither a dead drift nor a retrieved fly drew a look. To punctuate my puzzlement, big fish kept jumping both upstream and downstream.

Here is a fact on the Marabou Worm—I have fished it on an average of three days a season over the past nine years and yet in five of those years it has caught the biggest trout. Obviously, it isn't a random fly for me.

No one had to tell me that there were big trout in the Jefferson. I've fished it a lot and even guided on it a bit, mostly fall, streamer-pounding float trips. Still, it was nice to witness a spectacular show by three- to five-pound brown trout. It was nice to know a day was coming when those trout would be vulnerable. I had a name for this as a boy—it was a "worm rain."

August 21st came and went, and I still kept tying a few marabou worms every evening. It isn't a pattern with a lot of variations—the gray one, the main color for matching an earthworm, can be tied in sizes 8 to 18, but size isn't extremely critical with this fly. If it hadn't finally rained, I would have tied myself a lifetime supply in one fall.

Late on the night of the 26th the water started coming, not a scattered shower or a flash downpour, but the unremitting fall of big drops. It kept raining through the night and into the morning, finally stopping by 10:00 a.m. but leaving a covering of dark clouds.

By 10:00 a.m., I was already walking up the river to that run with the slack edge. The water was faintly stained, but not muddy, and the level was up a few inches. I held a screen in a riffle, just letting the drift collect, and in a couple of minutes there were three real earthworms in the mesh. The Jefferson, winding through rich bottomland, was definitely a "worm river."

How many times do fantasies come true? Even when a day is good it falls short of the wildest thoughts. This one didn't. Every trout in the river, refreshed by the spurt of cooler weather and treated with a feast of drifting fare, was gorging. The only problem to this fishing was getting the Marabou Worm past the 10- to 16-inch browns to the real brutes. The fly

Marabou Worm Log

was a magnet for any trout big enough to mouth it.

In the first run I caught eight fish, but none of them was the bull of the pool. Finally, standing chest deep and reaching across the main current to drift the Worm along the edge, I hooked the large, dark brown that had been in my thoughts.

He ran for his home among the tree roots in the slack water, but after nosing around there and failing to snag the leader he started leaping. He bounced up three times, then fought a long time underwater, and finally wallowed twice more. He measured out at 24 inches and weighed over six pounds.

That trout was the largest of the day, but the Worm caught the boss fish of three other runs. Those trout were over 20 inches, too, with incredible girths. There were plenty of fat, strong, fill-in fish between the big ones.

Natural Drift Stonefly Nymph

With any fly our underwater studies are designed to answer two questions—is the pattern effective and, if so, why? Sometimes the second question is a puzzler, but with most imitative flies the answer is usually obvious. It certainly is with the Natural Drift Stonefly.

A trout picking the drift can be very selective if any one insect is abundant, but when feeding generally on nymphs, lacking any specific picture as a search pattern, that same fish usually nips any likely bit of trash lightly with his lips. He uses the taste buds on the outside of the mouth to test objects, spitting out debris and sucking in food. He feeds so rhythmically that only one trait makes him absolutely refuse to touch an object.

Live insects don't tumble; pieces of inanimate trash do. Nymphs and larvae, as soon as they intentionally or accidentally break free from the bottom, establish their equilibrium, drifting with the current but staying in a vertical, hunched over position. Bits of trash, rolling and tumbling uncontrollably, are clearly not alive to a trout.

The Natural Drift Stonefly Nymph is effective on western rivers because it reacts to the current forces the same way as the natural insect. The balance between the buoyancy of the deer hair thorax and the sink of the lead-weighted abdomen keeps the fly drifting in the vertical position. The pattern behaves correctly.

Natural Drift Stonefly Nymph

Natural Drift Stonefly Nymph

step 1

step 2

step 3

step 4

step 5

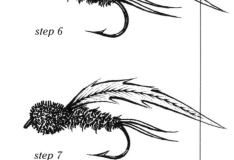

step 6

TYING STEPS

1. Bend the hook slightly downwards at the planned junction between the abdomen and the thorax. Wrap lead wire on the rear half of the hook shank; lacquer it.

2. Tie in two pheasant tail fibers; split them.

3. Tie in a stripped hackle quill; let it dangle for the moment.

4. Dub a thick abdomen (up to the bend).

5. Wrap the quill as a rib over the abdomen.

6. Tie in a hackle feather.

7. Spin a deer hair thorax.

8. Palmer the hackle through the deer hair.

Whip finish.

Hook:	4–8 (2X heavy and 2X long nymph, TMC 5262)
Weight:	lead wire (over the rear half of the hook shank)
Tail:	two pheasant tail or turkey feather fibers (split)
Rib:	stripped brown hackle quill
Abdomen:	dark brown fur (dubbed)
Thorax:	black deer hair (spun)
Hackle:	furnace rooster (palmered snugly through the thorax hair)

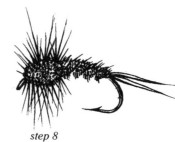

step 8

LOG ENTRY: MARCH 12, 1991
LITTLE BLACKFOOT RIVER

There is no stream more special to me in Montana than the Little Blackfoot River. Let me completely protect one drainage in the state, from ranching, mining, logging, and even over fishing, and this would be the one. Why? It is the classic freestone flow, a rich, pool and riffle gem, but it is badly abused by people who blithely destroy the greater economic potential of the stream as a tourist draw.

Wayne Huft told me why he likes this early season, before the run-off, so much: "Right now, we're sharp with nymphs, so sharp. Think about it. During the summer we're fishing dry flies, streamers, wet flies, and nymphs, switching around, and we're ragged with nymphs. Aren't we?" He didn't wait for an answer. "But in the winter we're bouncing nymphs every day. Every day. And we're hooking a great percentage of the strikes. During the summer we're probably not even seeing a lot of the strikes— we get spoiled because the fish hit harder. Right now if that line tip whispers, we're lifting the rod tip before we even know it's a take. And we're vacuuming the stream—trout, whitefish, and sucker, anything that nudges the fly into its mouth. Doesn't it feel great to be on top of it like this?"

Normally, in March on the Little Blackfoot, the best fly would be something matching the *Baetis* mayflies, probably a size 18 Olive Tear Drop, but the first few trout that we caught today were stuffed with brown stonefly nymphs (not *Pteronarcys* salmon flies, probably something from the Nemouridae family). These insects, with their fully formed winged pads, were migrating into the shallows for hatching.

One reason the Natural Drift Stonefly works better than other stonefly patterns at times is because it is not a "deep" nymph. It doesn't sink to the bottom in heavy flows. Most of these flies are designed to sink in the fastest water, but the Natural Drift is partially buoyed by the deer hair. Even with the lead wraps under the abdomen, it doesn't snag up in moderate flows.

The best drift line today was along the break, where the gravel shelf suddenly dropped into deeper water. The current wasn't fast on the inside of the curve. The fish weren't visible in the broken riffles, but from the way the line tip moved, always with a slight curl out towards the middle of the stream, it was clear that they were striking from the deep side.

Wayne was right. We were sharp today. Once we hit the Natural Drift Stonefly Nymph as the right fly, the fishing was furious. Down here, on the lower stretch of the river, all of the trout were browns. We had our winter reflexes working, but the fish, actively snatching these stonefly naturals (and our flies), were hitting like they do during a summer spree.

One strange thing was the size of the trout. They were averaging 13 inches, very good for the Little Blackfoot, but many of the fish were between 15 and 18 inches. None of mine were over 18 inches (my biggest here in spite of twenty years of hard fishing on the river), but two of the browns today matched that. This has always been a "numbers" river, and it gave the two of us over fifty trout and whitefish during the five hours.

Rollover Scud

The Rollover Scud is the perfect example of a pattern tied for a specific situation. A strip of lead wire is bound to the top of the hook shank, upsetting the natural balance of the fly. As the Rollover Scud sinks, the hook rides up, but as soon as the angler starts retrieving it, the fly flips over. That moment, the sudden roll, triggers a quick attack from even the most jaded trout if the fly is at the right spot. The Rollover Scud is a fine imitation for sight casting to cruising fish.

Rollover Scud

TYING STEPS

1. Lash a piece of lead wire along the top of the hook shank; lacquer the wire.

2. Tie down pieces of blue fluorescent spinning line; let them hang off the rear for the moment.

3. Tie in the blue fluorescent monofilament ribbing material; let it hang off the rear for the moment.

4. Use a dubbing loop to create a "rope" of sparkle yarn; wind the dubbing rope to form the body.

5. Wrap the rib, teasing out the yarn fibers during the process.

6. Pull the pieces of monofilament forward and tie them down.

Whip finish.

step 1

step 2

step 3

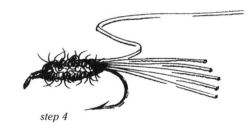

step 4

step 5

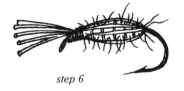

step 6

Hook: 8–16 (1X heavy wire)

Weight: a piece of lead wire (tied along the top of the hook)

Back: blue fluorescent monofilament spinning line

Rib: blue fluorescent monofilament spinning line

Body: sparkle yarn (fibers teased out between the ribbing; red, orange, pink, and olive are the best colors)

A size 8 scud pattern may seem large, but this is not an exaggeration in the Deer Lodge valley; many of the spring creeks and spring ponds hold Gammarus scuds that could pass as party appetizers.

LOG ENTRY: SEPTEMBER 22, 1991
BOHN LAKE

In the upper Clark Fork drainage, this twenty-five acre lake at the head of Dempsey Creek is reachable by rough jeep road into National Forest Service land.

The Rollover Scud was developed specifically for the Settling Ponds, the incredibly fertile complex of lakes and interconnecting seeps fourteen miles from my home. The fly proved itself there, but the method of fishing was sight casting. The angler put the fly in the path of a cruising trout and made the imitation "roll" right in front of the fish.

Did the rolling fly trigger strikes? Almost always, even on the prima donna trout of the ponds. Did live *Gammarus* scuds exhibit this rolling maneuver as they swam? Not in our observations. So why should this technique work so well? That was only one mystery with *Gammarus*.

In our underwater observations in lakes a trout rarely grabbed a swimming scud. A fish would spot the scud, scoot up behind it, and follow the

Rollover Scud Log

quick-moving quarry to the weeds. When the scud stopped on the leaf or stalk it blended perfectly with the green coloration. The trout would come so close to and stare so hard at the spot where the scud hid that the fishes' eyes seemed to cross. Then, with a powerful suck of water, it inhaled the luckless prey.

What good is a swimming imitation? How can the tier imitate a static food item?

The purpose of this trip was to answer a question: Can the Rollover Scud be fished blind?

Neither the date nor the place was by chance. The place had to be a rich lake, where trout didn't need to grab just any bit of fluff, and yet, oddly enough, it couldn't be one jammed with scuds.

Maybe the elevation, roughly 7,000 feet, makes the growing season too short for *Gammarus* in Bohn Lake. Or maybe the summer drawdown for irrigation destroys the cover they need. The trout are well fed in this lake, and subject to fits of snootiness, but with the right technique and fly there is no better place to catch one- to three-pound fish. Among the sixty or so high mountain lakes above Deer Lodge, it is second only to Rainbow (in the Gold Creek headwaters) on my list of favorites.

The date for the trip, late September, was aimed at a yearly phenomenon in lakes. The time varies in different waters, but in Bohn the vegetation starts to die with the first sub-freezing nights. The edges of the weeds turn brown and slough off. This shrinks the amount of hiding spaces and forces some of the insects and scuds into open water. This suddenly exposed abundance of organisms touches off the trout's first heavy feeding spree of the fall season.

Graham Marsh put on the scuba equipment, followed me and my float tube out into the lake, and slipped under the water for the first of two twenty-five minute experiments.

First period: The fly was cast, allowed to sink hook up, and then with the start of the retrieve rolled into the hook-down position. The retrieve was continued until the pick up for the next presentation.

The retrieve sequence was the same technique used on the Settling Ponds. But there was an important difference—on the Ponds, with sight fishing, the roll happened right in front of a trout, but in Bohn, with blind fishing, the roll happened randomly.

The Rollover Scud did catch two rainbows, 17 inches and 18 inches, but when Graham surfaced he said, "The fish were all deeper than the fly. When it rolled, they rushed up and behind it and when it swam away, they followed it. You might have felt a few nips, but except for the two that nailed the fly, most of the fish eventually got bored and gave up the chase."

Second period: This time the fly was cast, allowed to sink (hook up), retrieved for one foot (hook down), and then allowed to sink again (hook up) for at least a count of twenty.

The final long sink, with me patiently staring at the line tip, was the key to blind fishing. The technique caught five rainbows, best of 21 inches, but fighting those trout took up so much of the twenty-five minutes that this period was solid action.

We fished the rest of the afternoon. Without the advantage of a diver to pinpoint concentrations of trout, each move around the lake meant a bit of prospecting, but once the fly hit the first rainbow on the sink, there followed a flurry of five or six hookups. At each new spot we had to fan our casts until we found the edge of the weed bed. Frequently, once the spree began, both of us were connected to these running, jumping trout , making us kick furiously in our tubes to undo crossed lines.

The Rollover Scud, with the roll to draw attention and the sink to draw the strike, worked on a deep lake where it was difficult to spot trout. The fly became much more valuable as a lake imitation this afternoon.

What was the inspiration for the Rollover Scud? Except in my "Finding the Answers" column in Scientific Angler's Fly Fishing Quarterly, my writing rarely touches on saltwater subjects. And yet many of my early fishing experiences were along the coast, both in the Northeast for bluefish and striped bass and in southern Florida for snook, bonefish, tarpon, and permit.

Permit, of course, were the ultimate challenge. Very early in the morning a school of them would travel through a cut connecting two sunken humps. All artificials failed except one of my own crude concoctions, designed first as a lure and then later as a fly, the Rollover Crab.

The same concept helped me trigger inactive largemouth bass in lakes. The biggest fish, after feeding intensely for short periods of time each day, would hug some piece of solid cover, oblivious to any swimming fly. The one pattern that aggravated them enough to draw vicious, head-shaking strikes was a Rollover Salamander.

Naturally, confronted with those monstrous brown trout during the early days of the Settling Ponds, the idea of using motion to excite these well-fed, maddeningly indifferent trout crossed my mind. Rollover imitations of larger food forms did poorly, however—these trout demanded something closer to a staple item of their regular diet. In this fishery, a size 14 Olive Rollover Scud fooled six cruisers on its debut, all brown trout (with an average size of six and a half pounds and a best of eleven pounds).

Tear Drop Nymph

Tear Drop Nymph

Fifteen years ago my group started observing deep nymphs, but the focus was not as much on the fly as it was on the way the method of presentation forced the fly to the bottom. Each technique, whether it placed weight on the hook, on the leader, or in the line, needed to achieve the same end. They had to keep the imitation in the mixing zone between the dead water of the bottom and the fast water of the open current for as long as possible.

This mixing zone, or interface, was the only important layer for deep drifting nymph imitations. Entomologists discovered that 70 to 80 percent of the naturals drifting free in the stream were caught in the twisting, turbulent current band just above the tallest bottom obstructions. My group of scuba divers, charting more than a thousand feeding motions by trout taking deep nymphs, found that these fish captured nearly every drift item from that zone.

Frank Sawyer, on his English chalk streams, developed a nymph style for deep fishing. His flies were streamlined, lacking the appendages excusable on emergent, surface nymph patterns. Flies such as the Grey Goose and Pheasant Tail were the first imitations that purposely depended not on weight but on hydrodynamic design to sink quickly. These patterns reached the mixing zone on silky spring streams.

The goal with the Tear Drop Nymph was to create a pattern that would not frustrate the method of presentation on swifter waters. That is precisely what flies with a lot of realistic features did in our observations. The overdressed patterns, even weighted ones, rode the currents, spiraling upwards out of the mixing zone.

A riffle or a deep run in a freestone stream, flowing much swifter than a spring creek, required a weighted fly. The lead couldn't be just slapped on the hook shank, especially on smaller flies. Various weighting schemes were tested in actual streams. One shape clearly outperformed the others—and it made even the smallest imitations, size 20 mayfly patterns, plummet to the mixing zone, and it didn't occlude the hook gap. The lead was either squeezed, soldered, or, with flat lead, shaped into a tear drop on the hook. This method made an exaggeratedly robust thorax, but even if the trout minded the shape (and they didn't), the advantage gained in sheer weight with the tear drop would have more than compensated for any visual deficiency.

The Tear Drop Nymph works effectively with any method of presentation. A fine leader, 6X or 7X, is an advantage with any of the standard techniques. The thinner nylon doesn't drag the fly upwards as badly as a thick tippet. There is nothing on the Tear Drop itself to catch the current. The tail consists of a few strands of marabou, the only concession to action; the abdomen is fluorescent Uni-Glo, a very thin vinyl; and the thorax is dubbed fur. The extreme weighting carries the Tear Drop down and the fluorescent color grabs the attention of any trout feeding on the deep drift.

In one season the Tear Drop Nymph, in sizes 16 to 20, caught more large trout for me than all the other small nymphs in my boxes combined throughout my fly fishing life—and just as important, it caught large trout in spots where no other nymph stood a chance.

Tear Drop Nymph

step 1

step 2

step 3

step 4

TYING STEPS

1. Form the weight into a tear drop shape (either cut a thin strip of fat, adhesive-backed lead and wrap it in a radical taper, or slip a split shot over the hook shank and squeeze it into shape with pliers).

2. Tie in a sparse tail of marabou fibers.

3. Wrap a fluorescent Uni-Glo abdomen.

4. Spread head cement over the lead; use the Touch Method to dub the thorax (to cover the steep face of the lead, figure eight the fuzzy thread, front to back).

Whip finish.

Hook: 8–20 (1X long and 2X heavy nymph hook, TMC 3761)

Weight: flat lead (molded into a very robust, tear drop shape; or use split shot on the hook shank)

Tail: short strands of marabou

Abdomen: fluorescent Uni-Glo body material

Thorax: sparkle yarn and fur blend (dubbed)

The two main color recipes, with the thorax color listed first and the abdomen color listed second, are cream/fluorescent yellow, green/fluorescent green, and brown/fluorescent pink (the sparse marabou tail matches the abdomen).

LOG ENTRY: JULY 18, 1991
MADISON RIVER

What happened to Slide Inn? Ten years ago, if there were a half dozen cars at the pull out, we would drive past it. Today there were thirty vehicles there—and we stopped anyway. Welcome to the zoo. We ran into Gary and Nancy Borger and they told us that it had been a great morning on Pale Morning Dun imitations.

Jack Dennis, Mike Lawson, and I were going to fish; and Andy Anderson, Don Roberts, and Joe Burke were going to photograph us. So what did we do about the crowds? We followed Mike, who plowed right across the main channel. Andy, another strong bull, waded across with a load of camera equipment. Everyone else went. I couldn't be a wimp, so I danced it, overcoming normal fears about wading water I wouldn't want to take a boat on. There weren't any crowds on the other side (sanity be blessed).

Mike started right away, banging nice rainbows tight to the bank with a size 16 emerger. Later on Jack hit a streak with a nymph on a shallow riffle, taking seven trout from that one run. My trout were big, including a 21-inch brown from the main river and a 20-inch brown from a back channel.

That fish from the channel was in an impossible run. The water wasn't just deep, roughly four feet, but there was also another current sweeping into the slot from the side. The fish were there, taking naturals right in front of me, and I couldn't get a small imitation down to them. They snubbed a big fly.

It was time to christen the Tear Drop. This was what it was designed for—down and dirty. A size 18 *infrequens* imitation cut through that flow like nothing, but it took me a dozen drifts, and at least four muffed strikes, to fool that big brown trout. Andy photographed this one extensively.

There are two new products used for tying this fly. Uni-Glo is manufactured (along with Uni-Thread) in Canada by my friend, Jean Guy Cote. Petey's Sinker, a flat, adhesive-backed lead, is manufactured in Minneapolis, Minnesota, by C & D Trading Company.

I went upstream to the next run, where the currents weren't so damnably mixed, and the fish there were simple. The Tear Drop bounced the bottom nicely, taking rainbows and browns one right after another on this stretch.

It was Mike's day. He was nailing trout all afternoon. I'd pay to watch him fish.

Twist Nymph

Roger Thelen made up a bumper sticker for me after our trip into the high lake: Ban the Twist Nymph—Save Our Trout.

On those days it turned very tough trout into chumps. The Twist Nymph is not a miracle fly (none are), and even on these occasions it needed a particular technique, but in still waters it is the perfect "settling" nymph. The fly is really attractive to trout, looking both alive and vulnerable as it sinks.

That is the problem, by the way, with most flies when they are just sinking in the water—they don't look alive.

For me meetings and shows are as much a chance to learn about fly tying as a chance to teach the art. Mine is usually one of the faces crowded around the tables. My notebook ends up covered with crude drawings and indecipherable scribblings.

Larry Walker shows me techniques with his Dubbit, a tool for twisting a loop of thread. Spin deer hair? Make a hackle? Flare a synthetic collar? He does all these feats. Then it's my turn to go home and play with the tricks.

The Twist Nymph, strictly a still-water fly, is tied with a loop tool. The effects are wonderful; and they cannot be achieved easily without the loop technique.

Abdomen: The twist forms an amazing, fuzzy body of peacock herl and sparkle yarn (blended so tightly); it has to be seen underwater to understand the effect.

Crest: Two hackles are twisted together; this not only mixes the colors completely, but also makes the fibers stand up without the clockwise slant of regular hackling.

Twist Nymph

TYING STEPS

1. Wrap copper or gold wire along the entire shank.

2. Tie in two peacock herl tips as tails.

3. Tie in one strand of peacock herl; touch dub a section of thread with sparkle yarn (Antron)—form a dubbing loop and twist the peacock herl and sparkle yarn together; wrap this rope two thirds of the way up the shank for the abdomen.

4. Tie in two hackle feathers; tie in a loop of thread at the top of the shank—let these materials dangle for the moment.

5. Tie in three or four strands of peacock herl and wrap them in as a thorax.

6. Twist the two hackle feathers together in the dubbing loop—pull the hackle rope forward and tie it down as a crest.

Whip finish.

The crest of the hackle fibers over the abdomen makes the fly sink in an upright position (just like a real mayfly nymph).

Hook:	14–20 (1X long and 1X heavy nymph, TMC 3761)
Weight:	copper or gold wire (wrapped the length of the shank)
Tail:	two peacock herl tips
Abdomen:	peacock herl and yellow sparkle yarn (twisted together in a dubbing loop)
Thorax:	three or four strands of peacock herl
Crest:	grizzly hackle and golden badger hackle (twisted together in a dubbing loop)

Any color of sparkle yarn can be used in the first dubbing loop— favorites include pink (for the Rose Twist Nymph), brown, black, and white.

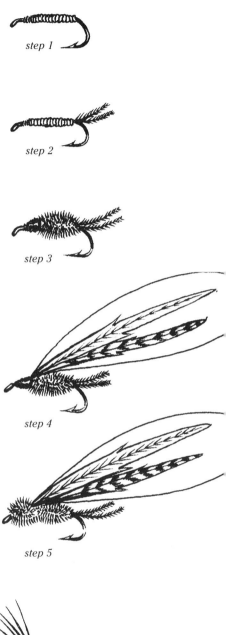

step 1

step 2

step 3

step 4

step 5

step 6

Twist Nymph

LOG ENTRY: JULY 1, 1990
RAT LAKE

This is one of those high mountain lakes famous for having large but difficult trout; John Gierach wrote a wonderful piece about this Gallatin River drainage lake in A View from Rat Lake.

It was a duck shoot. The big trout, which normally get their perverse pleasure from cruising close enough to touch but not to catch, went a bit goofy over this fly.

The trip really wasn't so much about catching trout anyway. It was more about having fun with one of Roger Thelen's challenges. This whole game started with a rash remark a few years ago, "There's no such thing as trout that can't be caught. The key is studying them long enough to be able to predict what they'll do next."

"That's my problem," Roger said. "I'm always reacting, never predicting."

He is not alone. He tries to catch a fish before he tries to know him; and that simple reversal condemns any angler to being an intruder instead of a participant.

Roger invites me fishing whenever he finds a particularly nasty situation. It could be a spring creek, a big river, or a high lake, but there will always be very big trout, one or more, in the spot.

Some new "twist" patterns are being tested in the summer of 1993. Other feathers, such as a strand of pheasant tail, can be twisted with various colors of touch-dubbed sparkle yarn. Strands of Krystal Flash (any color) can also be twisted, creating a very bright nymph. A Twist Damsel and a Twist Bead Head are two variations (minus the crest) that worked well in early fishing tests.

Rat Lake is shallow and weedy, about eighteen acres, and the only really open water is the bowl in the middle. There are smaller trout in the weed beds, but the biggest fish hang at the drop-off in the bowl.

It only took a few minutes of watching to know that they were spoiled by the abundance of food. Life was too easy for them to go chasing some odd-looking fly. Unless there was a flush hatch of insects—caddisfly, mayfly, or damselfly—they preferred very small items that took no effort to capture.

My advantage is that all the ponds around Deer Lodge are like this. My bag of still water tricks is slanted towards the slobs (simply as a matter of my survival). There is little use playing slog-and-flog with Woolly Worms for such trout. They want tiny flies that fall helplessly in front of them.

I backed my float tube twenty-five feet away from the bowl and started my Sloppy Roll approach. The first roll cast landed at the edge of the drop-off and almost immediately I rolled the nymph again. The fly plopped five feet or so further out and then I rolled it yet again. The fly plopped five feet further out and this time I let the nymph sink.

Any good roll caster could reach the full distance the first time. Any good roll caster wouldn't catch these trout. It is the multiple roll that creates an intriguing scene underwater.

The trout sees the fly land (and almost all of the fish in the area look in the direction of the splash). Then, magically to them, the nymph swims rapidly forward and disappears into the air. Almost immediately it lands again, five feet closer to them, and by now even the most jaded trout start swimming towards the fly. Of course, it swims up and disappears again. The trout stack up, and when the nymph hits the third time right over their heads they compete for the chance to snatch it on the sink.

On Rat Lake some of the credit belonged to the technique and some of the credit belonged to the fly. The Sloppy Roll strategy pulled the fish to the area and the Twist Nymph, with the crest balancing the fly on the sink, drew sure strikes. The tally for the day for the two of us was nine rainbows over four pounds on size 16 and size 18 Gold Twist Nymphs (even a size 14 failed on these fish).

This fly actually had a different name during the testing phase. Our fishermen called it "Double Magic" because for the first time a fly combined two proven, special materials in a way that did not diminish either one.

The tying method for the abdomen creates a startling effect. The technique is unique to these flies (no one else touch-dubs). Any other method of dubbing creates a pathetic, barber pole look when the thread is twisted with the strand of peacock herl. When the thread is touch-dubbed (explained in the section on the Emergent Sparkle Pupa), coating it with nothing but fuzz, and twisted with the herl, the rope shows the peacock perfectly, with no striping, but there is an aura of sparkle yarn fibers mysteriously and miraculously springing out around the body.

A scuba diver, Tom Poole, watched a Twist Nymph variation during a *Callibaetis* hatch in a lake and came out of the water more excited about this pattern than any other still-water fly he had ever seen. "If the Twist Nymph was anywhere near a trout, he always took it, every time, even if there were a half dozen naturals in the focus area."

Four

■

Emergers

Harry Ramsay, the old caretaker of the club water on Connecticut's Mill Brook, was my first fly fishing teacher. He never said a lot to me at one time; maybe he had a twenty-five word limit with all ten-year-old boys and not just me.

He watched me cast to a brown trout feeding on a nice hatch of mayflies. That fish refused the best floats of my Light Cahill, and finally Harry got disgusted waiting for me and snapped, "Spit on the fly."

On the next cast the imitation drifted half drowned and the trout sucked it in. "Why did he take it," I asked.

"You figure it out," Harry said and he left me there.

I used that trick for the next year on fussy fish and it worked often enough to keep me wondering about the why of it. My own observations didn't solve the mystery—it wasn't until my steady progress through Harry's massive library of English fly fishing books brought me to *Minor Tactics of the Chalk Stream*, the G. E. M. Skues classic, that the reason became clear.

The emerger fly and the dry fly are so closely bound that it is impossible to discuss one without mentioning the other. Only the slimmest of barriers, the meniscus (or surface film), separates the two types of flies, one mired in it and the other riding on top of it, but to a feeding trout the imitations are entirely different.

Without the surface film (a compressed layer of molecules created by the uneven electrical charges of water and air) nymphs and larvae could not emerge in open water. They would all have to crawl out onto the bank. The surface film helps in two ways; it gives the emerging insect something to grab onto, a roof that the rising nymph or larva can hump its back into to stabilize itself, and once the skin along the back splits and the insect starts to struggle out, the surface film holds and pins the skin while the adult pulls free.

The escape through the surface film takes only minutes, sometimes only seconds, but this brief stage in the insect's life is one of its most vulnerable periods. With mayflies, trout take as many emergers as duns during most hatches; with midges and caddisflies trout take many more pupae than adults.

There are three major things that distinguish the emerging nymph or pupa from the fully free, floating adult form. The emerging insect is half in and half out of the old skin. That "beast in transition" is larger than either the before or after forms, the skin or sheath is dangling below the surface film, and an emerger is bright with air bubbles inside the old skin.

In our underwater observations the divers observed how selectively trout feed on different forms of food (streamers the least; emergers the most):

Food Form	Most Important Characteristic	Second Most Important Characteristic
Streamer	Size	Shape

Minnow imitations are usually retrieved, and even slow movement obscures details of the food form or its imitation.

Wet Fly	Size	Shape or Texture

A moving wet fly is like a small streamer; a dead drift wet fly is like a nymph.

Nymph	Size	Texture of the body; the dangling soft parts

Visibility near the bottom of the stream is poorer than visibility at the surface—this by itself explains the lower degree of selectivity to drifting nymphs or their imitations.

Dry Fly	Size	Color

The surface film distorts the trout's view of anything above it; this is the feeding zone where light bathes an object and highlights its colors.

Emerger	Brightness	Size

The bright air bubbles inside the skin or sheath of the insect are a dominating characteristic—and if the natural insect is bright, the imitation must also be bright.

The imitation of an emerger has to have a trailing shuck, to match the shape and size of the insect in transition, and the bright body parts. It also has to float half in and half out of the water, and it needs to mimic the budding, unfolding wings of the natural.

The fact that trout typically feed more selectively on emerging insects than any other food form means that the imitations of them are the most

important patterns in this series of flies. Those imitations work in the most critical feeding situations—times when other flies not only fail but fail badly.

In my experience, the Emergent Sparkle Pupa outfishes a drab imitation six to one. The Halo Mayfly Emerger outfishes a drab imitation three to one. The Halo Midge Emerger falls somewhere in between these two. These rough figures are based on my experiences (a lot of them). The differences in these ratios are linked to the brightness of the naturals, the air bubbles surrounding the caddisfly being much more visible because the insect has a thin, transparent sheath, not the thicker, nymphal skin of the mayfly.

The major step in a fly fisherman's education occurs when he can tell the difference between the bulging and splashy rise forms of trout taking emerging nymphs or pupae in the film and the simple sucking rise forms of trout taking adult insects off the surface. He saves himself many hours of frustrating flogging over rising fish.

Cone

It is not unusual for my group to conceive a "counter pattern" during our testing. Such a fly, in some way opposite to another imitation, serves as a control. Typically, it is a failure—after all, it lacks the characteristic that makes the other pattern so good.

The Mess, spectacular as a mayfly dun imitation, has an exaggerated bunch of rooster hackle and mallard hackle fibers projecting forward over the eye of the hook. The Cone has the same overdressed mass of hackle, but the fibers slant backwards around the body.

The Cone didn't fail as an imitation for large mayflies. It worked at different times than the Mess, however. The Mess succeeded whenever trout were feeding on duns; the Cone succeeded whenever trout were feeding on emergers. The Mess exaggerated the upright wing; the Cone, inadvertently (our intent was only to rob the Mess of its strongest triggering characteristic), mimicked the disheveled appearance of the hatching nymph.

The Cone, again not due to any forethought during its creation, also blossomed as a "cripple." After the hatch, when the malformed duns trapped in nymphal shucks collected in the foam lines of the stream, the flush-floating, rough Cone took trout selectively mopping up the dying mayflies. The fly matched this aftermath stage of the insect so well that many of our fishermen tied the Cone in all sizes, not just on large hooks, as a cripple.

Cone

Cone

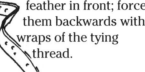

step 1

step 2

step 3

step 4

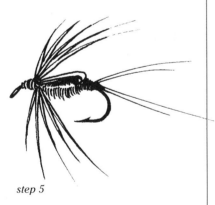

step 5

TYING STEPS

1. Tie in four hackle fibers; split them for tails (this is for the cripple variation).

2. Tie in a strip of foam; let it dangle for a moment.

3. Dub a body of synthetic seal's fur.

4. Pull the foam forward and tie it down.

5. Wrap two hackles, a rooster hackle in back and a mallard feather in front; force them backwards with wraps of the tying thread.

Whip finish.

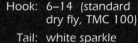

Hook: 6–14 (standard dry fly, TMC 100)

Tail: white sparkle yarn or split hackle fibers (the former for an emerger and the latter for a cripple)

Back: foam

Body: synthetic seal's fur (dubbed)

Rear Hackle: rooster (swept backwards)

Front Hackle: light-colored, soft-hackle fibers (swept back-wards)

Main color variations include the Vanilla Cone (cream body/light ginger hackle), Chocolate Cone (brown body/coachman brown hackle) and Pistachio Cone (olive body/cree hackle), but the tier is free to change the recipe to match any mayfly.

LOG ENTRY: JULY 17, 1991
BLAINE SPRING CREEK

The way to avoid the fishing crowd in Montana is to think small—this means small streams, not necessarily small fish. Blaine Spring Creek, especially below the old hatchery, holds plenty of large rainbows and browns, most of them untouchable unless a heavy hatch brings them out into open water. When there is a heavy emergence of insects, this tributary of the Madison River, entering near Varney, rewards anyone willing to fight the brush.

There's no doubt in my mind why streams like Blaine Creek appeal to me—most of my boyhood fishing was on the overgrown brooks of Connecticut. Those years of hunting smaller waters taught me techniques for tight places, but more important they taught me that these little flows always hold secrets.

The secret of Blaine Creek? This stream is hard fishing when nothing is hatching. But in July a large mayfly, the Brown Drake *(E. simulans)*, pops in enough numbers to bring the real reclusive trout to the surface. Emerger imitations, as usual with this particular insect, fool fish well during this hatch.

I was driving down anyway to meet Jack Dennis and Mike Lawson to fish the Madison tomorrow. I hit Blaine Creek knowing that it was probably too late in the year for the Brown Drake, but I was hoping that the cold, rainy spring had delayed the hatch a few weeks.

I wasn't in the water more than a few minutes before I was casting to rising fish, all of them slashing at nymphs in the surface film. A Were Wulff took a few rainbows, but when a larger trout rolled under the fly, missing it completely, I changed to a brown Cone.

I always thought that the Cone would be perfect for the Brown Drake. The *simulans* nymph, a fast swimmer, hits the surface film hard, with very little fooling around, and it escapes the shuck quickly for a mayfly. The adult gets off the water after a short drift on dry days.

The Cone, riding unkempt and prone in the film, was designed to match any large emerger; and, in theory, it should work wonderfully for the Brown Drake hatch. The fact that it had never been fished during Brown Drake time made my first casts a bit tentative—not crisp, not in perfect rhythm with the rises.

My clumsiness didn't bother the trout. Every presentation was made to a specific, rising fish, and with this hatch, heavy but not a blitz, the trout were pouncing on nearly every natural. Once the question was answered, once the Cone proved itself, my casting improved and every feeder became a marked trout. The fly caught big fish and little fish (from 8 to 20 inches). The afternoon didn't produce any monsters, but then none of the huge ones showed themselves.

My opinion of the Cone, after this wonderful day, is that it is so perfect for the Brown Drake that no other imitation in my experience equals it on this hatch. And given the rapid emergence phase of *E. simulans*, the Cone should always perform well with this insect. It will take more encounters with the Brown Drake to confirm this theory, of course.

What about other large mayflies? The Green Drake, the Gray Drake or even the Hex? The duns of those insects ride the surface for some distance with wings upright. The Cone might be important as either an emerger or a cripple, a critical imitation for certain stages of a hatch, but it probably cannot replace the Mess completely for those mayflies. It seems uniquely suited to the Brown Drake—that doesn't make it a universal pattern for all large upwings.

It won a place in my heart today.

Deep Sparkle Pupa

For twenty years the Deep Sparkle Pupa has been the fly to use before the main caddisfly hatch. It works well then because occasional strays cut free from the pupal cocoon all day. The insects hesitate at two levels, drifting along the bottom until they inflate the pupal sheath and struggling at the surface until they break through the rubbery meniscus. Later, during the actual hatch, trout concentrate more on the emergers in the film, but before the mass break-out they feed steadily for hours on the deep drifting pupae.

At last, after all these seasons of my being very much the robot in this situation, my summer of hard fishing with my own flies taught me something. The chance flailing showed me that the Deep Pupa, just like a steady food form on the surface (such as a beetle), makes an excellent teaser because it mimics one of those insects trout remember fondly. It became much more of a general searching pattern for me.

The Deep Sparkle Pupa is in the emerger chapter because it imitates an emerging insect. Many anglers fish this pattern with an active technique, such as a Leisenring Lift, that swims the fly up to the surface. My favorite method is a simple dead-drift presentation, but there is usually more than one way to catch a trout.

Deep Sparkle Pupa

step 1

TYING STEPS

1. Separate two plies of the four ply yarn; comb out a short piece of each ply and tie one in on the top of the hook bend and one in on the bottom (use less than a ply on top and bottom for hooks smaller than size 12); let the plies dangle for the moment.

step 2

2. Use the Touch Method to dub the underbody.

3. Pull the top ply forward, spreading it around the top half of the shank, and pull the bottom ply forward, spreading it around the bottom half of the shank; loosen the tied-down fibers until the overbody is a filmy, baggy sheath and then trim the stubs.

step 3

4. Tie in soft hackle fibers along both sides of the body.

5. Dub a head.

Whip finish.

step 4

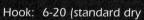

Hook:	6-20 (standard dry fly, TMC 100)
Weight:	lead wire (optional— all of my own Deep Pupa patterns have lead on the shank)
Overbody:	sparkle yarn
Underbody:	half sparkle yarn and half fur (chopped very fine and mixed in a blender; applied sparse and fuzzy to the thread with a method called Touch Dubbing described in Emergent Sparkle Pupa)
Wing Pads:	soft hackle fibers (on each side of the overbody)
Head:	fur or marabou fibers

The angler can (and should) carry colors to match the major caddisflies of his local waters. The four main variations are the Brown and Yellow (rusty yellow overbody and underbody/brown wing pads/brown head), Brown and Bright Green (green overbody and underbody/brown wing pads/brown head), Ginger (ginger overbody and underbody/ginger wing pads/tan head), and Dark Gray (dark gray overbody and underbody/gray wing pads/gray head). For my part of the country a size 8 Brown and Orange (orange overbody and underbody/brown wing pads/brown head) is indispensable in the fall when the Giant Orange Sedge (Dicosmoecus sp.) appears on our rivers.

step 5

Deep Sparkle Pupa

LOG ENTRY: MAY 12, 1991
ARMSTRONG SPRING CREEK

This stream is one of the famous fee fisheries of the Paradise valley near Livingston, Montana. During the summer the days are booked more than a year in advance, but in other seasons it is sometimes possible to arrange a day of fishing at the last moment. These spring creeks are worth the fee any time of the year.

The trout today were feeding continually, but all of us were struggling to find out what the mystery item was in their diet. My brother Jay, Steve Gayken, and Tom Trozera worked riffles above and below me; and there were other anglers spread out along the stream. Occasionally, someone would catch a fish, but no one was getting more than the stray. No one could (or would) keep a trout for a stomach sampling, and no one had a stomach pump with them.

My downfall was a preconceived plan. All last week I tied flies—for the Yellowstone there was an assortment of Emergent Sparkle, Deep Sparkle and Dancing Caddis patterns for the Grannom *(Brachycentrus* sp.) hatch; and for the spring creeks, our destination if the river blew out with the muddy flow of early runoff, there was a selection of Halo Mayfly Emergers and Duck Butt Duns for the *Baetis* hatch.

What fooled me here was that a size16 Olive Halo Mayfly Emerger was catching more trout than any other fly. After a lot of drifts, usually fifteen minutes worth or more, one of the porpoising fish would apparently pity the persistent angler and sip the Halo Emerger. It wasn't the "right" fly, obviously, but it was enough of a delicacy to make the selective trout sample the *Baetis* imitation.

There were some *Baetis* mayflies hatching, but with the bright sun there weren't a lot of them. There were also some Grannom caddisflies flitting about the creek, but few of them were on the water for serious egg-laying activity. Grannom for the Yellowstone—*Baetis* for the spring creeks; it was a formula that had worked for me for years at this time of the season.

So why didn't I see the problem? Other fly fishermen often miss caddis activity, but for me there is no excuse. Maybe it was the fact that the rises were soft rolls, not splashy, slashing moves in pursuit of the insects, but the Grannom is a slow caddisfly, a sluggard in every phase, showing little of the frantic panic of other species at the thought of being eaten by fish or birds. And this was a spring creek, where the trout expect such an abundance of drifting insect life that rushing is a lost art. The fish were taking Grannom emergers coming off the riffles.

I was sitting down on the grass at the lower end of the property, just above the fence, and with the lateness of the afternoon the fish were giving up on the fading hatch. I just had time to test my theory about the Grannom on two smaller trout still rising to insects. I put on an Emergent Sparkle Pupa and presented the fly dead drift on the surface. Both fish, a 13-inch and a 16-inch brown, took the imitation the first time they saw it.

The hatch was over for the day, but I still had to walk back upstream to the parking area and there might be a chance to salvage some dignity from my flogging. Since there weren't any trout at all working the surface, I picked out a size 14 Brown and Bright Green Deep Sparkle Pupa. On my way from riffle to riffle and pool to pool there were occasional fishermen, but even though they were all bouncing bottom now, too, with flies such as Glo Bugs, San Juan Worms, and Big Horn Scuds, they weren't hooking anything. The Deep Sparkle Pupa wasn't sweeping the stream clean, but it wasn't doing too badly. By the time I reached the meeting spot I had caught seven more browns and rainbows, between 14 and 19 inches.

One of the strangers I had given flies to had done well, also. He came over to tell me about a 21-inch brown he had landed on the Deep Pupa (and offered to trade me his first born child for a few more).

It never ceases to surprise me how many times I miss the fact that trout are taking caddisflies under my nose; and it never ceases to embarrass me.

Emergent Sparkle Pupa

Emergent Sparkle Pupa

The techniques for tying the Emergent Sparkle Pupa are not difficult—they are just different. Tied wrong, the Emergent looks like a chubby dragonfly nymph in a garish gown going to the school dance. Tied right, the fly looks like a shimmering caddisfly pupa struggling to escape through a backlit hole in the roof of the stream (the surface film). The difference between the good and bad versions is sparseness.

The underbody has to be "touch" dubbed. The dubbing mix of half sparkle yarn and half fur is hand-cut in 1/8-inch lengths, and then blended together in a mixer. The tier holds a puff of this specially prepared dubbing and pats the waxed thread lightly. He wraps the thread on the hook shank. No other method of dubbing—not noodle dubbing and not loop dubbing—creates such a sparse, fuzzy body.

The overbody, plies of sparkle yarn pulled forward to envelope the underbody, has to be loose and sparse. A size10 hook uses a full ply of yarn on top and a full ply of yarn on the bottom of the shank. On smaller sizes the tier pulls more and more fibers off of the plies. Each ply is combed completely out and spread over the top or bottom half of the hook shank. The tier loosens the overbody with a scissors point or a dubbing needle (the puffed out "ball" fills half of the hook gap). For the final test the tier holds the finished fly up to the light. He should be able to see the underbody through the overbody; he shouldn't be able to see any tight or solid bands of yarn.

Why am I so fussy about how the Emergent is tied? There is a tremendous difference in the effectiveness of good versus bad variations. The thick, overdressed version is still bright, the Antron filaments reflecting light, but it isn't translucent. The sparse version is translucent, and it also gathers a cluster of real air bubbles. This good version, floating in the surface film, is both an imitation and an attractor—and that makes it unique.

I am not nearly as fussy about how the fly is fished by my fellow anglers. People come up to me and tell me about their great days with the Emergent. Usually they describe their method of fishing it. The fact that they don't present the fly the way that I would might bother me, but that's no reason to tell anglers raving about terrific fishing that they are using the fly wrong.

Three methods (in addition to my favorite technique) seem particularly effective:

1. Don't grease the fly with any floatant. After a few casts, once it becomes waterlogged, cast it up or up-and-across and let it dead drift a few inches under the surface (usually with some type of strike indicator).

2. Cast the fly down-and-across stream, and, with constant mends, keep it twitching and struggling upstream against the current. Work it like this all the way across the stream, the fly struggling through prime lies.

3. Fish the fly with a 6-foot leader and a sink-tip line. Cast it down-and-across, and when it reaches a trout's holding spot, snug the line up, lifting the fly in a rising swim to surface (this is basically the Induced Take or the Leisenring Lift).

One thing might explain the variety of methods. Many anglers use the Emergent as a general all-around fly. Its ability to excite trout makes it a good attractor when nothing is hatching; that allure even makes it a hatch-breaker when some different kind of insect, a mayfly or a midge, is entrancing the fish.

My way of fishing the Emergent is simpler, and in my opinion, during a caddis hatch, it is more effective. The pattern is greased entirely and floated dead drift (from up, down, or across stream) over rising trout. The pattern rides half in and half out of the surface film, the deer hair wing quite visible above the water. Fished like this, the Emergent is a hackleless dry fly.

All of the other methods, by sinking or moving the fly, knock the natural air bubbles off of the Antron. Those bubbles, continually grabbing onto the body or breaking free from it, give the illusion of a squirming, living insect even when the fly is drifting drag-free with the current. From the underwater view it mimics not only the appearance but the movement of the caddisfly pupa.

In all my years of fishing the Emergent it has never failed during a caddis hatch. Not on any river or lake; in my experience, not even for a beginning angler. Once the insect is captured, and matched generally in

Emergent Sparkle Pupa

size and color, the dead drift fly turns a frustrating situation into an easy one.

What is the color and size of the natural pupa? The emerging insect is a fully formed, adult caddisfly inside a transparent sheath. The angler can usually find out the color and size of the emergent by capturing the most abundant adult from the brush.

How does the angler recognize a caddisfly hatch? The adults, once they escape the pupal sheath, fly away quickly. The angler wastes a lot of time staring at the surface looking for floating insects. The way the trout rise gives away the secret—they roll and even jump as they rush to take the emerging natural.

There is a well-known phrase in fly fishing: Presentation is 90 percent of the secret of success. But there is one case where the fly overwhelms presentation, and that is during the caddis hatch. The Emergent Sparkle Pupa, with its shimmering body of Antron fibers, catches more trout fished wrong than a dry fly or a drab pupal imitation fished right. The versatility of this pattern explains its popularity.

Hook: 6-20 (standard dry fly, TMC 100)

Overbody: sparkle yarn

Underbody: half sparkle yarn and half fur (a finely chopped dubbing blend)

Wing: deer hair

Head: dubbed fur or wrapped marabou fibers

The angler should carry the same basic selection for the Emergent as for the Deep Sparkle Pupa. Brown and Yellow (yellow underbody and overbody/brown speckled deer hair wing/brown head), Brown and Bright Green (bright green underbody and overbody/brown speckled deer hair wing/brown head), Ginger (ginger underbody and overbody/light tan deer or elk hair wing/ginger head), Dark Gray (dark gray underbody and overbody/gray speckled deer hair/gray head) are the most important color schemes. The Brown and Orange (orange underbody and overbody/brown speckled deer hair wing/brown head) version, in a size 8, is a great fly in the West in the fall when the Giant Orange Sedge appears on our rivers.

TYING STEPS

1. Separate two plies of the four ply yarn; comb out a short piece of each ply and tie one in on the top of the hook bend and one in on the bottom (use less than a ply on top and bottom for hooks smaller than size 12); let the plies dangle for the moment.

2. Use the Touch Method to dub the underbody.

3. Pull the top ply forward, spreading it around the top half of the shank, and pull the bottom ply forward, spreading it around the bottom half of the shank; loosen the tied-down fibers until the overbody is a filmy, baggy sheath and then trim the stubs.

4. Clip some of the yarn fibers directly on top of the shank (right in back of the tie-down spot) and let them trail off the back.

5. Tie in a deer hair wing, the tips extending to the bend of the hook.

6. Dub a head of fur or wrap a head of marabou fibers.

Whip finish.

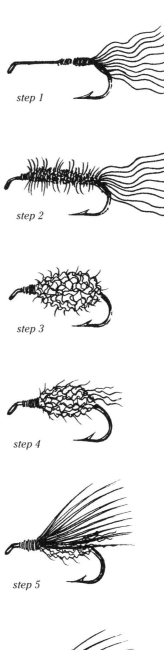

step 1

step 2

step 3

step 4

step 5

step 6

Emergent Sparkle Pupa

LOG ENTRY: JULY 20, 1991
MIDDLE CLARK FORK RIVER

Knowing the upper river around Deer Lodge doesn't give an angler any edge in the middle section. This water starts at the mouth of Rock Creek, the influx of cold, clean flow changing the character of the Clark Fork completely. It is no longer a total brown trout fishery, and no longer a twisting, meadow stream.

The middle river has an odd character. Usually it wouldn't be one of my favorite trout destinations, but since Powell and Tazun Swanser live on the Clark Fork at Turah, it ends up being one of my regular fishing holes.

The river bottom is made up of small stones. A fishing day starts at Powell's house and might cover two or three miles of stream, and in that entire stretch there is only one large boulder breaking the current. Most of the rest of the rocks range down from the size of baseballs.

What makes the Clark Fork odd is the combination of pea gravel and heavy current. There is a minimum of holding water for the larger trout. In the main river they either hug the banks or hang deep in the holes. There are shallow flats where small fish, 6- to 10-inch rainbows and browns, rise to insects, but there aren't many big fish sipping in these areas.

Small flies don't catch decent trout on this part of the river. It took me over a year to accept this fact. Powell would get big fish on big flies, usually on his size 6 Outlaw Hopper (a dry fly with a body of gray, high density foam and a white deer hair head), and I would stick to normal-sized offerings and never catch anything over 14 inches.

Even my stubbornness has its limits. After a while I was slapping an Outlaw Hopper or some other big dry fly on the surface and catching the nicer fish. After a while I started to appreciate my days on this middle section of the Clark Fork.

Powell knows my likes and dislikes. More important, he knows my fantasies. When he calls up and says that I have to come down to fish, it usually means that he has found a new place, and not just any place, but one that fits my dreams.

I was surprised then that we were going to fish the Clark Fork. We went down behind the house, but instead of starting right there we began walking fast upstream, crossing and recrossing the river as we went. It was almost dusk and soon Powell was running, and I didn't know why we were running but he was so excited that I was getting excited and before long we were far above where we usually fish.

We slogged across the river, rounded a rock cliff, and stopped at the mouth of a side channel. Powell held out his arms, presenting the water like a true treasure, and said, "There's a quarter mile of it," and then he left it to me.

It wasn't like the main river. Water tumbled in the classic pool-run-riffle sequence. Caddisflies were hatching and trout were rolling and jumping. It didn't take me long to tie on a match for the emerging insect, the Little Sister Sedge *(Cheumatopsyche campyla)*, and on the second cast, right there at the mouth of the channel, the size16 Brown and Yellow Emergent caught my first nice trout on a small fly from this middle section of the Clark Fork. It was an 18-inch slab brown.

The number of trout in the channel was amazing. It was no more than 20-feet wide, but there had to be more than a hundred browns and rainbows in the quarter mile of water. That was only a guess—with dark fast approaching there was no chance I'd get to see the whole channel. It took me a half hour to fish the first run above the mouth. Most of that time was spent fighting and releasing 14- to 20-inch trout.

I skipped past a hundred yards of rising trout and crept up to a large, corner pool. It was almost too dark to see the fish, but it was easy enough to hear them. Everything I'd caught on the Emergent so far was on a dead-drift, floating presentation, but I worked the fly on a taut line down and across through this pool. The active technique gave me another fifteen minutes of fast fishing.

Powell was waiting when I went down to the main river. In the black of the moonless night I don't think that I could have found my way home without him.

What makes the Clark Fork odd is the combination of pea gravel and heavy current. There is a minimum of holding water for the larger trout. In the main river they either hug the banks or hang deep in the holes. There are shallow flats where small fish, 6- to 10-inch rainbows and browns, rise to insects, but there aren't many big fish sipping in these areas.

Halo Mayfly Emerger

Halo Mayfly Emerger

The divers, after watching trout react to the Halo Mayfly Emerger, put this pattern into a rare category. They have a strict set of criteria for the best imitations. First, before the fly even gets a chance to qualify for their highest honor, it has to pass the normal tests:

■ The fly, entering the feeding circle at the right moment (and, of course, drifting perfectly) will be singled out and taken more than 50 percent of the time by a rising trout (this is tougher than it may sound—during a heavy hatch there may be as many as a half dozen real insects entering the window of vision with the fly).

■ The fly, once the trout notices it, and starts to rise for it, will rarely get that last moment, turn away refusal (this really isn't that tough—once a trout commits to a fly and expends any energy at all, he is reluctant to pass up an imitation).

A fly needs certain elements to pass these two tests. It gets singled out if the triggering characteristic (the first feature the trout notices on the natural) is exaggerated on the imitation. A fly rarely gets last moment refusals if the secondary characteristics (color, size, and shape mainly) are close to the natural's characteristics. Any imitation that grabs initial interest and passes close-up inspection is a very fine pattern.

What more could a fly fisherman want? There is a third test a fly must pass to be special. The fly must pull a feeding fish further than the real insect. A trout may be sliding a foot to his left and a foot to his right to take naturals, but he will move much more, as far as the limits of his vision, to take a special imitation. And he will not refuse that special fly like he might a strong attractor pattern once he gets close to it.

Tom Poole, the analytical person in our group, even set up a chart and listed many different types of insect imitations based on his hours of underwater study. The Halo Mayfly Emerger, shown for comparison with the Emergent Sparkle Pupa (the highest scoring fly in this system) and the floating Hare's Ear, a time-proven, hackleless mayfly imitation, rated high.

	Gets noticed	No refusals	Pulls the trout
Halo Mayfly Emerger	74%	96%	91% of its visual area
Emergent Sparkle Pupa	81%	94%	98% of its visual area
Floating Hare's Ear	41%	94%	50% of its visual area

Fishing a flush hatch of mayflies is easier once the angler understands how trout feed on insects in slow water. The trickiest part of this game is determining when fish are taking all emergers, a mix of emergers and duns (sequential selectivity) or all duns. Trout commonly feed on both emergers and duns, but extreme conditions favoring one form or the other can create a concentration of insects either in or on the surface.

A trout hanging just under the surface may be sipping either stage. One way of deciding which form a fish is selecting is by studying the spacing of the rises. A trout picking mayfly adults usually has a tight range, each break in the surface occurring in the same spot or slightly downstream each time. The same fish taking mayfly emergers not only moves slightly upstream on every rise, going forward to meet the insect, but he also sidles more to each side. This is because part of the emerger's body hangs below the surface. This lets a fish see his target further away and gives him time to advance on it. With the adult mayfly, especially a small one that doesn't press down that rubbery surface film much, the trout can't study the insect until it actually enters his window of vision.

The triggering characteristic on the Halo Emerger is the spike of fluorescent orange deer hair canting upwards. Never mind that it is a wild, improbable exaggeration of the budding wings on the emerging nymph. The spike is a great attention grabber.

This fly has another powerful visual characteristic—the translucent foam pieces overlapping the thorax. The mayfly laying in the surface film, struggling to climb through the bulging escape hole in the nymphal shuck, shows a brief halo of light. The aura is created by the edges of the stretched skin and the natural air bubbles surrounding the thorax. This feature on either natural or imitation not only attracts a trout but also seems to mesmerize him.

Halo Mayfly Emerger

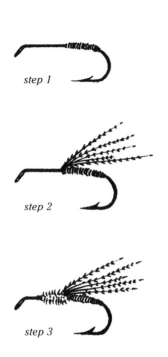

step 1

step 2

step 3

step 4

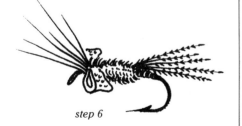

step 5

step 6

TYING STEPS

1. Wrap a tag of clear Antron.

2. Tie in a short tail of marabou fibers.

3. Dub an abdomen of synthetic seal's fur.

4. Wind the thread in a figure-eight motion, binding a strip of foam onto the hook shank; fold the strip back on each side and tie two loops of foam.

5. Dub a thorax of synthetic seal's fur (figure-eight the dubbed thread over the center area of the foam "halo," leaving the loops of foam overlapping the sides of the thorax).

6. Tie in a spike of orange deer hair.

Whip finish.

Hook:	10-24 (standard dry fly, TMC 100)
Tag:	clear Antron (optional; clear Antron is difficult to find in fly fishing outlets)
Tail:	marabou fibers
Abdomen:	synthetic seal's fur (dubbed thin)
Halo:	closed cell foam (common packing foam)
Thorax:	synthetic seal's fur (dubbed thicker than the abdomen)
Spike:	orange deer hair (extending out over the eye of the hook)

The tail, abdomen, and thorax of the fly are the same color—on a Brown Halo Mayfly Emerger those materials would be brown; the tag is always clear Antron, the Halo is always translucent foam, and the spike is always orange. The main colors for the Halo series are brown, olive, and cream.

LOG ENTRY: OCTOBER 24, 1991
CLARK FORK RIVER

The river below Missoula has a population of only 400 to 500 trout per mile. For such big water this is poor, but that number sounds worse than it is. The fish are very localized in the river, long stretches not worth much, but in other areas there are plenty of free-rising trout. It is a fine stream for the angler who knows where those pods of feeders are during the hatches.

This wasn't the best day with the Halo Emerger. It was the final moment of the fly this fishing season (a moment that verified all of my other experiences). What struck me was that when it came time to choose an imitation to show to the best fish of the day, I never hesitated, never considered any other fly, before tying on the Halo Emerger.

The weather broke earlier this week. There was a promise of a winter storm, the type of late fall nastiness that might finally make the *Baetis* hatch pop. It didn't come—it wasn't the beautiful seventy to eighty degree sunshine that has made this October fish more like September, but the sun broke through the patchy clouds and the insects hatched erratically. There were trout rising at 1:00 p.m., taking midges and the few *Baetis* duns from the surface. At 2:30 p.m. everything died. There wasn't a single dimpling trout even on the flats because there were no insects.

Justin Baker and I had nothing better to do or we would have left. I was disappointed because I wanted Justin to see and fish a flush hatch. This was going to be another lesson in his summer of learning. If he could catch a few nice trout on fine tippets and small matching flies, it would give him something to puzzle about over the winter.

Justin listens to my ramblings, probably out of politeness, but to my credit they're usually not too preachy. Today may have been the exception. "All the rest is fun," I told him. "Swinging streamers, bouncing nymphs, popping attractor dries—it's fun, but it's just fill-in between the hatches."

So there we were on a great dry fly stretch of the Clark Fork and not a thing was rising. We wandered upstream, chucking Woolly Worms, streamers, and crawfish patterns. I moved up to the bend, to the spot where a current brushed a backwater of foam, and sat on a log and watched for movement. It clouded over again and a few insects started hatching and with the subtlest of rises, takes on subsurface emergers, big trout started feeding.

There was a moment's thought about the leader, retying it to 12 feet and down to 6X, but there was no doubt about the fly. It was going to be the last size 20 Olive Halo Emerger in my box. The first fish it covered— and they were rising in a one-two-three and pause rhythm—wouldn't have a chance. A summer's fishing promised me that.

I waded in and the shifting foam on the right curled around me. On the edge of that foam a big nose poked out. There was also a nice fish just to my left, on the crease between moving and still water. I saved the one on

Halo Mayfly Emerger Log

the right—it looked like one of the slab cutthroats, almost 20 inches and shaped like a sunfish—because I wanted Justin to catch him.

The trout on the left took the Halo Emerger on the second drift. Even while he was jumping, I was forcing him to the left, away from the pod of risers. He bounced seven times. Between the jumps I was waving Justin upstream. The rainbow measured 17 inches.

After that Justin and I stood at the bend, staring alternately at the crease and the foam for fifteen minutes. Nothing else rose even once. We finally went back downstream to the original pods of rising trout (smaller fish, but more dependable).

Justin has never needed a formal lesson. He learns by watching either Powell Swanser or me (probably not the best influences), or by thrashing his way to his own conclusions. In this mad summer of fishing he has become incredibly good at general, riffle bouncing dry fly techniques, but he hasn't had the chance before this to work on a lot of feeding trout.

There were things that I was telling myself:

- Don't cast blind. Don't cast at all unless there's a rising fish in front of you.
- The line, leader, and fly can't slap down. Make the cast straighten out a few feet above the water, and let everything drift gently to the surface.
- Don't scatter shoot. Each drift of the fly should cover one prime fish.
- Watch the rise rhythm. One-two-three and pause. These fish are hanging just under the surface for three sips and then sinking back to the bottom.
- Hold the fly in the air, false casting off to the side. Then you're ready to drop it a foot or two above the fish, no more, right after the first rise and just before the second.
- The cast and drift have to be perfect, not an inch off, because the trout's window of vision is so small when they are holding just below the surface.
- Be ready to work in all directions. On the up and across fish or straight upstream fish you have to throw a curve cast to curl the fly off the line of drift; on the down and across fish you need slack, plenty of slack, so the fly can not only drift over the rise area but well past it.
- On straight downstream fish you don't cast to them. Lay the line off to the side, at least five feet from the pod. Let the fly hang in the current. Lift your rod and pull the dragging fly over until it's directly above the fish. Then drop the rod tip sharply, creating enough slack for the fly to drift over the fish in the pod.
- Don't make a "normal" pickup (wrong anytime). Roll cast the fly into the air and false cast well off to the side. Don't let the droplets of water fall on the fish.

The pods kept drifting away from Justin. They didn't spook outright. Soon he was either casting further and further or wading after them. The other alternative, waiting patiently for the trout to return to the original position, was hard for him to accept.

"I vote for dynamite," he said.

The hatch didn't last long enough, but even in the brief flurry he was figuring out these pods of trout. More important, he was fascinated with the game of stalking them. Maybe this appealed to the hunter in him as much as it did to the fisherman.

Justin will have the winter to think about the pods on the Clark Fork. It wasn't a flush hatch of insects by any means, but it was enough for me. A few more fish fell to the Halo Emerger, but nothing for either for us was as large as the first trout.

The cast and drift have to be perfect, not an inch off, because the trout's window of vision is so small when they are holding just below the surface.

Halo Midge Emerger

Every part of the Halo Midge Emerger appeals to the fish, but some parts do more than that on the stream. The pad of closed-cell foam diffuses light and creates an aura over the thorax for the trout, but it also stands out as a bright bit of white on the surface. The spike of orange deer hair looms into the trout's window of vision, an exaggeration of unfolding wings, but it also pokes out of the water, presenting a clear silhouette against any glare.

The Halo Midge Emerger appeals to the trout more than standard patterns. Even if it didn't, anglers would catch more fish with it. It is the only midge pupa imitation that they can see easily on the surface. It is the only one they can consistently present with a drag-free drift. It is adopted enthusiastically by fishermen because it is visible even with tough light conditions.

Halo Midge Emerger

On some streams, especially tailwaters with cold, bottom releases from a dam, midges are such a large part of the insect biomass that trout never ignore a hatch. They wait for drifting pupae, taking them with the classic bulging rise, only noses (or nebs) pushing the surface.

On lakes trout cruise and bulge. They usually face into the wind, swimming just under the top few inches of wind-blown water (in effect, upstream). After traveling maybe a hundred feet, usually the limit of a feeding beat, they return to their starting points and begin again.

The key on all waters is to watch for those bulging rises. Unlike a mayfly hatch, where bulges to emergers are mixed with simple rises to duns, the feeding on midge pupae is usually all just beneath the surface. When the trout are taking only inert insects from the film it is a good indication that they are selectively feeding on midges.

TYING STEPS

1. Tie in a strand of blue fluorescent monofilament; let it dangle for the moment (optional step—eliminate it on smaller sizes).

2. Dub a rough body of half sparkle yarn and half fur.

3. Wrap the monofilament rib.

4. Figure-eight in a strip of foam as a "halo."

5. Wind dubbing crisscross around the foam halo.

6. Tie in a spike of orange deer hair.

Whip finish.

step 1

step 2

step 3

step 4

step 5

step 6

Hook: 16–24 (1X fine wire, TMC 900 BL—barbless for quicker penetration with these small hooks)

Rib: fluorescent blue monofilament (optional—omit on smaller sizes)

Body: blend of half sparkle yarn and half fur (dubbed)

Halo: large-cell, closed foam

Spike: orange deer hair

The Halo Midge Emerger is the only emerger pattern without a trailing shuck. That feature is omitted on this fly because the natural curls its body up, tucking the transparent sheath underneath, as it hangs at the surface. Only the color of the body dubbing changes on this fly; effective patterns include green, red, black, yellow, brown, purple, and pink variations.

Halo Midge Emerger

LOG ENTRY: AUGUST 26, 1990
BIGHORN RIVER

For six years this tailwater river below Yellowtail Dam on the Crow Indian Reservation in southeastern Montana was closed because of a dispute over jurisdiction with the Crows. The Bighorn was wonderful during this span—for some of us, willing to risk arrest in order to serve as the test case in the courts, this was like a private river. Once it was reopened the publicity about the great fishing brought the crowds to the Bighorn.

The fishing is still good, although the number of truly large trout has declined. The hoards of people make any day on the Bighorn a social event now. My favorite times to visit the river are the cold months, and lately even that isn't a guarantee of solitude.

The real reason we came here was for the *Baetis*. That mayfly hatch is spotty this spring, and there is much more consistent fishing to the midge activity. The best trout are feeding on midge pupae, and they're in different positions than the ones taking *Baetis* duns. The midge eaters are tight to the banks, some of them in pods but most of them loners, and the mayfly-eaters are spread out on the flats.

Graham Marsh, Bob Aiken, and I walked up to the channel above the boat ramp. Surprisingly, no one was fishing the big flat above the island, and as we stood there watching a hundred or more feeding trout on this windless, overcast day it reminded us of the lonesome times of the closed years.

One thing, however, always happens to Graham on crowded rivers. As he started casting, and quickly hooking trout, two men appeared from downstream. "What are you using?" one of them asked.

"A Comparadun for the fish on the *Baetis* or a Halo Midge Emerger for the fish on the midges."

"We don't have any of those flies," the stranger said.

And that's when it happened. Graham or I would have gladly given these fine fellows some flies, but when Graham went over to talk to them, leaving his own fishing, and he figured out after a few moments that they were going to have trouble catching trout on any pattern, his mothering instinct bloomed and he adopted these lost souls.

In our group we call these people "Graham's Guppies."

Brad Raudin and Johnson Miller, young stockbrokers from Texas, watched Graham demonstrate the method. He lined up directly behind a bulging fish, no more than twenty feet away, and from a kneeling position put the fly above the rainbow, timing the cast to the trout's feeding rhythm.

Brad, full of awe as Graham released the big fish, said, "The guides have had us fishing shrimp patterns with a cork bobber. We can't get these trout like you do."

Graham took Brad and I took Johnson and we spread out on the flat. Johnson used my rod and started on the open-water, *Baetis* feeders. He put down one by flopping the line on top of him, another by simply dragging the fly over him on four successive casts, and a third by striking when the fish rose to an insect instead of the fly (which was 8 inches off the drift line anyway).

He didn't believe me when I told him that he was doing fine, but he was, slowly and consciously correcting all the little mistakes that become important with these fussy fish. The only thing that he couldn't do right was leave a trout after he botched him.

It is a simple rule: Don't nag the trout.

The first cast has the best chance of fooling a trout. If the fly is right, and the fish sees it, there is a great chance he will take it. Those odds drop sharply on the second presentation, and fade to a forlorn hope on subsequent casts. It is a waste of time showing the same fly over and over again to the same fish.

Johnson started hooking trout on a number of different mayfly patterns after he mastered the basics of presentation, but when we moved closer to the bank, and approached the fish feeding on the edge between slack water and current, a size 18 Black Halo Midge Emerger was the only fly he could catch anything with. At that point Johnson developed too much faith in the Halo pattern.

Every once in a while a trout would see the fly and turn away. Who knows why? A fish does the same thing to a real insect sometimes. Maybe the natural or the insect twists with the current suddenly, and the trout doesn't like the change in angle. Or, with the fly, maybe there's a moment of drag from the leader. Once the fish refuses a fly, no matter how effective it has been on other feeders, it is time to change patterns or move to another target.

Johnson stayed with one brown trout for more than a half hour. "He'll take it," he kept saying.

"Maybe if you nag him long enough."

"Right."

"No, it's not right. It's not efficient."

I understand how addictive rising trout can be, and Johnson could have stood there all day creating his hatch, lulling the trout's suspicion, but he was using my rod. He had such a happy mask of pain and pleasure on his face, a madman totally engaged in his quest, that I couldn't break his trance by asking for the rod.

I borrowed his outfit, a seven-weight rod unsuitable for midge fishing, and fished Plain Jane streamers (always a deadly fly on the Bighorn). I worked down the channel, taking browns and rainbows.

Johnson whooped loudly when he hooked his trout. The fish fought stupidly, uncharacteristic for a brown, never running for the cover of the undercut bank. Johnson waded upstream and downstream chasing the fish, spooking every other big riser in the feed line, but he didn't care

The Halo Midge Emerger triggered an interesting exchange of letters. One reader criticized the orange spike on the fly, writing, ". . . it's not only in the wrong place, but it's also the wrong shape and the wrong color to have any real imitative intent."

I put the letter in my Book Mailer newsletter (along with my usual defense for the odd appearance of any of my patterns, "The trout picked this version"). Immediately, an answer came from William Chappeler, a graduate student in entomology, "The orange color isn't far-fetched. Emerging insects pump fluids into the veins of the wings to expand them. On insects with clear wings (i.e., midges) the fluid gives the wings a momentary orange/red flush. The color is quite prominent."

Halo Midge Emerger Log

about them. He beached his fish, a hen brown over 20 inches long. He unhooked her for the release.

"The fly never fails," he said to me, holding the Halo pattern.

The whole subject of an effective imitation making a bad first impression on a selective trout is fascinating. Divers underwater see the last moment turn-away; and they know that the fish will recognize the fly and refuse it for a long time. Eventually, the trout's suspicion fades to indifference. He stops trying to find that annoying fraud among the naturals. Then he might take the fly.

What would I have done on Johnson's fish? I would have changed to another good midge pupa imitation, maybe a Suspender Midge Pupa or a CDC Midge Pupa, immediately with that first refusal. On a good trout it might be worth trying four or five different flies.

But for the next fish I would have tied the Halo Midge Emerger back on the leader. On a fresh trout it would have the best chance—better than any of the other flies in my box—on the first cast.

Five

■

Dry Flies

The dry fly is a strange creation, an impressionistic representation of an insect at best. It has to be—the alternative, a realistic representation, as true a copy as possible with natural and synthetic materials, is a proven failure. The effective dry fly works with the meniscus, which both distorts and amplifies the characteristics of anything floating on top of it. To a trout the meniscus makes everything on the surface a mystery.

A fisherman doesn't want a perfectly realistic copy of the insect anyway. During a heavy hatch, with adults covering the surface, a feeding trout may see thirty or forty naturals every minute. The perfect match, if that were possible, would simply be number forty-one in that parade of items.

The wise angler doesn't want a fly with a one in forty-one chance. He wants an imitation with characteristics that grab the trout's attention. He needs a fly that gets eaten before the real insect drifting right next to it. That is the only way he can ever be consistently successful on selectively feeding fish.

One moment a trout sees an object on the surface clearly. The next moment that object can be confused or indistinct, in rare instances even hidden entirely. Unpredictably the object can go back and forth between clarity and confusion as it drifts overhead.

This is what makes the floating insect or fly mysterious to a fish. Other food items, and their imitations—the nymph, wet fly, streamer, and even the emerger (the submerged portion)—remain clearly in sight once the trout focuses on them. Only the insect or the fly on top of the meniscus changes moment by moment, even as a trout struggles to get a view of it.

The meniscus creates this confusion because it is a barrier between water and air. Light rays either reflect off it, never entering the water, or refract (bend) as they pass through it. A trout looking upwards sees a silvery mirror where the light rays reflect off the meniscus. He sees a roughly circular hole, a window to the outside world, where the light rays penetrate the meniscus.

That window of vision, even under the best circumstances, is not a perfectly clear viewing area. The edge of it, where the light rays get squeezed as they bend, is four times brighter than the middle. There is also a burst of color, a rainbow effect (Snell's Circle), along that edge. This rim, where a trout has to separate a floating insect or fly from other items on the surface, is a chaos of light. Even the middle of the window is not a flat screen—any ripple caused by current or wind, turns the surface into quivering hills and valleys.

Effective imitation or attraction both depend upon exaggeration, more with the dry fly than with other types of patterns. Exaggeration makes it easier for the trout to not only see the floating object at the edge of the window but also to keep watching it as it drifts with the current. A strong characteristic, bolder on the fly than on insects floating overhead, makes a fish rise to the artificial instead of the natural right next to it.

There is not as much difference between an imitation and an attractor as anglers think. A good imitation has characteristics that are unnaturally exaggerated and attract attention. A good attractor has characteristics that are generally buggy looking and allay suspicion. All flies fall some-where on the scale between the predictable and the improbable.

Aft Sparkle

With a floating insect, the trout first sees the triggering characteristic. If the fish is feeding selectively, locked into a specific search pattern, then the imitation has to have that same prominent part. The characteristic, not the whole fly, triggers recognition (and, hopefully, a rise).

But on an attractor fly, such as the Aft Sparkle, the part the trout sees first is a hot spot or a focus point. The trout rests in a comfortable place, feeding sporadically if at all, and as he idly scans the surface there has to be something about the floating object that rivets his attention. With the Aft Sparkle it is the brightness of both the yarn and the natural air bubbles trapped in the yarn.

This pattern, with the hot spot at the bend of the hook, was just an afterthought in 1988. It looked good to us underwater; and the trout responded with the type of "hurry and kill it" rise that confirmed attraction. It went into my fly box.

Aft Sparkle

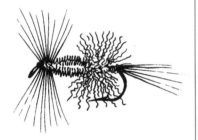

TYING STEPS

1. Tie in a tail of cream hackle fibers.

2. Tie in a rear hackle of sparkle yarn.

3. Wind a body of peacock herl.

4. Wrap a front hackle.

Whip finish.

Hook:	14–16 (3X fine wire, TMC 5230)
Tail:	cream hackle fibers (tied split or fanned)
Aft Hackle:	a "hackle" of colored or clear Antron or Zelon yarn (originally, this was an olive yarn, but there's no reason not to play with colors on this pattern)
Body:	peacock herl
Front Hackle:	cream

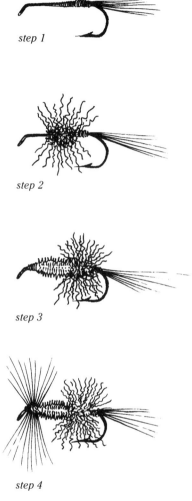

step 1

step 2

step 3

step 4

Aft Sparkle

LOG ENTRY: JULY 25, 1991
LITTLE BOULDER RIVER

This stream is a tributary of the Boulder of the Jefferson. The town of Boulder, site of the state institution for the mentally retarded, was where my wife and I lived and worked during the summer of 1970. The Little Boulder was my favorite fishing water that year.

The Aft Sparkle, like a lot of the new flies, has been just another pattern in my box. Until now it has had no "history," only a few random experiences. Suddenly, it is becoming one of my standby attractors. Three times in the last week it has topped the day.

I wonder if it is possible to choose flies based on water type? The angler takes a stream and finds a fly to match each particular type of flow. He develops his prejudices through trial and error (which means a lot of fishing).

This is what fly fishermen do subconsciously anyway. The prejudices develop quickly enough. For me with dry flies these aren't just broad choices (for example, a Mohawk on flats or a Double Wing on riffles), but very specific selections. Around rocks in fast water? An Air Head because of the way it fights the undertow currents. In backwaters? A Slider because of the way it cuts a clean line when drag pulls it out.

The Aft Sparkle is my favorite pattern for casting upstream tight to a bank. There's a band of slower current sweeping against rocks, grass, and brush. If the angler drops his entire line and leader on this current, he delays drag. He gets drifts of ten feet or more as the fly comes back to him.

This was a good afternoon for switching flies, testing one against another. Grasshopper imitations should have won any contest at this time of year, but they didn't—a Crowe Beetle did better than a Deer Hair Hopper and an Aft Sparkle did better than a Beetle. The real grasshoppers are so late this summer that the trout were still suspicious of big flies.

There was nothing very big, some fat brook trout and a few brown trout up to 14 inches, but the strikes came fast. It wasn't unusual to hit a hot stretch of bank and take a half dozen fish. It was important to lean back and get each hooked trout downstream before he spooked the run.

Why is Aft Sparkle an effective fly? It is predominantly green, and around grass and brush that is a strong color. But there is more to it. This pattern pulls fish from both sides, out from the bank and in from the channel. This probably happens because the back end of the Aft Sparkle forces the bright fibers of yarn below the surface. It looks pretty tantalizing from underneath, the strands at the rear waving and sparkling.

Air Head

The challenge with this odd pattern is getting an angler to try it. Even students in my fly tying seminars hold up their own finished copies in disbelief. The bolder ones accuse me of playing a joke on them. Why shouldn't they wonder? This fly was designed to fail.

The whole trial-and-error process of judging flies through underwater observation produces more failures than successes. New patterns that fail lack magic—they may catch as many fish as an existing fly, but that is not good enough. A new creation has to be special. The years of scuba diving have created forty or so successful innovations, but during that time more than 2,000 ideas have failed.

In science an experiment that fails can be as valuable as one that succeeds. It is important to know the limits of attraction. When is a fly too large, too colorful, too reflective? When does strangeness stop triggering the trout's curiosity and start arousing his suspicions?

The foam on the Air Head is a proven material. It is translucent, diffusing light. In small amounts, or when most of it is obscured by other parts of the fly, it mimics bright parts of an insect subtly and effectively (the Halo Emerger, the Mess, the Foam Ant).

The foam worked on imitations. What would happen if this bright material was tied to the hook with no subtlety, in a way that maximized instead of minimized the surface area? There was little doubt in our minds that such a fly would scare more trout than it would attract.

The scuba divers went underwater one July day with no prejudices. They had no knowledge of our expectations (and since they had never seen the fly above water they had no expectations of their own). At 6:00 p.m. they watched trout that were in a "pre-feeding" stage. The fish had worked heavily on an afternoon mayfly hatch from 12:00 noon to 4:00 p.m. and then settled into resting lies. By 6:00 p.m. a few trout were moving back to their feeding stations and

Air Head

Air Head

the others were exhibiting greater alertness.

The anglers in our experiment fished Air Heads dead drift down the main current. They started catching not just rainbows, the species actively looking at the surface, but also browns. The fishermen were pulling browns up through 6 feet of water.

The scuba divers surfaced and one of them, Graham Marsh, said, "That fly is the strongest attractor that I've ever seen."

We were so skeptical that we tested the Air Head five more times. At moments, basically during the middle of the day and on flat water, it was too odd for trout. They would swirl under it or jump over it. But usually fish would rush to the surface and take the fly cleanly.

To me the Air Head doesn't look like any living thing on the trout stream, but Graham disagrees with my conclusion. "I've seen it drifting next to insects, usually large stoneflies, beating their wings frantically, and from underwater the wild array of foam on the Air Head looks surprisingly like that commotion."

Maybe.

It is not unusual for friends to become bigger proponents of particular patterns than me. This is certainly the situation with the Air Head. One man especially, Joe Burke, uses it more and understands it better than me.

He told me about an evening on Flat Creek, the tough spring-fed meadow stream near Jackson, Wyoming, "The one place that I did get splashy refusals on the Air Head was on Flat Creek. The fly still got a lot of attention and it was fun watching the big cutthroats swim all around it.

"They wouldn't take the fly on a dead-drift, surface presentation, but when I started fishing it like a streamer at the end of the drift they didn't hesitate at all. Underwater the Air Head isn't too bright even on a spring creek."

The Air Head is becoming popular not just because of its power of attraction. It has other advantages. It is buoyant, so buoyant that at the end of the drift it can be worked with a retrieve and it will plane a few inches under the surface, a pulsing, struggling mini-streamer, and then with no false casting it can be fished as a dry again. And it is one of the easiest flies to see bobbing along on the surface, making it ideal for the wading or floating fisherman casting to broken water.

TYING STEPS

1. Dub the rear portion of the body one third up the hook shank.

2. Tie in a deer hair wing (the tips extending to the bend of the hook); clip the stubs.

3. Dub the forward portion of the body; leave the front third of the hook shank bare.

4. Tie in six strips of foam, extended forward over the eye of the hook; wrap the thread forward to the eye, binding down the strips.

5. Wrap the thread backwards to the original tie-in; pull the strips back and tie them down, forming the foam head; trim the strips, clipping the one directly under the hook completely off, the two at the sides short, and the three on top the length of the deer hair wing.

Whip finish.

Hook: 8–16 (wide gap, ring eye dry fly, TMC 101)
Body: mink fur (dubbed rough)
Wing: elk or deer hair
Head: translucent, closed-cell foam

The main variations are cream (bleached elk hair wing/cream body), yellow (brown deer hair wing/yellow body), brown (brown deer hair wing/brown body, and olive (brown deer hair wing/olive body). As an imitation, the Air Head can be tied to match any stonefly.

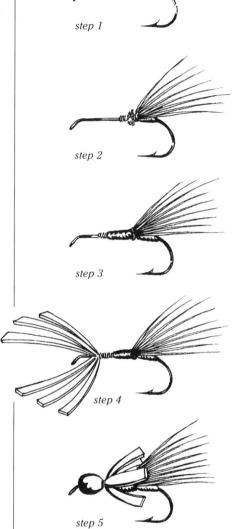

step 1

step 2

step 3

step 4

step 5

LOG ENTRY: AUGUST 6, 1991
ROCK CREEK

Few drainages define a category of trout water as well as Rock Creek. It is a superb example of a rich mountain stream. This tributary of the Clark Fork, the mouth near Missoula, is a state-designated Blue Ribbon Trout River. There are sixty or so miles of it, including the forks, and it holds brook, cutthroat, bull, rainbow, and brown trout.

My fascination with Rock Creek rests with the fact that it is a "balanced" stream. It is not a spring creek, so rich that the trout feed on a schedule, gorging during the hatches and otherwise ignoring available food, but it isn't an infertile mountain fishery, either, where the trout always look for food, snatching at anything drifting on or swimming in the current.

There are many fine waters within two hours drive of Deer Lodge. The main advantage of my home may just be its location in the middle of this abundance. The river right in the valley, the upper Clark Fork, will always be the stream I fish most, but one of the great rivers nearby—the

Air Head Log

Beaverhead, Big Hole, Blackfoot, lower Clark Fork, Missouri, or Rock Creek—is a "chosen destination" each season.

This chosen destination is important in my fishing. Each season something happens on one of these nearby waters that captures me. It is usually a heavy hatch of insects that shows me how many nice trout the stream really holds. And then suddenly I want to fish that water (not the whole stream; just that particular piece of water) as much as I can, every day if possible, to discover where those fish are hiding when they are not gorging on a hatch in plain view. Where will they be at dawn on a chilly July morning when nymphs are drifting? Where will they be on a warm August afternoon when grasshoppers are falling on the water? And so I fish the chosen stream whenever I can afford the time for the drive over from Deer Lodge.

This season a section of upper Rock Creek is my prime spot. It is nearly an hour trip, by way of Montana Route 1 through Anaconda and past Georgetown Lake, then left on route 348 near Philipsburg, to reach the upper end. There has been so much late rain this summer that the stream level is not falling as fast as usual; and where the larger rainbows would normally migrate back downstream soon after spawning, they are staying in this section of the creek.

Today is my thirty-fourth trip to this water this year.

By now this part of Rock Creek should be very predictable for me. It is predictable with most dry flies—a Joe's Hopper will work through the afternoon hours and a Poly Caddis will take rainbows and cutthroats at dusk. This late in the summer there aren't any heavy hatches, maybe a smattering of caddisflies just before dark, and when trout aren't rising to insects, attractor dry flies will do better than imitations.

The one dry fly that will probably never be predictable is the Air Head. Even on the half-mile stretch of Rock Creek, where I know the feeding and holding spots of every pool, run, and riffle, this pattern does funny things. I can look at a current sweeping under a grassy bank and say, "A hopper will bring up a couple of nice fish out of there," but I can stare at the same water and wonder, "I might get nothing or every fish in the hole might come boiling up after an Air Head."

The mystery is that I don't know what factors control success or failure. The sunlight, in all its variations of color and intensity, plays strongly on the foam, and it must be an important part of the answer, but there is no consistency—one bright afternoon the Air Head works wonderfully and the next day, same weather pattern, the fly is too strong, getting splashy, curiosity refusals.

Is there any doubt why the Air Head is usually the first dry fly I try on a stream? I can't wait to see what is going to happen.

With the low, clear water of late summer the Air Head has been mediocre on this part of Rock Creek. Eight days ago, on a sunny afternoon, nothing even rose to it, which is unusual, and yet trout sipped a size 16 Green Mohawk with confidence. Three days ago, on a partially cloudy morning, fish slashed at it, but most of them never hooked up.

Larry Solomon came up with me. By the time we had the rods strung, it was almost five o'clock. It was another nice day, and with no rain in the drainage for the last few weeks the water was still low. I hung a thermometer in the creek and it was 64 degrees F.

Larry tied on a size 16 Delta Wing Caddis and asked, "Will this work?"

I knew the fly and I knew the angler and with the caddis that would be bouncing around soon enough I knew exactly what would happen, "You're going to get a lot of fish, rainbows and cutts up to 14 inches, with maybe a few bigger ones."

I went down a few pools and put on a size 12 Olive Air Head. I was sure that the fly wouldn't catch as many trout as the smaller, imitative Delta Wing, but I thought that it might catch bigger fish, 17 to 19 inches, from the deeper, rougher water. I greased the Air Head up, more out of habit than necessity, and cast straight upstream.

This evening there were no doubts about the pattern. Even in the first riffle, a 1½-foot deep run, every trout sucked the fly down on the dead-drift float. These fish ranged in size from 4 inches up to 14 inches, all of them apparently wanting that Air Head badly. In the next run, in faster water, two rainbows and one cutthroat, all over 14 inches, grabbed the fly.

By the time that I caught up to Larry it was 8:30 p.m. The Air Head (same fly, never greased again and still floating well, but quite tattered and torn from teeth) had taken over forty fish, with a couple of 18 inches. My prediction for the evening for Larry and the Delta Wing was right—a lot of trout up to 14 inches; my prediction for the Air Head was half right—it brought up bigger fish, but it also vacuumed the stream, small, medium, and large trout taking it with an odd, sure rise.

The strangest moment happened at a deep, slow bend pool. A nice fish was holding at the tail, his nose a few inches under the surface, sipping small insects (maybe midges). He was the unlikeliest of targets for the Air Head, but I tossed the fly up into his drift line anyway. On the first pass that 15-inch rainbow sipped—not sucked, not grabbed—just sipped the fly in as if its arrival was perfectly natural. There was no way that that fish should have taken the Air Head like that (many times a big attractor will put a feeding trout down).

When trout aren't actively feeding on the surface, I'll try the Air Head first as my "tell-tale" fly. How fish react to it tells me what to use that day. If trout won't rise to an Air Head, to splash if nothing else, they won't rise to any dry fly. If they rise and refuse the Air Head, a more subtle attractor, a Mohawk or a Double Wing, will usually work.

The soft foam does get ripped up by the teeth of trout. In our tying the fly is whip finished twice, once after the body is dubbed, before the foam strips are tied in. Then, if fish destroy the foam, we take the fly home, cut away the tatters, and tie a new bullet head and spikes. An Air Head usually survives fifteen to twenty brown trout (toothy fish) and twenty-five to forty rainbows.

Buzz Ball

Midges are the primary dry fly insect on great winter rivers such as the Bitterroot, Madison, Bighorn, and Missouri. On these tailwater rivers pods of trout feed on drifting pupae and adults. The fish key on emerging and egg-laying insects.

The mating and egg-laying usually occur over slower, flatter water. On the Madison, for example, mating swarms form next to the banks. The insects stay close to the surface on windy days, clumps buzzing over the surface in a circular frenzy.

These mating groups sometimes number hundreds of insects, spreading in a dark mass, but a fish feeds rhythmically on single insects flush on the surface. Then, when a clump comes near, the trout can't resist the opportunity to grab a mouthful of adults and he busts the swarm with a splashy, rolling rise.

The Buzz Ball, in sizes 12 or 14, was created to represent a small clump of midges. In our testing, the bigger versions, on size 6 hooks, imitating a much larger swarm, did not do nearly as well as the size 12 or size 14 fly. That smaller Buzz Ball seemed to perform, just like the mass of insects, as a special treat, a prime chunk of food, that made a sipping fish suddenly break his rhythm, leave his lane, and smash the offering.

Buzz Ball

step 1

TYING STEPS

1. Tie in all three hackles at the bend.

2. Wrap a blue dun hackle and an orange hackle together; trim them.

3. Wrap a grizzly hackle; leave the sides long, but trim a V into the top and bottom.

step 2

step 3

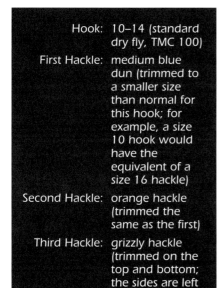

Hook:	10–14 (standard dry fly, TMC 100)
First Hackle:	medium blue dun (trimmed to a smaller size than normal for this hook; for example, a size 10 hook would have the equivalent of a size 16 hackle)
Second Hackle:	orange hackle (trimmed the same as the first)
Third Hackle:	grizzly hackle (trimmed on the top and bottom; the sides are left long)

LOG ENTRY: APRIL 16, 1991
MISSOURI RIVER

Take three major trout streams, the Jefferson, the Madison, and the Gallatin, put them together at Three Forks, and then run the river through four dams, each one clearing and enriching the water, and finally push the flow out onto a plateau below Holter Dam, between Helena and Great Falls, and the result is a giant spring creek.

It's wrong to call this winter, or even spring, fishing. This has been one of the mildest years in the records of Montana weather. The river has been ice-free, midge hatches have been heavy and trout have been feeding on the surface since January. The water near the dam, as usual, has been great, but unlike most winters the lower river has also been consistently good.

There are two sections of this tailwater fishery. The top part is roughly the fifteen miles below the dam. This water unintentionally gets "stocked" with trout. The state fisheries people put hatchery rainbows, mostly a

Buzz Ball Log

short-lived Arlee strain, into Holter Lake. Thousands of these fish either flow over the dam during high water or survive the trip through the turbines, and populate the river. They grow quickly in the rich environment, but after a few years, at a length of 18 inches or so, they die of old age.

The lower part of the river, from fifteen miles below the dam all the way to Cascade, has a greater percentage of naturally spawned fish. The Dearborn River, for one, is a major source of wild trout. These rainbows, while not a great strain, are better than the hatchery product. They grow bigger, and are still free-rising, in this bottom section.

Bill Fortune has never caught a 20-inch rainbow from the river. There are many reasons for this, but basically it rests on the fact that Bill doesn't have the slightest idea how to catch large trout on small flies. He has years of fishing experience, including many trips on the Missouri, but his angling methods are the scattergun variety.

"You're a hard man," he said to me.

"I'm getting blunt in my old age."

We met at his trailer at the Craig campground and drove downriver, past the mouth of the Dearborn. We only took one outfit, my 8′ 9″ three-weight rigged with a gray line and a 15-foot leader (6X), and walked the banks together. "So what is this simple secret for big trout?" Bill asked.

"You have to catch them one at a time."

We moved upstream along the high bank, passing four pods of rising fish in the half mile, and at each group of feeders Bill wanted to cast. I wouldn't let him. I kept urging him farther up the river, stopping at moments to watch trout. Finally, I handed him the binoculars and pointed at a pod.

Bill studied the lead rainbow in the V-formation, "That is a very big fish."

"You cast to her and only to her."

Bill was shaking even as we crept up for a presentation. Maybe, if he had been calm enough to float a fly four or five times over the trout, my choice of pattern would have been a midge pupa or a midge adult imitation, but with his nerves he needed a larger, easier-to-see fly. Also, the Buzz Ball might pull the fish a little way if the drift wasn't exactly on the feeding lane.

Bill, with the tippet cut back to 5X, made a fine cast, the fly landing two feet above the trout. The Buzz Ball, more colorful and bigger, floated down with a scattering of naturals, but the fish surged forward and took the fly.

One cast, one large trout. Bill landed her and we measured her quickly at 21½ inches. We slid her back into the river (hoping that she would spawn a larger-growing flock like herself).

We hiked six miles of river this afternoon, stopping four times and casting to four large trout. The fish, one more for Bill and two for me, did not fall as quickly as the first one, but they all finally took a size 14 Buzz Ball. Two of the trout were browns, one 19 inches and one 20 inches, and the other one was a 19½-inch rainbow

Clear Wing Spinner

This fly was baptized on one of the most demanding rivers in the country. A size 18 Black Clear Wing Spinner, the only version of this pattern in my box for two seasons, was tied to match the Trico spinner fall on the Missouri.

One factor that makes the Trico hatch so demanding on the Missouri is the sheer number of insects. From August until October the spinners drop to the water in blankets. Pods of whitefish and trout (rainbows starting at 9:00 a.m. and browns starting at 11:30 a.m.) slide up onto the weedy flats and sip the spent mayflies. They hold just under the surface, each fish pushing his nose out in an exactly spaced series of feeding movements.

Any fly has to compete with millions of naturals. The only thing an angler can do to increase his chances is pick one fish and put his imitation time after time on the exact line of drift. It's no use trying to match the feeding rhythm of any trout—the movements are too close together. Even with a perfect series of presentations, a fish takes the adequate imitation roughly one out of twenty casts.

Only two patterns tip those odds significantly—a Clear Wing Spinner and a Poly Wing Spinner. The Clear Wing has a slight edge over the Poly Wing. Other flies, such as a Parachute Trike, CDC Trico, and Crystal Flash Trico, all fall into that one in twenty response range. The Clear Wing Spinner, the brightness and size of the spent wings slightly exaggerated, gets eaten at a greater rate than the real insect (always the goal of our imitations).

Other flies do poorly on the Missouri River for another reason. The anglers cannot see them on the water. If they can't follow the drift and detect the strike, they have little chance of catching a trout even with a good presentation.

I thought that George Senger was joking when he said about his Hackle Spinner, "I don't have any trouble seeing these flies in Wisconsin." Why should

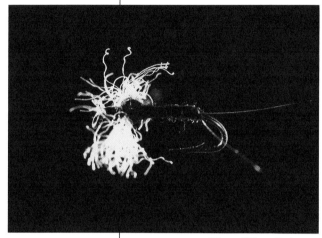

Clear Wing Spinner

Clear Wing Spinner

Wisconsin trout streams be different than Montana rivers? But then a week later Will Koukkari, after a disastrous morning with Crystal Flash Spinners, said exactly the same thing about his Wisconsin fishing experiences.

It is difficult to see a small fly on many western rivers, not just the Missouri, because of the glare on the water. There is no canopy of trees to break up the sunlight. The surface itself shimmers with reflections. Any drab or flush fly is lost—among mayfly imitations, only the Clear Wing Spinner, with the sparkle off the Antron fibers, sticks out at twenty feet or more.

Other colors and sizes of the fly were slowly added to my carrying collection, starting with a size 14 Gray Clear Wing for *Callibaetis*. The pattern worked in other areas of the country (even in Wisconsin) for me and my friends, and it became popular in a full range of imitations.

The big change for me with the Clear Wing Spinner occurred in 1979. Until then it was a fly that came out of the box for specific situations. That year it found its place as an everyday pattern. My total catch on the Clear Wing for 1978 was less than thirty trout; for 1979 it was more than ninety .

The shift happened one morning on Big Spring Creek. Particularly fussy feeders refused every dry fly, even though they were obviously sipping something. I crawled over to the bank edge, and stared at the water. All along the edge of the stream, piled thick in the indentations of the shore, were dead mayfly spinners. Occasionally a clump of them would get caught by a wisp of current and peel off into the stream. The trout were lazily rising to these morning leftovers.

This is a mid-summer phenomenon. Many species of mayflies molt into spinners, lay eggs, and die in the night. Daytime fly fishermen never see this activity, but the following morning the mayfly bodies still litter the stream and trout look for them.

For July and August, months with regular nighttime mayfly activity in Montana, the Clear Wing Spinner is the most consistent morning searching fly for me. The best hours are from 8:00 a.m. until 10:00 a.m. If there are no other hatches, the trout hang close to their holding lies, near or in quieter water, and these areas were where the spent mayflies collected. A size 12 Cream Clear Wing Spinner, drifted on the foam lines, next to the banks, was the best general color.

step 1

TYING STEPS

1. Tie in two hackle fibers; split them.

2. Dub a thin abdomen.

3. Tie in a wing of clear Antron fibers; pull both wings back and clip them so they are even with the bend.

4. Dub a thicker thorax.

Whip finish.

step 2

Hook:	8–22 (3X fine wire, TMC 5230 in available sizes)
Tail:	two hackle fibers (split)
Body:	synthetic or natural fur
Wing:	clear Antron fibers

step 3

step 4

LOG ENTRY: SEPTEMBER 21, 1991
POINDEXTER SLOUGH

The state of Montana purchased a large part of Poindexter Slough, a spring creek that enters the Beaverhead River just outside Dillon. They fenced off the cattle, stabilizing the banks, and a good fishery has just kept getting better.

I lost the first half hour of fishing today. I sat down to wait for the spinner fall of Tricos, and was watching the water when a baby muskrat came up the bank, sniffed around my wader boots, crawled into my lap, and fell asleep. He didn't mind me petting him and he seemed perfectly healthy, not sick or starving. He must have been an orphan, but I've never known anyone who has raised a muskrat. At 10:30 a.m. he woke up and clambered back down into the stream.

There were plenty of visible trout holding in the weed lanes, suspended just under the surface, sipping spinners. In the big pools there were even pods of fish working. There weren't blizzards of insects. It wasn't one of those situations where there were too many spinners for good fishing—now, at the tail end of the Trico season, there were just enough females on the water to trigger a steady rise.

The feeders fell to a size 18 Black Clear Wing Spinner. The procedure was exactly the same for each fish—wade upstream directly behind it, usually within fifteen feet, and false cast off to the side, keeping line

Clear Wing Spinner Log

shadow off the water until it was time to drop the fly in time with his feeding rhythm.

Even with the pods of rainbows it wasn't difficult to take the fish on the back end. These were such strong trout, however, that as soon as they were hooked they bolted upstream, scattering all of the other fish in the feeding group. The standard, upstream-stalk method never once took the biggest rainbow in a pod, the one typically at the head of the V-formation.

I started playing a new game with the pods. I would hunt and find the fish, and then circle on land away from the water. I'd come towards the bank on my hands and knees, and while still ten feet back from the edge, I'd drop a cast, with the line on the grass and the leader on the water, to the head fish. If he didn't take the fly, I'd roll cast the line into the air, trying not to spook the group. Frequently the line would snag in the grass and the game would be over.

On the first five pods I caught the lead rainbow twice (both fish in the 16-inch to 18-inch range). As the hatch petered out, I searched for one more bunch of trout, hoping for a chance to raise my "catch-average" with this strategy to 50 percent.

> The procedure was exactly the same for each fish—wade upstream directly behind it, usually within fifteen feet, and false cast off to the side, keeping line shadow off the water until it was time to drop the fly in time with his feeding rhythm.

On the next pod the leader was a brute, more than likely a fish up from the river. It wasn't just his length, over 20 inches, that made him different from the others—it was his girth, too. On every sipping rise his nose broke the surface and tiny ripples washed over his back.

I crept into position and was about to start false casting when that baby muskrat swam upstream (this was his first appearance since this morning). I stuck my head up and began clicking my tongue and calling him. This got his attention and he came up on the bank towards me.

While my muskrat was coming to me I made a cast to the big trout. The fly landed by luck at the perfect moment, just as the fish was looking up for another insect, and he took the Clear Wing Spinner with no hesitation. He ran and I jumped into the stream.

The trout was disoriented in the shallow water. He swam in zigzags from bank to bank, and then dove and buried himself in a bed of weeds. I waded over and booted him out of the vegetation. He ran in zigzags again, and after one crossing, buried himself in the weeds again. He did this four times in all. Although the fight lasted many minutes, the trout didn't swim all that much, and he was still fresh when I netted him. The 5X leader tippet should have broken with the gobs of weed hanging on it, but it held. I never measured the fish, but he weighed 4¾ pounds without the weeds.

I really puzzled over that baby muskrat. In the end I left him in the stream.

Cricket

Lenny Moffo, who guides in the Florida Keys, told me about the time two clients climbed into his boat for a day of bonefishing and one of them turned and asked, "What elevation are we at?"

My own lesson about elevation came in 1988. Until then the only cricket imitations in my boxes were leftovers, some of them twenty years old, from eastern fishing. Crickets never seemed important on Montana trout streams, even during the summer when four of us fished fifty-seven nights. On streams such as the Big Hole, Missouri, and Madison, there were no great chirping choruses of these insects.

My first encounter with crickets in Montana occurred in 1988, during a day of floating on the middle reaches of the Clark Fork River. Every fish that August morning, mostly browns, had at least a few crickets in their gullets. At one campsite that night, right across the river from the town of Drummond, the insects were so loud that it was hard to sleep.

One of the controlling factors for crickets in Montana is elevation. Along the upper Clark Fork, at my hometown of Deer Lodge (over 4,500 feet elevation), there are not any crickets to my knowledge, but fifty miles downstream and hundreds of feet lower they are abundant. On that middle stretch of river they are also important enough for trout to look for them. The fish acquire the taste for them each summer.

Cricket

Cricket

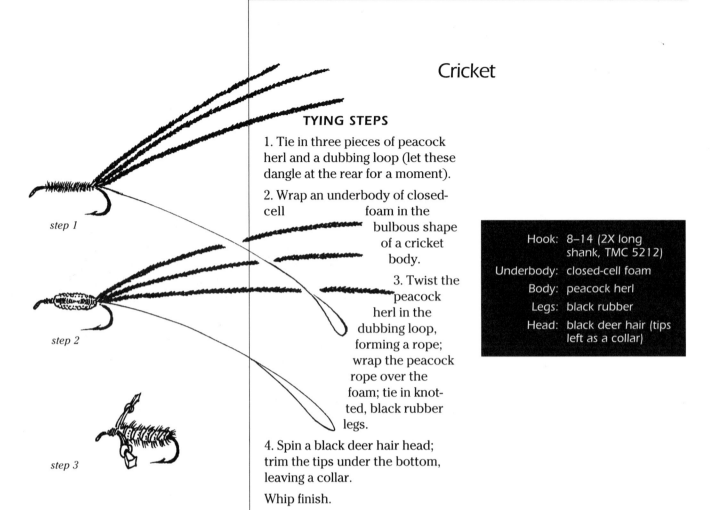

step 1

step 2

step 3

step 4

TYING STEPS

1. Tie in three pieces of peacock herl and a dubbing loop (let these dangle at the rear for a moment).

2. Wrap an underbody of closed-cell foam in the bulbous shape of a cricket body.

3. Twist the peacock herl in the dubbing loop, forming a rope; wrap the peacock rope over the foam; tie in knotted, black rubber legs.

4. Spin a black deer hair head; trim the tips under the bottom, leaving a collar.

Whip finish.

Hook:	8–14 (2X long shank, TMC 5212)
Underbody:	closed-cell foam
Body:	peacock herl
Legs:	black rubber
Head:	black deer hair (tips left as a collar)

LOG ENTRY: SEPTEMBER 23, 1991
FLINT CREEK

It is hard to find any tributary of the Clark Fork that hasn't been dewatered, straightened, and beaten down. Flint Creek suffers from all of these agricultural abuses, but there are stretches of it that aren't as badly degraded as others and in these sections there are surprisingly good numbers of trout. In the lower few miles, before it enters the Clark Fork across from Drummond, there is a population of brown trout that moves up from the river in the fall even prior to the spawning migration.

Powell Swanser called up and said, "Go hit the last mile of Flint." He didn't have to say anything more because anyone who fishes with him knows that he only gets excited by big trout.

Joe Zderick and his nephew, Greg Quinn, came with me and we camped on the river. Three other friends, Peter Juvan, Lou Bovee, and Dick Ravetta, met us at dawn (but they wouldn't be fishing—their job was to handle the trout). The plan for the day was to start early and sample fish with stomach pumps, hopefully Joe, Greg and I catching enough of them from dawn to dusk for Peter, Lou, and Dick to put together an hour-by-hour menu of terrestrials.

Joe landed the first trout right at the mouth of Flint Creek. It wasn't even light yet, the first tinges of color edging the mountains. Dick gently put the pump into the 17-inch rainbow's mouth and took out the last few items the fish had eaten (a stomach pump really only takes food from the gullet). The trout gave up three crickets and a few smaller insects.

In all of my stomach samplings on Montana streams (including the work on the Missouri River for *Caddisflies*, a study with more than 2,000 trout), these were the first crickets I had ever seen pumped from a fish.

I put on a size 12 Cricket and started walking up Flint Creek. At the first bend, where the fallen tree protects the bank, there wasn't anything rising, but the fat Cricket hit with a plop and brought brown trout out from the limbs. Two of the four fish sampled had crickets in their stomachs.

The question for the day quickly became not, "Will the Cricket catch fish," but "How long will it keep catching fish?" All of us used it, and even when Joe and Greg switched occasionally to a deer hair version of the insect, it did better than any other fly. This was not a solid conclusion, just a feeling from the enthusiastic way trout rushed the pattern.

By 7:30 a.m., after nineteen fish, my first Cricket was torn up. A fresh one lasted for another twelve trout, until 9:00 a.m., when the action on the fly petered out. No one fished with the Cricket after 10:00 a.m.

September is the ideal month for terrestrial fishing. There are beetles, grasshoppers, crickets, leafhoppers, and ants (including flying ones) around, and on warm days plenty of them get on the water. At this time of year, when the weather is nice, there aren't a lot of heavy hatches (the Baetis mayflies preferring nasty conditions), just a smattering of different species. During the fall the trout feed opportunistically on all but the richest rivers.

There was a definite menu for terrestrials over the course of the day. We sampled a total of sixty-three trout (all of these over 14 inches) in twelve hours of hard fishing. There were forty-nine browns, thirteen rainbows, and one cutthroat in the group.

Over the twelve hours, broken down hour-by-hour, the most prevalent terrestrials were (first and second) as follows:

6:30 a.m. to 7:30 a.m.— 1. crickets, 2. beetles
7:30 a.m. to 8:30 a.m.— 1. beetles, 2. crickets
8:30 a.m. to 9:30 a.m.— 1. beetles, 2. ants
9:30 a.m. to 10:30 a.m.— 1. beetles, 2. ants
10:30 a.m. to 11:30 a.m.— 1. beetles, 2. leafhoppers
11:30 a.m. to 12:30 p.m.— 1. leafhoppers, 2. ants
12.30 p.m. to 1:30 p.m.— 1. leafhoppers, 2. grasshoppers
1:30 p.m. to 2:30 p.m.— 1. leafhoppers, 2. grasshoppers
2:30 p.m. to 3:30 p.m.— 1. leafhoppers, 2. ants and beetles (virtual tie)
3:30 p.m. to 4:30 p.m.— 1. ants, 2. beetles
4:30 p.m. to 5:30 p.m.— 1. ants, 2. leafhoppers
5:30 p.m. to 6:30 p.m.— 1. beetles, 2. ants
6:30 p.m. to 7:30 p.m.— 1. beetles, 2. ants
7:30 p.m. to 8:30 p.m.— 1. beetles, 2. ants

This sampling only covered one day; and there were those oddities that distort any brief study. The dominance of ants in the 3:30 p.m. to 4:30 p.m. time period was caused by a fall of small, flying red ants. Normal ants were common most of the day. Moths, spiders, true flies, and one bumble bee were also found in the fish. Only beetles showed up in every time period.

Surprisingly, the Cricket wasn't a great fly at dusk, even when the real insects were chirping lustily. It caught a few fish, but it wasn't the "prime chunk" that the trout had been looking for early in the morning.

Dancing Caddis

Any pattern can be dragged on the surface. But the typical dry fly, so heavy and squat that after a few drifts it sits flush in the water with hook and materials piercing the film, doesn't "drag" very well. Over-dressed flies don't even look like adult aquatic insects. Living mayflies, caddisflies, stoneflies, and midges rest lightly on the surface, not in it.

Thoughtful innovators have always recognized the role of stiff hackles, light wire hooks, and sparse (or no) body materials in imitating the living, active insect. The English angler, Dr. Baigent, developed the high-riding Variant style dry fly. Edward Hewitt created the all-hackle Bivisible and the Skating Spider. Leonard Wright tied the Fluttering Caddis with a wing of long, quality hackle fibers. These flies stood so high on the surface that the hook remained above the water.

Dancing Caddis

The Dancing Caddis solves the problem of hook and materials piercing the film in a different way. It has no parts hanging down—everything, including the hook, is up. The fly rests flush on the surface and presents the proper silhouette, but with the slightest tug of the leader it skates effortlessly across the water.

There is an advantage with this style—a big one. A high-riding fly has to be fresh to sit properly. After a few fish, or after too many drifts and dunkings, it sinks into the film. The upside-down design of the Dancing Caddis can catch trout after trout, and it still floats entirely on top of the water.

The Dancing Caddis was one of those flies that took a long time, over ten years, to really gain my favor. Other good caddis adult imitations, such as the Elk Hair Caddis and the Poly Caddis, caught more trout for me season after season (because they were used more). Then, in the winter of 1990, a friend, J. A. Ankey, tied up a large supply of the Dancing Caddis for me, and the next summer the pattern tallied fine performances. My confidence in the Dancing Caddis grew, and before long it was no longer the last caddis imitation out of my box.

A comparison of the 1989 and 1990 ranking of my flies for the number of trout caught on each pattern shows the jump in ranking that the Dancing Caddis made in one year:

1990 Rank	Pattern	1989 Rank
1	Emergent Sparkle Pupa	1
2	Halo Mayfly Emerger	17
3	Double Wing	21
4	Foam Beetle	4
5	Deep Sparkle Pupa	3
6	Clear Wing Spinner	2
7	Dancing Caddis	43
8	Plain Jane	15
9	Deer Hair Wooly	7
10	Diving Caddis	9

Making a fly look alive is not the same as dragging a fly. Drag is uncontrolled, a belly in a taut line and leader pulling the fly downstream faster than the current. That action discourages a trout from rising.

Why? Conditioning. A trout that rushes after and tries to grab an insect moving faster than the current misses the mark too often. After enough of these futile pursuits, beginning with the earliest feeding experiences, a trout learns to avoid items on the surface that race downstream.

An insect, or a dry fly, that moves against the current is a much easier target for a trout. When the angler makes a down-and-across presentation, the fly does twitch upstream when the line and leader draw tight.

The biggest mistake most anglers make with the active fly is over exuberance. They move the pattern in 1- or 2-inch hops. The purpose of action is to grab the trout's attention—a twitch is better than a hop, a quiver is better than a twitch, and a shiver is better than a quiver. The movement, for best effect, should occur at the upstream edge of the trout's window of vision, just before the fly slides into clear view.

On large expanses of flat water, a lake or a big pool in a river, the angler can "run" the fly. He strips the pattern as steadily as possible across the surface, mimicking the way certain species of adult caddisflies travel across the water.

Dancing Caddis

step 1

step 2

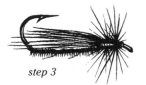

step 3

TYING STEPS

Put the hook in the vise with the hook point up.

1. Dub a fur body.

2. Secure a deer hair wing on the underside of the hook shank (make sure that the hair tips don't cover the hook point).

3. Wrap a hackle; clip the bottom hackle fibers.

Whip finish.

Hook:	8–12 (wide gap, ring eye, 1X fine, TMC 101)
Body:	natural or synthetic fur
Wing:	deer hair
Hackle:	rooster

Change the colors of the body, wing, and hackle to match major caddisflies. Brown wing/yellow body, brown wing/bright green body, gray wing/gray body, ginger wing/cream body are important color combinations.

LOG ENTRY: OCTOBER 14, 1991
SNOWSHOE LAKES

There are ranch ponds, spring-fed and rich, in the Little Blackfoot drainage. Anyone fishing them needs the permission of the owner. The limited pressure makes these small waters good.

There are irrigation ponds of varying size on most of the creeks in the drainage. Throughout the state there are ponds and small lakes on ranches and farms—most of them provide fine fishing. On many of them, the owners give permission to anyone who asks politely.

It has been a long, warm fall. Many other years these ponds would be frozen this late, but the water temperature is still in the fifties. The trout are feeding heavily, taking advantage of the strange weather. The browns do not even look close to spawning.

At the top pond Powell Swanser and I ducked under the fence at the outlet and started walking around the smaller, lower bowl. This was not a thought-out decision—it was habit. In this pond, shaped like an hour glass, the trout were always in the deeper, upper bowl.

I stopped right at the narrow waist, the channel separating the lower and upper sections, and started casting. This was from habit, too—the deeper slot was the first spot that might hold a fish and it was hard for me to pass it. I was on one side of the pond and Powell, already up to the upper end, was on the other.

It was turning to dusk and we would be lucky to get in an hour of fishing. It was obvious, however, that it was going to be a fast hour of fishing. Powell was already fighting his second trout when I hooked my first one on a red/orange Woolly Bugger. All of these early fish, Powell's and mine, were the fat, 18- to 20-inch rainbows that dominate the fish population.

That's when I heard the splash in the lower bowl. I stared at the water and soon enough another fish broke water. In a full season on this pond, these were the first trout I'd ever seen in this small, shallow section (except for a few spawning rainbows right at the outlet pipe in the spring). There weren't just a few of them—trout were slashing and jumping all over. It wasn't hard to leave the sure fishing on the upper bowl. Whatever was happening on the lower end was too exciting to miss. It was the first surface activity that I had ever seen on this pond.

As I walked back down to the lower bowl, I studied the water for insects. Large caddisflies were running on the water, the rear edges of the wings leaving a sharp V on the surface. Cruising trout, all too visible over the weeds, were crossing each others' paths, darting after the insects. There were no territories. It was every fish for himself in this normally empty bowl.

I put on a Dancing Caddis and cast out as far as possible. I held the rod under my arm and pulled in line hand over hand, drawing the fly back in a steady run across the surface. A brown caught the Dancing Caddis on my third retrieve. In the shallow water he had to go into the air, and he did, a 24-inch fish thrashing as wildly as any rainbow.

He did something that I have seen bass do but never a trout. He rose out of the water, only his tail buried, and with bends of his body walked eight feet across the surface. He jumped twice more, but they were the normal rise and fall sort. It was that first slide that stayed with me.

There were more trout on the Dancing Caddis, everyone a brown (odd for this pond), everyone a leaper, and everyone at least 20 inches. There was even a revelation about fishing a fly with a Run Retrieve, one of those minor insights that justify the day: Even the fish feeding against the bank wanted the fly to run at least ten feet. They would circle out to meet it and attack it sideways. Fish cruising in the center would follow the trail and rush up behind the moving fly. No fish took the fly during the first five feet of the retrieve.

Nothing else this evening meant as much as that tail-slapping trout. His crazy walk across water etched a memory—even while it was happening I was telling myself that here was the greatest jump by any trout in my lifetime of fishing.

> An angler should strike slower than normal with any upside-down fly. He has to give the trout time to close his mouth and turn down.

Deer Hair Hornet

The various black and yellow members of the bee family end up on the water in significant numbers during a rain storm. At other times a matching pattern is a very undependable fly, drawing more splashes than solid strikes. Even on wet days the Deer Hair Hornet usually doesn't fool the most fish. It is an exciting fly, however, because it draws out some of the biggest surface feeders in any stream.

The clear Antron wings, spreading out to the sides, make this a better imitation than standard patterns. The sparkling fibers attract trout, but unlike the bright color contrast of the body, there is nothing frightening about the brightness. The allure of the Antron counteracts some of the reluctance trout have about snatching even drowned bees.

Deer Hair Hornet

Hook: 12–14 (standard dry fly, TMC 100)

Body: yellow and black deer hair (five alternating bands; spun and clipped—a narrow waist for imitating a hornet or a fat waist for imitating a bumble bee)

Wing: clear Antron (fastened at the waist of the fly)

TYING STEPS

1. Spin four alternating bands of black and yellow deer hair; clip to shape.

2. Tie in the clear Antron fibers as wings, laying them flat over the back.

3. Spin a short band of deer hair; clip to shape.

Whip finish.

step 1

step 2

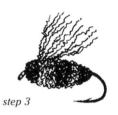

step 3

Deer Hair Hornet

LOG ENTRY: JULY 21, 1990
SOUTH FORK OF THE MILK RIVER (AND LIVERMORE CREEK)

The area within and around the Blackfoot Reservation is so famous for its still water fisheries that the streams, even superb ones such as the South Fork and its tributary, Livermore Creek, get ignored by visitors— and this is fine with me.

Our plan was to park at the dirt road where it crosses the mouth of Livermore and fish down the South Fork of the Milk together. Tory Stosich saw those deep undercuts upstream and couldn't resist casting along the run; and as soon as he hooked that first fat cutthroat he was on his way up Livermore in the rain.

He put up the hood on his yellow slicker and asked, "Do you have any extra Hornets?"

He deserves the credit for my good fishing as well as his. The Hornet is just not the type of fly that occurs to me on a small stream—the average length of the fish it catches is over 15 inches.

Various dry flies did wonderfully on the mile of hiking and casting down the South Fork. The Lady Heather, Were Wulff, and Shroud all caught a dozen brooks and cutthroats. That was my rule: A dozen fish and change. There was nothing discriminating about these eager feeders. Most of them were between 8 and 11 inches, and the biggest was 13 inches.

My bet with myself on the walk back upstream was that for the entire distance the Deer Hair Hornet would not catch a dozen trout. The goal was to lose the wager, of course—and just barely it was lost. The Deer Hair Hornet fooled fourteen trout. The difference with this fly, however, was that two of the fish were slightly over 15 inches long and the smallest one was almost 13 inches long.

Tory had an even better day up Livermore on the Hornet. His catch included a 16-inch brook and a 15-inch cutthroat, monsters for such a small stream. The big fish came out to play in the rain.

Deer Hair Wooly

This pattern became a favorite of mine in the 1950s, not for trout, but for bluegills and bass. There were always a few in my box of general, "junk" flies, and inevitably one day on the Housatonic River, my regular Connecticut stream, the Deer Hair Wooly caught some trout.

Later, on Montana rivers, it really became an important pattern for me. It is often the first fly out of my box during the middle hours of the day in the summer. On rough, riffle water the Royal Trude rules as my favorite attractor, but on smoother flows the Deer Hair Wooly, a large meaty chunk, is my most consistent searcher.

It's silly to speculate on what the fly might imitate. Most anglers would immediately label it a caterpillar pattern, but it is too thick to realistically represent most common types of moth or butterfly larvae. When actual caterpillars are falling onto the stream in significant numbers, it isn't a great fly. The Double Caterpillar pattern catches more fish in those fussy situations. When there is nothing specific happening, though, the Deer Hair Wooly looks enough like a vulnerable insect to pull trout up from the bottom. It doesn't specifically imitate any land bug, but if fish need to think of it as something (not a proven supposition), then the fly, with its bulk and its buzz of hackle fibers, probably passes as the perfect, all-around terrestrial in their minds.

Deer Hair Wooly

Deer Hair Wooly

step 1

TYING STEPS

1. Tie in a grizzly rooster hackle at the bend; let it hang for the moment.

2. Spin a body of deer hair.

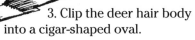

3. Clip the deer hair body into a cigar-shaped oval.

4. Palmer the grizzly hackle.

Whip finish.

Hook:	8–12 (standard dry fly, TMC 100)
Body:	natural gray deer hair (spun and clipped)
Hackle:	grizzly rooster

step 2

step 3

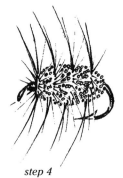

step 4

LOG ENTRY: SEPTEMBER 17, 1990
LITTLE BLACKFOOT RIVER

So many cold, spring seeps enter the Little Blackfoot River that even during the hottest summer days it never tops 60 degrees F. in my favorite stretches. There are cutthroats, brooks, and rainbows scattered throughout the upper watershed, but oddly enough it is almost entirely a brown trout and whitefish stream from the town of Elliston down to its mouth at Garrison. Maybe because of the cold water, the browns in my experience are not night feeders, hitting flies all day, every day, throughout the summer.

The fishing this evening provided a revelation. The truth wiped out twenty years of failure at dusk on this stream; and at the same time the experience made me look like a fool. Wouldn't the rankest beginner have seen the problem? Wasn't the solution to hundreds of mediocre evenings on the Little Blackfoot obvious? Call me a slow learner.

This has always been a great midday stream. It's the place for me to take friends to show them how to catch brown trout. The secret is to slam the fly, any aerodynamic terrestrial pattern, deep under the tangles of branches hanging over and trailing in the water. This is not the place for tentative casters, fishermen who peck at the edges, too afraid of snagging a fly to risk going into the cover. The open water gives up only small trout, 8- to 10-inch browns. The closer to the bank the fly gets, as much as two feet into and under the thickets, the bigger the fish. Aggressive casts catch the 14- to 18-inch browns.

This has always been a great midday stream. It's the place for me to take friends to show them how to catch brown trout. The secret is to slam the fly, any aerodynamic terrestrial pattern, deep under the tangles of branches hanging over and trailing in the water. This is not the place for tentative casters, fishermen who peck at the edges, too afraid of snagging a fly to risk going into the cover.

When evening comes the stream has fine hatches of mayflies and caddisflies. It is possible to match an insect and catch large numbers of trout, but the fish are mainly those 8- to 10-inch tiddlers. Apparently the larger browns don't feed on the hatches (or so I thought).

I didn't even get to the stream until 5:30 p.m., just about the end of the midday terrestrial fishing. I tied on a Deer Hair Wooly and started fishing under the brush anyway, using a Skip Cast to make the fly bounce deep into the shade.

The fun started when a large trout took the fly. Giving slack would be a mistake. The only way to get the fish out was to set the hook and drag the trout into open water. Any fish over 14 inches was strong enough to resist the pull. So for the first few seconds the battle was usually a standoff, the fish on one end thrashing wildly half in and half out of the water and the angler on the other end holding a rod hooped in a dangerous semicircle.

A hatch of mayflies started at 6:00 p.m. The fish began rising to them, sporadically at first and then with more and more enthusiasm. And then something happened that never happened before, not in twenty-five years of fishing the Little Blackfoot. I ignored the hatch.

Whether or not the big trout were feeding on the emerging insects was irrelevant. The Little Blackfoot was different—the fish didn't have separate holding lies and feeding lies. The two spots were one and the same on this stream. The big brown trout didn't need to come out to feed on a hatch.

I used the Deer Hair Wooly until dark. It was so black when I quit that I couldn't see the fly in the sticks and had to strike whenever something splashed. I caught trout, landing browns up to 18 inches. It was my best evening ever on this stream.

Double Caterpillar

Caterpillars are a very sporadic food item for trout. To make fishing imitations even more chancy, some caterpillars are so bad tasting, or even toxic, that trout develop an aversion to certain species (the black and orange Wooly Bear of autumn is an example).

The Double Caterpillar, presenting a nice long outline on the surface and flexing in the center, matches the tasty caterpillars that find their way to the water in great numbers. The Double Caterpillar is not a general, random fly for me, though. It comes out only when real caterpillars are obviously a part of the trout's menu.

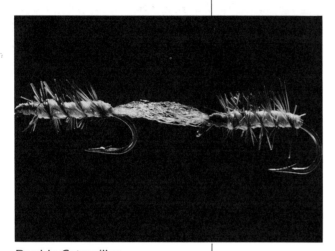

Double Caterpillar

Hook:	12–16 (standard dry fly, TMC 100—two of them)
Connector:	white macramé cord (color with felt tip marker)
Rib:	green thread
Body Hackles:	grizzly (palmered separately on each body; clipped short)
Body:	foam (color with a waterproof marker)

TYING STEPS

1. Tie in a piece of green tying thread; let it hang off the back for the moment.

2. Tie in a grizzly hackle; let it hang off the back for the moment.

3. Tie in a piece of white foam and wrap it to the front of the hook—do not compress out the air by winding the foam too tightly; color the foam with a permanent marker.

4. Wrap the green thread, segmenting the foam.

5. Wrap the saddle hackle; trim it all the way around.

6. Tie in a piece of white macramé cord the length of the hook shank, binding it securely by doubling over the butt and wrapping the fold down with the thread; color the macramé cord with a permanent marker.

7. Put the second hook in the vise; connect it to the first hook by binding down the macramé cord securely.

8. Repeat steps 1 through 5.

Whip finish.

step 1

step 2

step 3

step 4

step 5

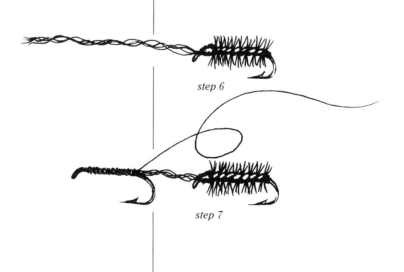

step 6

step 7

step 8

Double Caterpillar

LOG ENTRY: JULY 22, 1990
FOUR HORN LAKE

This Blackfoot Reservation lake is in a valley that funnels the wind. Even on days when other Reservation waters are fishable this one can have whitecaps.

The fascinating aspect of Four Horn is the inlet stream. This creek is too shallow and open to support much of a fishery, and it may even go dry at times, but it passes through miles of high, windswept grassland and collects all kinds of terrestrial fare for the lake. Where it dumps in and spreads out, the trout line up in a fan to feed on the soup of the day.

Harry Patman told me about his best day of fishing on Four Horn. He wasn't catching anything, or even seeing anything, until a rainbow at the inlet finally grabbed his fly. The trout's stomach was stretched and knobby, bulging with grasshoppers. But none of these insects had been taken on the surface. They were drowned ones dumped into the lake by the stream. For the rest of the afternoon Harry cast a wet hopper and banged big rainbows.

The problem with Four Horn is not just that the special of the day keeps changing. My logs show plenty of frustrating hours casting grasshopper, beetle, and ant imitations. No fly is going to work unless it is at the perfect depth. The stream is going to sink under the lake water if it is colder; it is going to spread out on the top of the lake water if it is warmer. All of the food concentrates somewhere between the surface and a depth of fifteen feet.

Today, for the first time in my experience, the trout at the inlet were rolling and taking something on top, but Dave Kinne and I, bobbing in our tubes, kept changing flies and neither of us could find anything those rainbows would touch. An hour failed to produce the Judas fish we needed to tell us what the pack was doing.

Dave hooked something and it scorched out into the lake and snapped him off. He reeled in his backing and fly line, "How big do the fish go here?"

"This is not like Mission or Mitten. These rainbows mostly run between two and four pounds."

"Not that one. He eats trout that weigh four pounds."

We both put on big streamers, like the fly he lost, and stripped them fast. We stuck with this technique, even after a half hour without a nip, because nothing else seemed more promising. Finally, tormented too long by those feeding fish, I gave up on the flogging and said, "Why don't we go in and check the stream?"

The answer to the mystery was obvious. The clues were in front of us. What those fish were taking hadn't been washed down miles of stream—the food would only be floating if it had dropped onto the water in the last 300 or 400 yards. The stream, in a final rush to the lake, ran through a pine forest. The surface was covered with small caterpillars.

The Double Caterpillar, the only reasonable imitation in my box, took those rolling fish. The rainbows were filled with brown mush, the caterpillars identifiable only by the more sclerotized head sections of the insects. The fishing was suddenly steady, if not spectacular, for the rest of the afternoon. Neither of us hooked anything over four pounds.

Three factors control how well the angler sees any fly. The drabber it is, the smaller it is, and the flusher it is on the water, the harder the pattern is to spot. The Double Caterpillar is neither drab nor small, but it does float very flush. A tuft of orange poly yarn tied in at the lowest blood knot of the leader helps the angler follow any hard to find fly on the drift.

This is not like nymph fishing. The angler doesn't watch the tuft as an indicator. The yarn lets him locate the end of the leader and track the monofilament out to the fly.

Double Wing

The Double Wing is not one fly. It is a series of color variations designed for my Theory of Attraction. The concept behind the pattern style is based on simple physics. Each one of the Double Wing series is supposed to work under specific light conditions.

It isn't necessary to know the physics, only the effect of light on color. The light falling on a stream isn't always the same. Sometimes it can be redder than usual (in the evening), and sometimes it can be yellower than usual (at midday). It can have more green, orange, or blue rays in it than usual, too.

Here is the whole theory behind the Double Wing: A red fly is brightly colored in red light (and conversely, dull in green light); a green fly is brightly colored in green light (and conversely, dull in red light). This rule is true for all of the colors on a dry fly.

With this theory the angler can always pick out the brightest attractor pattern. The primary color of the fly will be so intense that it will act as a beacon that fish will notice immediately (or so the theory says).

There is no disputing the physics behind this Theory of Attraction; under the right light conditions the variations of the Double Wing are an intense color. The only question is whether or not the theory works on the stream. Does the bright attractor catch more trout than the dull attractor?

My opinions changed about many of my flies after fishing them hard for couple of years. My basic beliefs about the Double Wing changed the most. In my mind the Theory, even it if was based on scientific fact, had not been completely proven in actual fishing situations.

Part of my skepticism came from my opinions about color in general. For imitations, color is usually the fourth or fifth most important characteristic. For attractors, even on a fly with an intense hot spot, such as the Double Wing, color would have an effect on trout, but shouldn't be a powerful feature.

Double Wing

The Double Wing surprised me on all kinds of water. Time and again the fly that was bright in a particular situation completely outfished a fly that was dull. But there was another oddity—the correct Double Wing easily outfished other attractors, even when they were the correct color, too. The Double Wing was designed feature by feature to maximize the impact of color, and apparently the long process of testing created a fly that boosted the attracting powers of color.

The real confirmation for the series, plus some fine observations, came from professional guides. They saw the comparisons between the Double Wing and other patterns almost every day. Many of them either wrote or told me about their experiences.

Frank Obrist, guiding out of Great Falls, wrote, "From 12:00 noon to 4:00 p.m. the Royal Double Wing was the best fly on the Missouri River all summer. My clients racked up more big trout with it than they did even with streamers, fish up to 6½ pounds. I kept saying to myself, 'Maybe it imitates this or maybe it imitates that.' I couldn't believe that a pure attractor would work on the Missouri, but finally I had to admit that it did."

Graeme McDougal, guiding out of Dillon, told me, "I've noticed that even minor differences in the light effect the performance of the flies. A Gray Double Wing works great on the Madison as soon as the day gets the least bit overcast, but on the Big Hole it only works great when there's a heavy overcast."

Bob Eaglen, guiding out of Augusta, said, "I disagree with you about the Yellow Double Wing. You call yellow a 'dangerous' color, and that may be true in a pure form, but on the Yellow Double Wing there is a lot of variegation. On the Sun River trout never seem shy about rising to the Yellow Double Wing on a bright day. It is the most valuable color variation in the series for me and my clients."

Double Wing

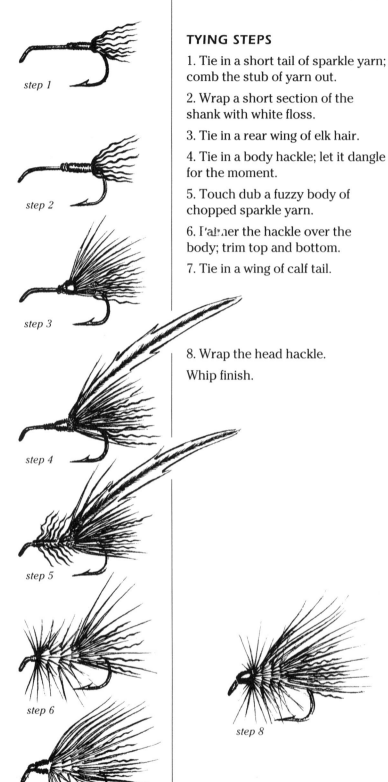

step 1

step 2

step 3

step 4

step 5

step 6

step 7

step 8

TYING STEPS

1. Tie in a short tail of sparkle yarn; comb the stub of yarn out.

2. Wrap a short section of the shank with white floss.

3. Tie in a rear wing of elk hair.

4. Tie in a body hackle; let it dangle for the moment.

5. Touch dub a fuzzy body of chopped sparkle yarn.

6. Palmer the hackle over the body; trim top and bottom.

7. Tie in a wing of calf tail.

8. Wrap the head hackle.

Whip finish.

Hook:	8–18 (standard dry fly, TMC 100)
Tail:	sparkle yarn (combed-out stub)
Tip:	floss
Rear Wing:	elk hair
Body Hackle:	rooster (palmered and clipped flat top and bottom)
Body:	sparkle yarn (touch-dubbed rough and fuzzy)
Front Wing:	white kip tail
Hackle:	rooster

There are eleven color variations of the Double Wing in The Dry Fly. A basic carrying selection would include the Lime (lime green tail/white tip/lime green rear wing/olive-dyed grizzly body hackle/lime green body/white front wing/grizzly hackle)—midday and around green vegetation; Orange (burnt orange tail/white tip/brown rear wing/brown body hackle/burnt orange body/white front wing/grizzly hackle)—dawn and dusk; Gray (dark gray tail/white tip/rust rear wing/cree body hackle/dark gray body/white front wing/grizzly hackle)—overcast days; Yellow (yellow tail/white tip/pale yellow rear wing/golden badger body hackle/yellow body/white front wing/grizzly hackle)—rainy conditions; and Royal (green tail/red tip/brown rear wing/coachman brown body hackle/peacock herl body/white front wing/coachman brown hackle)—sunny days.

LOG ENTRY: SEPTEMBER 19, 1990
ROCK CREEK

There couldn't be any better place for me to learn something about a fly than on Rock Creek. The stretch above Gillies Bridge has been my regular water, my study area. I've watched it change day by day over the season. The fishing has been like a chess game—my moves designed to counter the daily variations of the stream.

For me photography is almost as fascinating as fly fishing. The problem is that I cannot do both at the same time. Neither one lends itself to casual pursuit. I either have to put away the rod and take pictures or put away the camera and fish. Guess which one usually wins out?

That's why I admire someone like Don Roberts. Don loves to fish, but he doesn't even bring a rod when we go out. He carries a 40-pound backpack full of photographic equipment and follows fishermen all day. Obviously, he enjoys taking pictures for a living.

Don and I went to upper Rock Creek for the scenery, the wildlife and the trout. The limestone cliffs above Gillies Bridge, looming over the stream, made a great backdrop. The weather, sunny, but with the softer, warmer light of autumn, promised wonderful colors.

The only thing that we needed for a successful photography session was a decent-sized trout. It didn't have to be a monster, just a nicely proportioned fish in the 17- to 20-inch range, something to highlight, not dominate, a picture of the stream. On this stretch of water, which has kicked out so many good rainbows and cutthroats this season, this seemed like an easy task.

The fishing was great, trout rising freely to dry flies all afternoon. Not one of these fish was over 14 inches, however. I would come to a spot and say to Don, "There's a big cutthroat in that notch in the bank. Justin Baker caught him last week and I caught him in July," and then I'd put a fly down the drift line and a 12-inch rainbow would jump all over the pattern.

I wasn't too worried because there was so much good water ahead of us. I kept moving upstream, catching lots of small fish. I was changing flies, looking for something to tease up a big trout. Finally, with only a half hour of good light for pictures left, we reached the Junction Pool.

The Junction Pool, where two braids of the stream come together, always holds large fish. It is also reliable water, with a center slot nearly ten feet deep that funnels trout up to the feeding line. Even the biggest fish in the pool watch the surface for insects.

I started casting with confidence, but in the first ten minutes nothing, not even a small fish, rose to my drifts. I tried Humpies, Wulffs, and Trudes in a number of sizes and colors—and still nothing. I covered the current lanes methodically, working left to right in 1-inch increments—and still nothing.

There were only a few minutes of good light left. The sun was nearly down, sitting bright orange over the cliffs. I took out a size 10 Orange Double Wing and said to Don, "According to the theory, this should be the fly," but by now I didn't have much confidence.

Double Wing Log

I cast, floating the Double Wing down a current edge I had already covered more than twenty times. A big rainbow rose as if he had been waiting all day for that fly. He took solidly and after a series of jumps and runs I landed him. He was fat, brightly colored, and maybe 18 inches.

When Don finished taking pictures of the fish, there were still a few minutes of light left. I made one more cast and this time the fly only drifted a foot. A big cutthroat, with slab sides, grabbed the Orange Double Wing. I landed this fish, an inch longer than the rainbow, and Don photographed him, too.

Don said, "Next time, let's try that fly first."

Note to myself:

Stamp this in blood: The theory of color attraction works.

I have doubted this for too long. It would be easy for me to call tonight a fluke, but the last four times I've used a Double Wing have been in impossible situations just like this one. I've put the fly on after other dry flies have failed.

These desperation times usually aren't a fair test for any pattern. If nothing is catching fish, changing to another dry fly isn't going to work. But a Double Wing, matched to the color of the ambient light, has brought up non-rising trout four trips in a row.

This is the day my skepticism died.

Aft Sparkle

Bread

Air Head

Bristle Leech

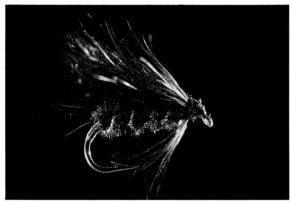

Black June

Buzz Ball

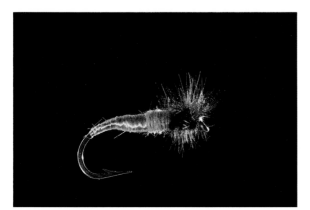

Blackfly Larva

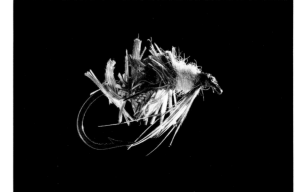

Cased Caddis Larva

Cat's Ear

Creature

Clear Wing Spinner

Cricket

Cone

Dancing Caddis

Cranefly Larva

Deep Sparkle Pupa

Deer Hair Hornet

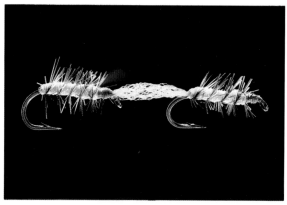

Double Caterpillar

Deer Hair Wooly

Double Wing

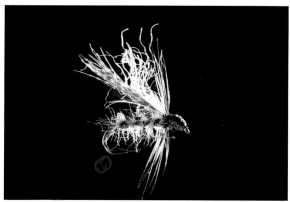

Diving Caddis

Duck Butt Dun

Diving Water Boatman

Emergent Sparkle Pupa

Firecracker

Flex-Stone

Flame Thrower

Floating Caddis Larva

Flex-Cicada

Floating Damselfly Nymph

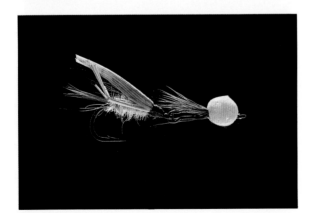

Flex-Hopper

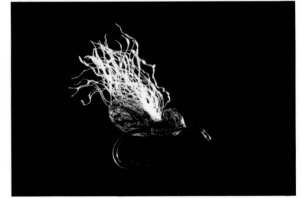

Flying Ant

Foam Ant

Free-Living Caddis Larva

Foam Beetle

Gray Coughlin

Foam Inch Worm

Hair Sucker

Foam Spider

Halo Mayfly Emerger

Halo Midge Emerger

Marabou Worm

Lady Heather

Mess

Marabou Single Egg

Mohawk

Marabou Spawn Sac

Natural Drift Stonefly Nymph

Occasion

Silver Bi-Color

Plaine Jane

Slider

Rollover Scud

Snow Stone

Shroud

Spruce Moth

Stub Wing Bucktail

White Deer Hair Moth

Tear Drop Nymph

Wiggler

Twist Nymph

Were Wulff

Butt Dun

This v   the result of a
search   rial. There
were nu   up to test,
includin   the Shroud,
pulling th   omparadun
didn't wo   tron sparkle
yarn (perf   a, but too
bright for t   eeded was
a material t   marabou
and sparkle   to have
some sparkle

There was   person
in our group, a   nd observing fly patt   w the
ideal material fo   ita-
tion. But no one   the
problem.

Cul de Canard (g the
preen gland of a du   saturally saturated with
water-repelling oils, had the softness and, with the
tendency to gather air bubbles from the meniscus, the
muted sparkle.

A Comparadun tied with a tail of Cul de Canard
(translated from the French, "duck butt") fibers,
looked superb drifting in the water. The shuck moved
with every deviation of current; and it shimmered just
enough, like the mayfly's shed nymphal skin jammed
with air bubbles. This variation caught the most selective trout. Like any Cul de Canard pattern, the Duck
Butt Dun caught three or four of them before it was
ruined forever.

These feathers are not new to fly fishing. Patterns
tied with Cul de Canard fibers have been the cher-
ished weapons of fly fishermen in Switzerland and
France since early in this century. Professional anglers
in those countries, supplying fish for the hotels, used
Cul de Canard flies to fool the wary trout of the spring
creeks.

Duck Butt Dun

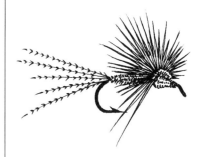

Duck Butt Dun

Cul de Canard feathers long ago proved their worth as one of the magical materials, not just providing bulk and color to a fly but adding some special attraction. Still, patterns tied with the fibers never swept the fishing world like most other good flies do. Instead they remained a curiosity. The disappearance of their special properties after even a few hours of normal fishing made them impractical.

The feathers themselves have no inherent buoyancy. But they have tiny barbules that absorb the oil of the preen gland. The duck preens itself, taking oil from the source and carefully coating the feathers of its body. The layer of oil is not permanent. Renewing it is an unending process for a waterfowl.

The Duck Butt Dun would have remained just a promising but impractical oddity, but then, during a trip to Europe, fly fishing friends showed me a new, synthetic duck gland oil that perfectly mimics the water-repelling qualities of the real stuff. With this oil it was possible for the first time to renew the magical properties of Cul de Canard flies. The flies could be taken home and restored after a day of fishing.

It took me a few attempts to learn how to use the oil (now available in this country). Simply wiping it onto the fly out on the stream, and then casting the soggy pattern to a fish, failed completely. All of the oil immediately washed off and the fly sank.

The oil has to be applied hours before; and it has to be put on as lovingly as a duck preening its feathers. The fly must be clean, all slime and dirt washed out of the fibers. The best way to work in the oil is to take a pin, dip it in the bottle, and stroke repeatedly from the butts to the tips, leaving the fibers glistening but not soaked.

TYING STEPS

1. Tie in a tail of Cul de Canard (duck butt) feathers; make the tail the length of the hook shank (don't try to make the tips even).

2. Tie a wing of deer hair (flared in an 180 degree fan).

3. Dub an abdomen and a thorax (make the thorax more robust).

Whip finish.

step 1

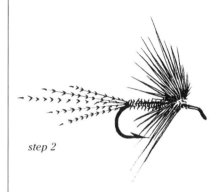

step 2

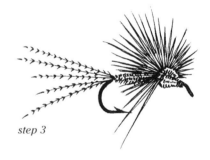

step 3

Hook: 14–18 (3X fine wire, TMC 5230)

Tail: Cul de Canard fibers

Body: synthetic or natural fur (thicker around the thorax)

Wing: deer hair (from the face of the animal)

Important color variations (the first color describe tail and body, the second describe the wing) are white/white, pale gray/ yellowish olive, pale gray/cream, cream/yellow, slate/olive, gray/ yellowish gray, dark gray/brown, mahogany/brown, and pale gray/black.

LOG ENTRY: MAY 13, 1991
MADISON RIVER BELOW BEAR TRAP CANYON

This lower section of the river gets almost too warm for trout during the summer months. The high temperatures make fish sluggish, retarding growth rates. The problem starts at Ennis Lake, a shallow expanse of old reservoir where the water heats up. But the lake is not the only source of trouble. The canyon itself, a famous piece of Class IV whitewater, is also a heat sink.

A solution to the warming problem would turn the lower river, already rich water, into a top fishery. There are technologies available that can make the water coming out of Ennis Lake cooler than when it enters (counteracting the effect of the canyon area on the lower river). The economic value to this part of the state would make any such project cost effective.

Until this happens the lower Madison will remain an early season and late season fishery. The trout, for the most part, aren't big, 8- to 16-inch browns and rainbows the typical range, but the great hatches of insects always make this a fun piece of fishing water.

Duck Butt Dun Log

Steve Gayken, Justin Baker, and I are traveling towards Deer Lodge, leaving the Yellowstone region and fishing rivers on the way. This is the second season in a row that Steve, here from Massachusetts, has hit this section of the Madison at this time of year. It is Justin's first time on this water.

So what is the attraction? This is not a trophy river down here, but it is a place where a fisherman can cast to rising trout for hours on end on an overcast day like this one. And it is a place where a few friends can spread out, wading the easy riffles below the canyon, and holler and wave to each other with each hookup.

It was easy fishing most of the day. At one point Justin was above me, practicing his nymph fishing, hooking trout and whitefish one after another on a Hare's Ear Bead Head. Steve was below me, drifting a small dry fly, and his rod was always hooped over.

The only touchy bit of fishing occurred at 4:30 p.m. There were blankets of insects on the water, but not just one kind. There were Grannom (*Brachycentrus* sp.) caddisflies, *Baetis* mayflies, and even caterpillars. The bushes and trees along the river were infested with tents of gauze-like webbing, and each tent was filled with hundreds of caterpillars. Enough were falling into the river to attract feeding fish. The Grannoms were both emerging and egg-laying, but the trout seemed to prefer the pupa over the adult from 3:00 p.m. to 5:30 p.m. The *Baetis* were just beginning to thin out a bit, after a 1:30 p.m. peak, but the duns were still the most numerous insect on the water.

For almost an hour we had to watch each rising fish to find out what he was eating. A few trout near the banks were hunting caterpillars, taking them with arching, rolling rises. A size 16 Brown Double Caterpillar caught these fish. Almost all of the trout out in the river were feeding on caddis pupae. A size 14 Brown and Bright Green Emergent Sparkle Pupa worked well on these slashing fish. The whitefish were working in pods on the *Baetis*, but we weren't trying to catch them.

The only exceptions to this range of feeding preferences were stray trout, always larger ones, feeding on the flats right in the middle of the whitefish. It was simple enough to spot these browns, their sipping rises very different from the quicker flashes and turns of the whitefish, but they were finicky.

One brown trout fell to a Comparadun, but only when the fly hit the edge of his window just as he was opening his mouth. On the two casts prior to this lucky drift he took naturals instead and whitefish snatched the Compardun.

I only had two Duck Butt Duns in my box that matched the *Baetis*. I was sure that these flies would compete with the flood of naturals on the water very well, the shuck of Cul de Canard fibers adding a strong element of attraction to the imitation, but I had to keep them away from the whitefish.

I spotted a nice brown, and cast to him. The fly landed softly right at the front edge of his window and, maybe because the splash grabbed his attention, he passed up two naturals already in the window and then sucked down the Duck Butt Dun. Surprised, I struck too hard and broke off the fly.

I did better on the next two trout, sneaking a 14-inch and a 16-inch brown out of the middle of the whitefish. And then I muffed everything, hooking a whitefish on a cast to a third trout. There was no excuse for it. I just threw a bad cast, two feet off to the right, and before I could pick up the fly a whitefish snatched it.

I played out the fish, but the Duck Butt Dun was already coated with its slime. Any fish slime would have hurt the oils on the fly, but the slime of the whitefish, much worse than the slime of a trout, destroyed any water-repelling qualities of the Cul de Canard fibers. There was nothing I could do except wash off the fly and stick it back in my box.

Maybe this flub destroyed my confidence, or maybe I didn't have enough faith in other mayfly imitations, but I never caught another trout that was working the *Baetis* hatch. Finally, I went back to fish feeding on the caddisflies.

So what is the attraction? This is not a trophy river down here, but it is a place where a fisherman can cast to rising trout for hours on end on an overcast day like this one. And it is a place where a few friends can spread out, wading the easy riffles below the canyon, and holler and wave to each other with each hookup.

Flame Thrower

The distinguishing feature of the Flame Thrower, a variant-style dry fly, is a fluorescent orange hackle. Even that bit of brightness, however, is muted by winding the orange hackle with a cree hackle—and that feature symbolizes my former ambivalence towards fluorescence on dry flies as well as anything. That ambivalence has changed after a string of successes with this fly.

It is easy to make a surface pattern too odd, too bright, with fluorescent materials. On wet flies, nymphs, and streamers fluorescence is an important facet of attraction, one that has not seen enough experimentation on trout, bass, and saltwater patterns, but on dry flies it does nothing most of the time and adds a bit of mystery in the low light of evening. It does not make a dry fly much better in the low light of overcast days; it doesn't help a surface fly at dawn, either, but that may be because dry flies in general don't do particularly well at dawn unless the fish are already feeding steadily on surface insects (and then a matching fly is a better choice than an attractor).

The reason fluorescence doesn't add anything to a dry fly during the middle of the day is that there is very little increased contrast. The fluorescent part of the pattern is bright, but every other part of the fly is bathed in enough sunlight to radiate color, also. It is in the weak light of dusk, when fluorescent materials convert ultraviolet rays into longer rays visible to the human eye, and those parts of the fly reflect more rays of a given color, that a pattern such as the Flame Thrower proves valuable. A fluorescent fly, depending on how the bright materials are used, is going to have a little or a lot of contrast.

It wasn't until the spring of 1992, after getting advice from Peter Ingraldi and Sam Merkins, two friends with a lot of experience with the Flame Thrower, that the fly became special to me. On three consecutive evenings on the lower Clark Fork below Missoula, the Flame Thrower averaged more than twenty trout a trip.

Flame Thrower

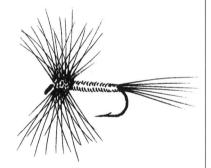

TYING STEPS

1. Tie in hackle fibers for a tail.

2. Dub a body of cream dubbing.

3. Wrap a cree hackle and an orange hackle together.

Whip finish.

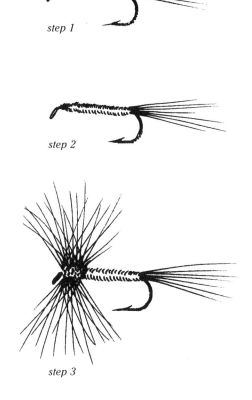

step 1

step 2

step 3

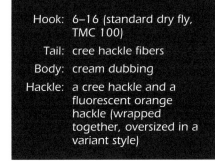

Hook: 6–16 (standard dry fly, TMC 100)

Tail: cree hackle fibers

Body: cream dubbing

Hackle: a cree hackle and a fluorescent orange hackle (wrapped together, oversized in a variant style)

LOG ENTRY: OCTOBER 8, 1991
GALLATIN RIVER

This is a stream that usually teases me with a lot of small trout. It holds better fish, and occasionally during a heavy hatch or fall of insects, it gives them up even to me.

My guiding partner out of West Yellowstone, Gordon Seese, used to come over to the Gallatin on his days off. He fished the river with weighted Girdle Bugs and always caught larger trout than me with my dry flies. Even my best attractor patterns, proven on plenty of other rivers, couldn't bring decent, 14- to 18-inch fish to the surface when they didn't feel like rising in the Gallatin.

Peter Ingraldi might be able to have a good day with a Flame Thrower. He only carries four dry flies—a Gray Fox Variant and a Flame Thrower for upwings and a Henryville and one of his own variations, an Elk Hair Caddis with a fluorescent body and hackle, for downwings. He believes in the power of fluorescence and, of course, that confidence makes him a better fisherman with any "hot" dry fly.

Peter used a size 12 Gray Fox Variant early in the afternoon. He ignored trout feeding on the smaller mayflies. He worked the riffles instead,

Flame Thrower Log

where nothing was rising, and pounded up plenty of trout, the largest only 13 inches He was waiting until 3:00 p.m. to use the Flame Thrower, and he still seemed confidant that he could bring bigger fish to the surface.

He said something that was odd, "This has always been a much stronger pattern in the spring and the fall than in the summer."

I had never used the Flame Thrower enough to notice that.

Peter has an uncanny touch with the Flame Thrower. He decided not to use it at 3:00 p.m. because, in his words, "The water doesn't look right," but by 3:30 p.m. the conditions must have been better because he passed out size 12, 14, 16, and 18 Flame Throwers to the rest of us.

There was no rigid plan for the fishing. The four of us—Tom Poole, Clint Lere, Peter and I—would try various upwing dry flies, including the Flame Thrower, and count and measure all of the trout caught throughout the evening. This rather random flogging might indicate something about fluorescent patterns.

Peter's faith in fluorescence in general and the Flame Thrower in particular was inspiring, "It'll work because it always works." Then he said something else that was odd, "It's a better fly for browns than it is for rainbows, so float it near the cover."

I fished hard and measured everything. I alternated the Flame Thrower with a Royal Wulff, changing flies every twenty minutes. The action was steady with both patterns until 5:00 p.m., and from then on the Flame Thrower caught a few more trout. Neither fly fooled any huge fish, but the Flame Thrower did take some browns up to 15 inches.

> It wasn't unusual for me to bring in someone like Peter Ingraldi, a fisherman who had more experience with one of my patterns than me. There was a bit of pressure on Peter, however. There were times when the Flame Thrower had caught trout over the past few years, but it had not caught bigger or more fish in those situations than other flies. My plan was to take Peter on a five day jaunt, hitting various rivers, hoping to find him great fishing somewhere with the Flame Thrower. His performance with this fly on the first day of the trip set a pattern of successes—on the Big Hole, Clark's Fork of the Yellowstone, Boulder of the Yellowstone, and Stillwater it was easily the best evening fly, both for numbers and size of trout.

At dark, back in the parking area, Peter was like a dealer showing a crowd card tricks. He predicted the results as we tallied our counts. He knew what the flies had done in this match of Flame Thrower versus the non-fluorescent, upwing dries (mainly the House & Lot, Royal Wulff, and Humpy).

"Forget the numbers," he said. "Look at the average size of the fish you caught."

The brown trout the Flame Thrower caught averaged 12½ inches; the ones the non-fluorescent upwings caught averaged 10¾ inches. The rainbow trout the Flame Thrower caught averaged 11 inches; the ones the non-fluorescent upwings caught averaged 10 inches (a much smaller spread). These averages were for all of our fish, more than seventy trout, but the deviation was roughly the same for each of us individually, too.

Peter predicted all this exactly and we were like rubes at the carnival watching the man perform his card tricks and wondering, "How did he do that?"

Flex-Cicada

The real cicada is a large, cyclically abundant insect, a member of the order Homoptera (meaning "similar wings"). It is important to fly fishermen on the tailwater trout rivers of the arid Southwest.

My experiences with it have been on the Green River in Utah (below Flaming Gorge). It has never been my good fortune to see the cicada in all of its glory, at the peak of the seventeen year cycle, but being on the water when just a smattering of the huge insects slapped the surface was exciting enough for me. A pool in a hatchery couldn't boil as much as that river did when a scattered flight landed on a large hole.

Flex-Cicada

Flex-Cicada

TYING STEPS

REAR SECTION

step 1

After wrapping the thread on the hook do not cut the excess—it will serve as the ribbing material.

1. Tie in the hackle; let it dangle with the ribbing thread for the moment

step 2

2. Wrap a body of dense, polycelon foam.

3. Wrap the thread as a rib, segmenting the foam; palmer the olive-dyed grizzly hackle; trim it.

4. Tie in a wing of gray fox squirrel tail hair.

5. Dub a thicker fur front over the stubs of the wing base.

Whip finish the rear section.

step 3

FRONT SECTION

6. Spin a collar of deer hair tips.

7. Wrap a foam head.

Whip finish the front section.

step 4

Hook:	8 (Flex Hook, TMC 80B)
Rib:	black thread
Body Hackle:	grizzly dyed olive (palmered and clipped)
Wing:	fox squirrel tail
Front:	dub a thicker front over the stubs of the wing base
Head Section:	the head section of the Flex Hook can be cork, foam, balsa, or deer hair. My favorite head for a cicada imitation has a foam base for buoyancy and a flare of deer hair tips.

Feel free to get fancy with this fly. Rubber legs, an overwing, and an extended body are just a few of the optional body parts possible on this big fly.

step 5

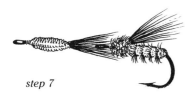

step 6

step 7

LOG ENTRY: OCTOBER 11, 1990
KOOTENAI RIVER

This huge tailwater in the northwest portion of the state has fluctuating flows. When it is good it is very, very good, and when it is bad it is unfishable.

There are no cicadas in this state. The Cicada pattern had never touched a Montana stream until today. And even now it wasn't a situation where someone said, "Wow, what these trout are really going to want is a cicada imitation."

It was just the opposite. "Is there any fly that these trout won't eat?" W. J. Witts asked.

The Kootenai is an incredibly rich river, growing Kamloop rainbows over thirty pounds (a fish of this size was found dying in the shallows). It can be impossible to take trout on a fly rod effectively when the gates of the dam are wide open, but at other times, when the water level is ideal, the fishing can be (and usually is) so furious that eventually the inquisitive angler wonders which flies won't work on these free-rising trout.

That is how the Cicada, a very large dry fly tied on the Flex Hook, debuted on a Montana river. Who knows what those fish thought? There was no reluctance like there normally is with an unusually large fly. Many times even active trout swirl around and nip at big patterns if they are not conditioned to accept them by a steady supply of big naturals.

The Cicada did not catch more trout than other flies, but, oddly enough, it did bring up bigger ones. The flows were perfect for good fishing, but even so the main holding runs in the river were heavy and deep. So maybe the fly, not only large but flexing on the surface, made an attractive meal, not just a meal. Other dark flies on regular hooks, the same overall length as the Cicada, did not pull up as many big fish.

> Interestingly enough, the next day the water seemed the same in every respect—temperature, level and clarity—but the trout were no longer in a giddy mood. They preferred small dry flies, and they reacted very suspiciously to anything over size 16.

Flex-Hopper

Flex-Hopper

My box is full of grasshopper imitations. It isn't a random collection. Each one of the main flies has a specific purpose. This assortment reflects the importance of grasshoppers in the semi-arid Rocky Mountain states. The need for the right fly, not just any imitation, during years of grasshopper abundance is important.

The flies include:

■ Nymph Hopper (Gerald Almy)—for early in the season, before trout see many of the full-sized adults;

■ weighted Joe's Hopper—fished dead drift subsurface like a nymph;

■ Henry's Fork Hopper (Mike Lawson)—matches the shape of a real grasshopper; also a very aerodynamic fly, perfect for bouncing with a skip cast deep under overhung banks;

■ Shroeder Parachute Hopper (Ed Schroeder)—excellent visibility on broken water or in tough light situations;

■ Flex-Hopper—for trout that are suspicious of large food forms.

From an observation blind on the banks of the Clark Fork we watched brown trout feed on grasshoppers (sometimes on the random, natural victims and sometimes on our chum line). Fish showed two distinct feeding styles—the reaction and rush by trout to the splat itself, and not to the actual shape, size or color of the the natural; or the studied rise, the speed of ascent depending on the speed of the current, to an already drifting grasshopper. By the end of the summer, the trout were really looking close at the largest insects, the ones matched by size 8 and 6 hooks.

One day we tossed in a dozen packaged, freeze-dried grasshoppers, along with some live specimens, and the trout refused to eat every dead one. They would drift back, peering intently at the stiff shapes, and eventually return to their holding stations. The dead grasshoppers lacked something. Their bodies did not bend, or flex, like the bodies of live naturals.

The ideal imitation of a living insect was not a dead one (and there is the most valuable lesson in fly design).

The solution to stiff imitations was the Flex Hook. It took me a few weeks working with steel wire to devise a prototype. The finished one had two advantages. Not only did the sections bend without binding but the rear part snapped on and off the clip of the head.

The new grasshopper imitation, tied on the Flex Hook, took the brown trout on the upper Clark Fork late in the year. The fish reacted well to a variety of head styles, including the spun and clipped deer hair, the wrapped and trimmed hackle, and the high density ball of foam. Often, an odd color on any of these types, pink or orange or white, attracted trout to the fly, and then the flexing body teased them into striking. It was even possible to put on a sinking head section, and then a tug would make the fly dart underwater in a short, undulating swim and then pop to the surface.

[The illustration on page 184 shows only the rear section of the Flex-Hopper.]

Flex-Hopper

step 1

step 2

step 3

step 4

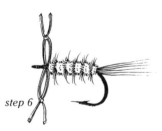

step 5

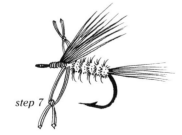

step 6

step 7

step 8

TYING STEPS

REAR SECTION

1. Tie in cree hackle fibers for a tail.

2. Tie in a dark ginger hackle; let it dangle for the moment.

3. Tie in a piece of foam, wrapped as an underbody for flotation.

4. Dub a body of yellowish green synthetic fur.

5. Palmer the dark ginger hackle; clip it.

6. Tie in knotted, yellow rubber legs.

7. Tie in brown bucktail as an underwing.

8. Tie in a piece of turkey feather flat, trim the back edge round.

Whip finish the rear section.

FRONT SECTION

9. [not shown] The angler should tie a variety of head types—foam, deer hair, cork—and mix and match them with the rear section.

Hook:	8 (Flex Hook, TMC 80B)
Tail:	cree hackle fibers
Body Hackle:	dark ginger hackle (palmered and clipped)
Underbody:	a strip of closed-cell foam (optional—wrapped as an underbody to add buoyancy)
Body:	yellowish olive sparkle yarn (dubbed thick; color can be varied to suit the naturals in an area)
Legs:	two pieces of yellow rubber on each side (knotted)
Underwing:	natural brown bucktail
Overwing:	turkey feather section (laid flat over the back)

LOG ENTRY: OCTOBER 2, 1991
BIG HOLE RIVER

The Big Hole is a diverse river. First, there is its length. It flows free of dams from its headwaters above Wisdom as a brook trout and grayling stream to a brown trout and rainbow trout fishery between Wisdom and its juncture with the Beaverhead below Twin Bridges. It passes from meadows, through canyons, and into twisting runs. Parts of it are free-stone, but many sections are influenced by rich springs.

The Flex Hook is so large that for most of the season the Hopper imitation has been too big. It was a cold, wet spring and the whole grasshopper "hatch" was three weeks late. Until now the Flex-Hopper has been kind of a dud.

It is valuable now. On the Big Hole today, below Maiden Rock, the fly banged rainbows and browns. John Petsley, who has been doing great with a size 10 Parachute Hopper all summer, went up the run and caught trout between 10 and 15 inches. He borrowed a Flex-Hopper, worked the same piece again, and took six fish over 15 inches, including a 24-inch brown.

The fly did well all afternoon for me, too (but no 24-inch trout in my tally). Oddly enough, for what is supposed to be a "big fish" fly, it also took a lot of browns in a range of sizes. Even 10- to 14-inch trout pulled it down confidently.

I have no solid data on one of my conclusions, but just looking back over my experiences guiding and fishing on the lower Big Hole, it seems as if rainbows aren't nearly as keyed on grasshoppers as browns. They take them but usually with a rise and suck in-stead of a rush and roll.

Why? Maybe it's because rainbows don't orient to structure, especially banks, the way browns do. The grasshoppers they see out in the open currents are frequently drowned or drowning, drifting along without much kick and fuss, and the rainbows rise cautiously. They may be suspicious about a large food item simply because they do not see as many of them.

I had a bet once with Graham Marsh that a size 16 Mohawk, which probably passes for a generic, beetle-like terrestrial, would take twice as many rainbows from the riffles on the Big Hole as a number 10 Hopper, a size that matched the naturals in the grass. Two other anglers fished the flies and the Mohawk won easily.

The Flex-Hopper, while not as good as a Mohawk for rainbows, is a better than average pattern in open currents, where fish come up underneath it instead of coming at it from the side. The fish see the bending movement of the hook and that natural looking flex usually conquers any last moment doubts that they might have.

I knew the spots where I could take the larger rainbows today. Right at the head of a bend, where the main current sweeps into and under the

> I have asked a lot of western anglers which fish, browns or rainbows, take a grasshopper pattern more aggressively. Their answers were different for different rivers, and were even different for different sections of certain rivers.

Flex-Hopper Log

bank, rainbows staked out the fast water. Almost coincidentally they were snug to an overhanging bank where a number of grasshoppers hit the water.

At each one of these prime pieces of water I caught nice rainbows, between 16 and 21 inches, boating six of them on the float section below Maiden Rock. Not one of the classic "curves" failed to yield a fish.

The combination of a head section with a tightly wrapped, brown-dyed grizzly hackle and a rear section with the standard yellow and brown colors caught the bigger trout, browns in slower water near the banks and rainbows from the deeper, rougher runs. Even in open currents the fly was a good choice, not taking great numbers out there but fooling nice-sized fish.

Flex-Stone

In eight seasons of guiding, my favorite period was always the salmonfly hatch. The clients needed me most then. On a river like the Big Hole, with no dam on it to moderate the runoff, people couldn't wade and fish effectively in the high water and they always appreciated rowing skills. They also needed help understanding the dynamics of the blizzard hatch of huge insects.

The stonefly emergence normally advances upriver three to five miles each day. Every day there is a head, a middle, and a tail to the hatch and every day the location of these segments shifts. At the head of the hatch the trout feed eagerly, with just enough insects landing on the surface to trigger a competitive urge among the fish. In the middle of the hatch, especially during a great year for salmonflies, trout and birds actually get glutted by the abundance of large, easy victims. At the tail of the hatch, once they digest the food already in their stomachs, fish start searching again for the occasional insect.

Flex-Stone

The middle section of the hatch is the toughest fishing, but during a day of floating it comprises most of the water. The head may stretch over a mile of river; the tail might be two miles. That middle covers from three to five miles of the trip.

One season I studied one trout for two days on the Big Hole. It took that long for the middle section of the hatch to pass through his area. This fish started rising as soon as the egg-laying females began hitting the water in the early afternoon. He came up roughly once every two minutes for twenty minutes; then his feeding pace slowed to a rise every five minutes for the next half hour; and then for the rest of the afternoon he fed sporadically, taking a salmonfly adult four times over a three and one-half hour span. His feeding pace had no correlation to the abundance of insects—it was linked to his appetite.

After the first half hour this large brown trout had to be teased. He became very fussy about imitations,

189

Flex-Stone

refusing cruder, general flies. He wanted the insect, or a matching pattern, moving on the surface, but he wouldn't charge after a jumping or skittering item, real or fake. From his position under an overhanging willow he had to see every adult salmonfly passing on the current, but he let many of them go downstream. Then, when the perfect performer came by, one mired in the surface and struggling, he would rise up confidantly and engulf the insect.

This was the fish that inspired the Flex-Stone. That second afternoon he took the imitation, a variation of the proven Flex-Hopper, without hesitation. The trout, a 24-inch brown, was gorged with natural adults, his stomach distended so badly that the condition looked painful. The large belly didn't stop the fish from running and jumping during a spectacular battle.

The Flex-Stone, particularly with a subtly colored foam head, worked well all afternoon. It had to be cast accurately, within a foot of a trout's holding position, and twitched gently if at all, but even the most erratic feeder would take it eventually.

Hook: 8 (Flex Hook, TMC 80B)

Tail: two rubber strands (tied split)

Body Hackle: rooster hackle (palmered over the body and clipped)

Body: synthetic seal's fur (dubbed rough)

Legs: six rubber strands (three on each side; not overly long)

Wing: elk hair

Head: balsa, deer hair, foam, or hackle of any color

The main variations are the Orange Flex-Stone, matching the salmonfly (white rubber tail and legs/brown body hackle/orange body/brown elk hair) and the Ginger Flex-Stone (yellow rubber tail and legs/dark ginger body hackle/cream body/light tan elk hair).

TYING STEPS:

REAR SECTION

1. Tie in two pieces of rubber equal in length to the gap of the hook; split them in a forked tail.

2. Tie in three sets of rubber legs at the thorax.

3. Tie in a hackle feather; let it dangle for the moment.

4. Dub an abdomen.

5. Palmer the hackle; clip it.

6. Dub the thorax (thicker).

7. Tie an elk hair downwing.

Whip finish.

FRONT SECTION

8. Create head sections of balsa, foam, deer hair or hackle.

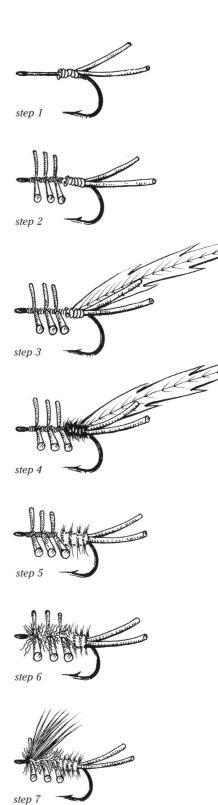

step 1

step 2

step 3

step 4

step 5

step 6

step 7

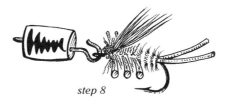

step 8

Flex-Stone

LOG ENTRY: JUNE 5, 1991
BIG HOLE RIVER

Some anglers love the Big Hole and others hate it. Count me among the former, of course. In my four years of guiding on it, mainly the sections below Wise River, there were very few days that weren't fascinating— and this included the frustrating fishing.

The people who don't like it are the ones who expect a river to yield trout predictably to their regular tactics. This river doesn't yield trout predictably to my regular tactics and, in many years, the Big Hole is my home water.

It is easy to spot someone who is going to have problems. He arrives on the river already committed to a favorite technique—nymph, wet fly, dry fly, or streamer—and if the trout don't take his fly he rates the day as an insult instead of a challenge. He lacks the ability to adapt to the moods of a most fickle piece of water, and in the end his only recourse is to blame the fishery.

I wrote once in an old log, "The only time guides from other areas of the state crowd the Big Hole is during the salmonfly hatch. The river always runs clear, even in a highwater year, and the bugs hatch profusely. The Big Hole is almost predictable (which in part explains its popularity with the outsiders now)."

I have regretted that smugness a few times. The problem occurs when I make promises to friends, "The Big Hole is the best salmonfly river in Montana." The river punishes me when I take it for granted.

The plan was for Brant Cozzie to share the rowing with me and for Rick Vezina, who didn't know how to row, to fish all the way. The purpose of the float trip was to show Rick a western river, and the fun for me was the guiding.

Just like most other days for the past few weeks it was raining, and the Big Hole was not just high, it was pushing over the banks. Amazingly, it wasn't mud soup, but it was stained a dark tea color. The weather kept the female stoneflies in the trees anyway and that, combined with the

heavy flow, put a damper on the dry fly fishing.

Brant could dead drift a nymph from a moving raft, but Rick couldn't. Brant used a Brooks Stone in the middle of the river and, at my suggestion, a Natural Drift Stonefly Nymph against the banks. He cast down and across, letting the strike indicator pace the raft, and he kept the fly moving naturally for 20 or 30 feet. Finally, the indicator would dive and Brant would strike, sometimes snagging the bottom and occasionally hooking a fish. His best trout was an 18-inch brown, but the day wasn't full of furious action.

Rick listened and he tried to sling nymphs. Chucking weighted, size 4 flies intimidated him (and scared the hell out of whoever was rowing—his rod didn't have the power or length to handle heavy flies well). He probably had a few hits, but he was slow on the strike.

Finally, I said to both Rick and Brant, "Let's switch to dry flies."

We were in the prime hours for the egg-laying females, 1:00 p.m. to 3:00 p.m., and also right at the head of the hatch, but surface patterns did poorly. In an hour, dry flies caught three fish, nothing huge (and Rick still didn't have a trout, but, God bless him, he kept saying what a beautiful river it was). We all wanted Rick to start hitting fish.

I handed him the box of Flex flies, a mix-and-match of head styles and body types. He put on the basic combination, a deer hair head and a salmonfly rear, but it didn't do any better than the ordinary dry flies, getting one hit in fifteen minutes.

Rick was having fun with the Flex-Stones, hooking the body onto all the different styles of heads. He had a nice strike on the hackle head variation, the first big fish of the day rolling on the imitation, but Rick pulled the fly away too soon.

Then he clipped on a black, scooped-face popper, the head for a bass fly, and threw it against the bank. He chugged the Flex-Stone once and let it drift dead. On the third cast he missed a fish, pulling back with a sweep of the rod but never setting the hook in the trout's mouth.

Rick's 7½-foot rod, for a 5-weight line, wasn't enough stick for this fishing. Brant gave him his 9-foot for an 8-weight line and a few minutes later Rick hooked his first trout solidly. All of us started catching browns on the poppers, but no one hit a rainbow all afternoon. The chug of the fly brought brown trout rushing out from the banks. A very poor day turned suddenly into a great one (especially for Rick).

Was it the fly? Or did the fish just start feeding? There were very few rises that entire afternoon to real stoneflies. At the take-out for the boats, the other guides and their clients all grumbled about the slow day.

The Popper Head, a scooped-faced chugger, didn't always work during the salmonfly hatch. Once, on Rock Creek, when that stream was a chocolate wash, the Popper Head caught a lot of trout on what looked like an impossible dry fly day. Two weeks later on the same water my favorite combination, the brown, cone-shaped foam head, did much better when the creek ran clear.

Flying Ant

Flights of ants don't fall on a river or pond all that often. In my years of fishing, over forty, it has happened to me less than a dozen times. It would hardly seem worth the trouble carrying flies to match such a rare phenomenon, but when flying ants do hit the water, fish go so berserk that it would be a shame to be unprepared for the frenzy.

My box contains red and black versions of the Flying Ant in a range of sizes. The pattern has a foam body (colored with a permanent marker) and a wing of clear Antron fibers. This imitation and a few other types, winged versions of the McMurray Ant, Deer Hair Ant, and Fur Ant, are always in my terrestrial box.

Different characteristics of the fly are important at different times. Early in the feeding madness the distinctive shape of the ant is enough for trout. The clear, bright wings of the insect are often held above the surface, and fish don't see them. Once those wings droop, they spread out flush on the water and trout key on them.

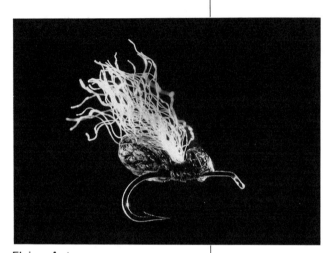

Flying Ant

step 1

TYING STEPS

1. Lash a piece of foam to the middle of the hook shank.

2. Fold the ends of the foam over into the middle; tie to the shank; color the foam with a permanent marker.

step 2

3. Tie in a wing of clear Antron fibers in the middle (slanting up and back at a 45 degree angle).

step 3

Hook: 10–18 (3X fine wire, TMC 5230)

Body: a strip of foam (colored with a waterproof marker)

Wing: clear Antron

Flying Ant

LOG ENTRY: AUGUST 29, 1991
BIGHORN RIVER

In mid-summer the Bighorn gets crowded, fishermen in boats and fisher-men on foot combining in an assault on the trout. It is hard sometimes to find a good piece of water to work at all. The only salvation is that the regular army of anglers moves in lock-step, wading fishermen in one wave and drifting fishermen in another. There are areas that are aban-doned at odd hours.

I was driving past the river and I stopped to look at the water. It was after-noon and I decided that as long as I was there, I might as well walk the left bank for a mile or so below the Afterbay. I like to carry a strung-up rod and wear my vest on a stroll like this, even if I have no intention of fishing. Then I saw a few trout sipping, and thought that I might make a cast or two.

A few hours later, near 4:00 p.m., the big fall of flying ants hit the river. They were large, matched with a size 14 fly, and black. The fish didn't "rise"—they never simply rise to a heavy fall of ants. The fish churned up that river; and, as always, the frenzy of the feeding amazed me.

The trout seem to know that the ants are only going to be over their heads a short time. When there is a fabulous hatch of mayflies, with as many duns on the water as there are flying ants during a heavy fall, the fish rise to the mayflies with a rhythm. With flying ants, they slop and roll, taking as many naturals as possible.

The choice of imitation probably didn't matter in the first twenty min-utes of the spree. Anything close to the size, shape, and color of the natural would have caught plenty of trout. A size 14 Black Flying Ant drew a strike nearly every drift over the fish. The only challenge was picking out the largest feeders, those 21- to 23-inch slobs mixed in with the other rainbows and browns.

After a while the rises petered out, but there were still a few nice fish taking the ants caught in backwaters or along the grass banks. These trout were tougher, maybe because the insects still left on the water were drowned, completely mired in the surface film.

One brown tore up the foam body on my fly. I cut that fly off (the third one ruined this afternoon) and put on a fur-bodied pattern with some kind of clear, plastic wing. This new fly caught one rainbow, but other trout snubbed it with turn-away refusals. I tied on my last Black Flying Ant, re-touched the body with a felt tip marker, and showed it to the same rising fish. It fooled two of the three sippers before the surface feeding stopped completely.

Foam Ant

Ants tied with closed, large cell polyurethane foam are better than other patterns, even ones made with dense types of foam. The translucence of this material is important on imitations of black and brown ants (although they seem relatively opaque to the casual observer). It is absolutely critical on imitations of red ants. When the foam is colored with a red marker, it radiates fire under sunlight just like the body of the natural.

My revelation with ants came during a massive feeding study on trout in the Missouri River. This work, done for *Caddisflies*, sampled over 2,000 fish. The stomach pumpings showed that while most of the trout ate a few ants, some fish consumed a lot of them.

The difference in the diets of these trout was connected to the habits of the insect. Ants were not like beetles (clumsy enough to fall in anywhere) or leafhoppers (agile enough to jump in anywhere). They were such surefooted little beasts that they didn't drop into the water randomly. There were very well defined spots where ants hit the stream. My group of observers labeled these places. Any fish with a feeding lie below one of these spots sipped ants from the surface continually all summer.

There was one willow tree along the edge of the Missouri that stood just a bit taller than the high bank behind it. The bank protected most of the tree from the wind; and it also sheltered all of the other bushes and trees growing next to the river. Nearly every ant that fell onto the water in that stretch was blown off of the top section of the tall willow on gusty days. The exposed portion of the tree fed enough ants onto the river to keep a line of fat rainbows and browns busy.

Foam Ant

Foam Ant

step 1

step 2

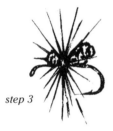

step 3

TYING STEPS

1. Lash a piece of foam to the middle of the hook shank.

2. Fold the ends of the foam over into the middle; tie ends to the shank; color the foam with a permanent marker.

3. Wrap a hackle one turn in the middle.

Whip finish.

Hook: 10–18 (3X fine wire, TMC 5230)

Body: foam (colored with a marker

Hackle: rooster hackle

Red, brown, black and (surprisingly) white are the major colors.

**LOG ENTRY: JULY 15, 1990
BLUBBER CREEK**

A tributary of Elk Creek in the Sun River drainage

Blubber Creek, near the Augusta horse camp my daughter used to go to each summer, is more a series of beaver ponds than a stream. There are hoards of brookies and rainbows up to 10 inches in any opening. In the few holes in the actual stream connecting those ponds there is the occasional boss trout up to 15 inches.

After a few days of fishing the Sun River, it was time to break the brush on Blubber. Once, in a terribly ambitious mood, I spent a week slogging the beaver ponds, averaging over a hundred trout a day. Today, I was just going to fish the afternoon.

Everything was normal, beaver pond flogging for a few hours. I was using a soft hackle wet, casting the fly and letting it settle on the silt. After a few moments, when the fish forgot about the commotion, I would start a hand-twist retrieve and strike if the line tip twitched. The catch was nearly two brookies for every rainbow, the typical ratio, and the biggest fish was only 11 inches.

At my favorite stretch of overgrown channel, I put on a Blonde Wulff and began popping fish on the surface. Surprisingly, there were a number of swirling refusals. By the time I reached a big pine laying across the stream, few fish would respond to the Wulff.

The trout were too small to stomach pump (about 14 inches is the minimum size). I gave up on the fishing for the moment and went up to the tree, walking into the stream to get a closer look at the rough bark.

The leaning tree was a danger point for the ants, wind or no wind, feeding insects onto the water continually. There was a war of survival going on between two types of ants, a dozen battles taking place at any moment. Small red ants ran along the tree gathering food, with one particular muscle man toting a dead caddisfly. Just as many large brown ants scurried back and forth, but they didn't seem to be collecting anything. They moved much more randomly.

When a big ant crossed paths with a small ant, the brute chased his tiny cousin, but even if he caught him, the outcome wasn't certain. The big one just held on until more of his kind discovered the struggle, and then the group of attackers worked together, tearing the smaller worker apart. When the fight appeared hopeless, a red ant had one more trick. He pushed away and fell, sometimes carrying his tormentors with him.

This instinctive defense undoubtedly worked better on an upright tree, dropping the ant to the ground. On the tree over Blubber Creek, the maneuver dumped him on the water. One red ant lifted three of his attackers and pulled them onto the stream with him.

I went back downstream and waited a full hour for the trout to return to their positions below the leaning pine. Once they began rising I showed them a size 18 Red Foam Ant, each fish accepting it with a confident sip. I carefully worked the four hundred yards from the head of the beaver pond to the fallen tree, getting a couple of 14-inch brook trout, trophies for this stream, along with nine smaller ones.

> When the fight appeared hopeless, a red ant had one more trick. He pushed away and fell, sometimes carrying his tormentors with him.
>
> This instinctive defense undoubtedly worked better on an upright tree, dropping the ant to the ground. On the tree over Blubber Creek, the maneuver dumped him on the water.

Foam Beetle

A fisherman needs two types of beetle patterns. There are subtle flies, such as the Crowe Beetle and the Marinaro Beetle, which succeed simply by mimicking such an important food form, and there are strong flies, such as the Foam Beetle, which adds an element of attraction with a translucent foam wing.

The Foam Beetle, especially with the wing free over the back instead of tied down, pulls trout further than the simple imitation. It seldom gets refusals during morning or evening hours. It is only during the brightest hours of midday that it appears a little unnatural to fish. Those subtler flies, the Crowe Beetle and the Marinaro Beetle, prove more reliable during the middle of the day.

A beetle imitation can be the rarest of all flies—a hatch breaker. A trout, if not totally locked into a selective snit, will slide away from a natural mayfly or caddisfly and sip either a real beetle or a matching pattern.

An ant breaks a hatch sometimes. A grasshopper breaks a hatch rarely. Why does the beetle do it so consistently? The very act of selective feeding is a game of numbers. Ants end up on the water but not in overwhelming numbers and grasshoppers, no matter how conspicuous on land, splash onto the stream sporadically unless the conditions for blundering are ideal. Beetles are much more prone to watery disaster than either ants or grasshoppers.

Beetles, all hours of the day and all seasons of the year (even in the dead of winter), form a significant part of the trout's diet. They are such a constant component of the drift in streams and lakes that they inspire a form of general preference in fish. The numbers are so steady that trout usually see a helpless beetle as an acceptable food item.

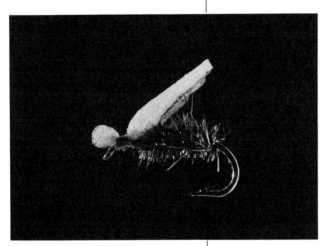

Foam Beetle

TYING STEPS

1. Tie in a hackle; let it dangle for the moment.

2. Wrap a body of peacock herl.

3. Palmer the body hackle; trim it top and bottom.

4. Tie in a foam wing; color the bottom of the foam with a black waterproof marker, but leave the top of the foam white; leave the back end free.

Hook:	8–18 (standard dry fly, TMC 100)
Body:	peacock herl
Body Hackle:	dyed-olive grizzly (palmered; clipped flat top and bottom)
Wing:	closed-cell foam

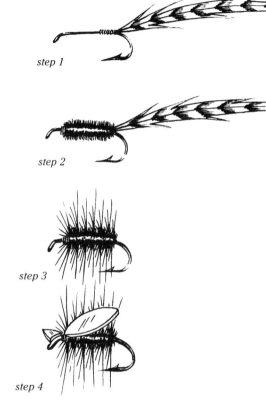

step 1

step 2

step 3

step 4

LOG ENTRY: SEPTEMBER 30, 1991
BASS LAKE

This is a high mountain lake of approximately 100 acres in the Bitter-root-Selway Wilderness Area; it nestles right below the peaks that divide Idaho and Montana.

It would be a rough one-day hike with fifty-pound packs for real backcountry walkers. For Rich Macomber, Jim Dipisa, and me it was a lei-surely two-day trek (as leisurely as possible climbing the final half mile of jumbled boulders). The mystery of any new mountain lake, as muscles get sorer with every step, becomes more like a nagging question—is the fishing going to be worth it?

Last night after setting up camp we rushed out for a bit of casting in the dying light. There was no time for intelligent decisions. It was slog and flog frantically with Twist Nymphs and Wooly Worms on an unknown lake. None of us even knew what species of trout were in Bass Lake. It took less than an hour to find out that it had cutthroats, very silvery and lightly spotted, up to 13 inches, and rainbows, fewer in number, up to 20 inches. We kept a few of the smaller fish for supper (everything else for the trip was kiss and release).

The supper trout provided something just as important as a meal. The stomach contents gave us a blueprint for the next day's fishing. Surpris-

Foam Beetle Log

ingly, considering the plumpness of the trout, there weren't any large aquatic forms in the stomachs—no damsel nymphs or scuds or leeches. For the most part, the contents were a black mash of midge larvae, pupae, and adults. The only substantial forms were grasshopper pieces in one trout and a number of beetles of various size and color in all of the trout.

So what flies did Rick and I start with the next morning? Wooly Worms. The only excuse for this choice was that the lower part of the lake was choppy. It would be hard to see any pattern on the surface. Our plan was to work around to the upper end, a sheltered dogleg at the inlet, and save the dry flies for there.

For every trout we caught on a Wooly Worm there were a half dozen short strikes. Even large fish would follow the fly into the shallows, nipping at the tail end. Maybe because of the paucity of big swimming organisms in Bass Lake, the trout were stuck between curiosity and suspicion.

The upper end was not only protected but also shallower and richer. The lake was drawn down this late in the fall, leaving an edge of boulders. My tactic was to climb up one of these big perches, sit down and stare into the water, and wait for cruising trout.

In this blissful cross between meditation and fly fishing, the trick was to simply put the fly in the path of every passing cutthroat and rainbow trout. Various dry flies caught fish, including grasshopper, ant, and midge pupa imitations, but no pattern pulled trout further than a Foam Beetle. And there wasn't a single refusal to this fly all afternoon.

The pattern obviously was matching a common food form. Beetles were so prevalent in the routine of these high mountain trout, not in vast but in steady numbers, that the visual image of one of these insects on the surface triggered immediate recognition. The fish were so sure of the imitation, apparently a good one for this time of year, that even in clear, flat water there wasn't a last moment hesitation in the rise, that critical bit of inspection, that occurred with other patterns.

Rick caught trout on a small Royal Trude, but some of the visible fish that he casted to snubbed the attractor. When he took my rod and worked the Foam Beetle, he began taking every trout in the cruising lane, also. Even Jim, returning from rock climbing, caught a trout (his first on a fly rod) with the Beetle.

Until we started back to camp, along the far shoreline, the largest fish of the day was a 17-inch rainbow. It was late and Rick said, "We're not going to stop for anything under 15 inches."

That should have been an effective curse, but within a hundred yards he spotted a fish. He refused to try for the trout, a case of beginner's buck fever, "He's too big for me."

"She is too big," I said.

> The pattern obviously was matching a common food form. Beetles were so prevalent in the routine of these high mountain trout, not in vast but in steady numbers, that the visual image of one of these insects on the surface triggered immediate recognition.

The trout at first glance really didn't look that large to me. It was hard to tell how deep she was swimming in the clear water, however. My hurried roll cast put the Foam Beetle in front of her and she started slanting up to the fly. The swim took a long time.

Rick muttered, "He looks as big as a bass."

"She looks as big as a bass," I said.

The rainbow sipped the fly, felt the set of the hook, and jumped twice in a bouncing run out into the lake. The leaps were all the more impressive considering the pot belly on this overfed lady. She rolled, dug and splashed. At the finish she lay still only for a quick measurement, 20 inches in length but more impressive for her incredible girth.

The total catch for Rick and me, including the angry lady rainbow that came up through so much water, was roughly sixty trout for the day. Over half of those fish, and all of the biggest ones, took a Foam Beetle.

Foam Inch Worm

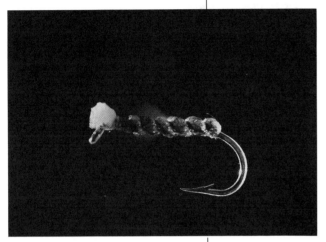

Foam Inch Worm

When I was a boy, the green inch worm gave me my first bonanza days on Connecticut trout streams. Until then my flogging had produced a fish here and a fish there, the occasional sacrificial victim to my mad rush along the banks. For me there were none of those big catches described so often by my heroes writing in the outdoor magazines.

I was getting tired of asking myself, "What would A. J. McClane do right now?"

After a few seasons puzzling over the green inch worm "hatch," I came up with my own answers for the when, where, and how of this summertime event. My way was different from everybody else's approach, but this was not due to any great burst of original thinking on my part.

The other anglers on my streams marched up or down, covering all of the water. My approach was to find the "home trees"—usually there was only one in a couple of hundred yards of bank with an infestation of inch worms. The trick was to tie a ribbon on the best trees, the ones hanging over good trout holes.

The other anglers stood on the shallow side and cast across to the deep bank. On these overgrown streams they spent as much time with a fly in the trees as on the water. My presentation was dictated by my horribly inept casting style. My only chance was to wade upstream along the deep bank, the water as high as my chest sometimes, and throw sidearm to curl the fly for an easy, drag-free float down the entire length of the prime run.

Other anglers just cast randomly, and without knowing where the fish were holding they often ruined a spot without getting a single rise. My weakest virtue, patience, was severely tested, but my plan after getting into position below a good home tree was to always wait until a trout rose to a real inch worm, and then cast ten feet above him.

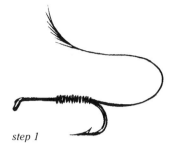

step 1

TYING STEPS

1. Tie in a piece of floss; let it dangle for a moment.

2. Tie in a piece of foam on the hook shank; leave a stub of foam in front of the tie down.

3. Bind the foam around the hook shank with the floss.

Whip finish.

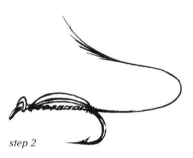

step 2

Hook: 16 (standard dry fly, TMC 100)

Rib: chartreuse floss

Body: a piece of closed, large cell foam

The foam is colored green with a permanent marker, but the front stub is left white for better visibility.

step 3

LOG ENTRY: AUGUST 3, 1990
BLUEWATER CREEK

This tributary of the Clark's Fork of the Yellowstone is an aberration—a small, brushy stream that is great for large trout.

There are no inch worms along Montana streams, but my travels take me around the country each summer, at least a few times to Connecticut, and there are always inch worm imitations in my box. They are useful occasionally even in the West.

Wayne Huft, one of the superb fly fishermen in the country, came with me to Bluewater, but he was skittish right from the beginning. "You always take me to these streams that have rattlesnakes."

"Little Prickly Pear? Sixteen Mile? Hound?"

"Right."

"This one's a lot worse. It's my favorite."

"Damn you to a fishless hell."

His curse worked for both of us. He did poorly because he twitched everytime the wind rustled the burnt grass. Finally, after a mile and only a few small trout on nymphs he put away the rod and took out the camera. He stayed close, letting me break the trail.

My fishing was ruined by the drought. The stream was too skinny in the lower stretches and it didn't get wider until our upstream flogging

Foam Inch Worm Log

took us past a few diversions and closer to the source at a state fish hatchery.

I saw a trout rising, sporadically but enthusiastically, a long way off. While I debated which fly to put on, all the time working into position, two more fish showed themselves along that left bank. I took a beetle imitation out of the box. (I always take out a beetle imitation when trout are mysteriously rising to some unknown item.)

Then I noticed first one and then a few more little, dark green caterpillars on the water. I tied on a Foam Inch Worm, my closest match, and waited for the nearest fish. When he rose, I drifted the fly over him and he took it. I forced him out of the slot and netted him.

We intended to release him, but sometimes a fish runs back up into a hole when he is let go and spooks everything else in the spot. Wayne kept the 14-inch brown in the net, holding him comfortably in the water. That second trout in the chain of risers was too big to take a chance on spoiling his mood.

He was really tight to the bank, under an overhanging bush, and it took a curve cast to hook the fly onto his feeding line. He let the Foam Inch Worm pass by twice, both times right after gulping a real caterpillar.

He stopped moving for a few minutes, possibly nervous from the commotion of the line landing. This quiet period lasted long enough for me to put on two more feet of finer leader tippet. After another ten minutes the fish rose again, a head and tail roll. This time he was greedy enough to ignore my casting, slurping what he thought was a second caterpillar. With the set of the hook the trout immediately burst across the stream.

Wayne went wild with his camera, crashing in the brush and rolling in the grass to get into position for his pictures. It would have been cruel to remind him of the rattlesnakes at that moment.

There was no playing the fish. He was a very big trout on a very small stream, a bad combination, and there was nothing for me to do except hang on and follow him. He wore himself out with a series of blind rushes. Except for a dangerous jump, when he almost looped the leader over a branch, he never came close to running through cover.

That brown trout measured 23 inches in the net. He wasn't my best fish ever from Bluewater Creek. There were others in previous seasons, many on minnow and mice imitations and thicker leaders, that were as long as 25 inches. This was my biggest trout from the stream on a light tippet and an insect imitation, but even he wasn't the biggest one I had hooked on fine terminal tackle—others had snapped me off easily in the brush, leaving me feeling helpless and frustrated.

There was no playing the fish. He was a very big trout on a very small stream, a bad combination, and there was nothing for me to do except hang on and follow him. He wore himself out with a series of blind rushes. Except for a dangerous jump, when he almost looped the leader over a branch, he never came close to running through cover.

Foam Spider

Mike Lawson made me aware of spiders as a food source for fish. He told me how they not only scramble around the banks but also blow out over the Henry's Fork. They sail onto the water and trout snatch them avidly.

There is always a question with these ubiquitous food forms. Do they get on the water frequently enough to be recognized by the fish? They are not worth imitating specifically unless trout are almost waiting for them to drop on the surface. That happens throughout the season with ants, beetles, and leafhoppers; and it happens during periods of abundance with grasshoppers, crickets, caterpillars, bees, and moths.

But what about spiders? Mike has successfully used spider patterns on the tough Railroad Ranch section of the Henry's Fork. Imitations have worked for me and my friends on other western rivers. A good, matching fly catches trout and sometimes these trout have real spiders in their stomachs. All this is strong circumstantial evidence.

Foam Spider

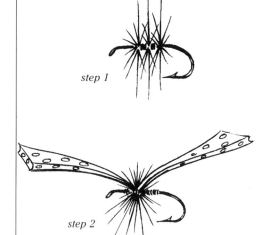

step 1

TYING STEPS

1. Tie in two packs of deer hair tips, ends extending out on each side of the hook; flare the hair with the thread; trim all stubs.

2. Tie in a strip of foam on top of the deer hair stubs.

step 2

3. Pull the ends of the foam into the middle, forming a larger hump at the rear and a smaller hump at the front; color with a brown marker.

Whip finish.

step 3

Hook:	14–16 (standard dry fly; TMC 100)
Legs:	deer hair tips (one pack extending out on each side)
Body:	foam (a large hump at the rear and a small hump at the front; colored with a brown marker)

LOG ENTRY: AUGUST 20, 1990
WISE RIVER

This is a wonderful tributary of the Big Hole, especially during the low water of mid-summer when the trout get not only fussy but also very spooky.

There is one great line that divides all of my fly fishing days. They are either without a plan—and on these days we just go somewhere and adapt to the problems; or with a plan—and on these days a group of my close friends come with me and we fish in a way decided upon long before the first cast. The unplanned days outnumber the planned ones nine to one, but somehow both types of trip are essential for my summers to feel complete.

This is just one more day in the experiment with the Foam Spider. Usually this fly gets tied on for only an hour or so, but it has caught trout on fifteen of the last twenty-one days. It looks different enough from an ant, a leafhopper, or even a beetle that there should also be a difference in the fishing results.

Time after time—and this has been verified over years, not just this summer—trout will show a preference for one terrestrial fly or another.

Foam Spider Log

One day it will be a red ant pattern; on a different day somewhere else it will be a leafhopper (jassid) imitation. Many times, when one fly is an overwhelming winner, one of us will study the surface and count drift items to see if there is a correlation. Seldom is there a clear link.

Today, the Foam Spider, a size 16, was the winner in this game. The victory couldn't have been more absolute. Four of us split up, each carrying a box of terrestrials, and the only plan was to fish all the flies an equal amount of time. My order of use was beetle, grasshopper, leafhopper, spider, caterpillar, bee, and ant, but everyone else had their own, random schedule. When Ken Drobbs, Graham Marsh, Larry Enos, and I met up afterwards the best fly for each of us was a Foam Spider.

The odds of this happening, considering that the flies were used at different times, were slim indeed. It could only happen on a stream like the Wise River, where the fish seldom get enough food to disappear to resting holds for long periods of the day. The trout were apparently willing to rise to a Foam Spider anytime.

These opportunistic rainbows, cutthroats, and brooks apparently liked the size, shape, or color of the Foam Spider better than other patterns. Does this mean that the Foam Spider was a great imitation today? Not necessarily. It was a great fly, but whether or not the fish in the Wise River were looking for real spiders is unknown.

> The combination of deer hair and foam created an odd, parachute shape on the water. That strange silhouette, combined with the translucency of the foam, seemed to trigger the curiosity of fish on all parts of the stream.

There were plenty of those little, brown spiders, moving with incredible quickness along the stream banks. A sampling with a stomach pump on fish big enough to survive the process, a cutthroat, brook trout, and two rainbows over 14 inches, turned up as always a few spiders (along with a few of nearly every other type of terrestrial). There was no glut of any single food item, even aquatic forms, in the stomach contents of the fish.

None of us believed that the trout were taking the Foam Spider only as an imitation. The combination of deer hair and foam created an odd, parachute shape on the water. That strange silhouette, combined with the translucency of the foam, seemed to trigger the curiosity of fish on all parts of the stream. The fly caught trout along the banks, where spiders were common, and in the heaviest riffles, where spiders were rare.

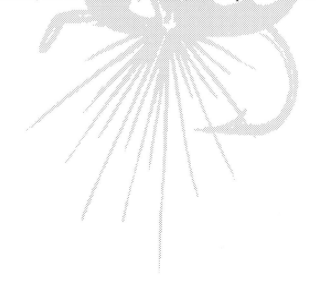

Gray Coughlin

There are many patterns that could serve as the "drab searcher" in my fly box. An Adams fills that niche for most anglers, but the Gray Coughlin is my favorite dry fly when trout are feeding on a general variety of insects.

This isn't one of my original patterns, but it is strongly associated with me through my writings. It represents an entire category of flies—my favorite drab searcher could just as easily be an Atherton or a Gray Ugly. The important point is that one of these patterns belongs in an angler's carrying selection. My reason for choosing the Gray Coughlin over some other drab fly (including the Adams) is that the brown color scheme worked better for me day in and day out than a gray color scheme did.

The Gray Coughlin didn't bump the Adams from that top position in my fly box. Over thirty years ago the Adams lost favor to a different fly. That pattern, an Atherton Dark, had a powerful theory behind it—all of John Atherton's creations, following his preferences as an artist, were impressionistic. The patterns in *The Fly and the Fish*, from nymphs to dry flies, were not "solid" colors. The patterns were variegated, parts of a fly made with many different specks, or points, of color to create an overall effect.

My family rented a cabin for four weeks one summer in Vermont on the Battenkill River. This was long before I started tying my own flies, so my allowance money was spent on flies at a local sporting goods store. "What's good?" I asked the clerk.

"On the Battenkill?" He sold me three size 16 Adams and three size 16 Atherton Darks, "These are the best."

My small stream skills were no match for the brown trout of the big Battenkill. The fish were too critical; the expanse of river was too overwhelming. The best I could do was peck at the edges, catching small brook trout. Even those tough, little snits snubbed my coarse leaders and heavy lines—or maybe it was my

Gray Coughlin

Gray Coughlin

sloppy casting and clumsy wading. Five brookies over ten to twelve hours was a fine day for me.

I bought size 16 Adams and size 16 Atherton Darks as often as my allowance allowed me to. They were the only two flies that I used on the Battenkill that summer, changing them hourly until I either caught something or chased away all rising fish. By the fourth week of the vacation my terminal tackle and my on-stream skills were both a bit more refined, but the river, low and clear in the August heat, was at its toughest, too.

The Atherton Dark outfished the Adams that week, although my logs noted that they were both used roughly the same amount of time. The totals for six days were:

- size 16 Adams—caught eight brook trout
- size 16 Atherton Dark—caught twenty brook trout and two brown trout.

I didn't begin tying my own flies until years later. My faith in impressionistic patterns, with few solidly colored parts, especially for general imitations, never left me. My tying was haphazard, the recipes coming from books such as J. Edson Leonard's *Flies*. I could have tied up a selection of Atherton Darks , but I stumbled upon the Gray Coughlin, a fly with a body of naturally variegated hare's ear and a hackle blend of brown and grizzly.

After one season the Gray Coughlin was permanently added to my carrying stock, escaping my large, jumbled collection of "test" flies. It always seemed to catch trout consistently for me that first year on my home waters of Connecticut, doing well on a wide variety of trout waters. Starting one May evening on the Housatonic and finishing one September morning on Salmon Brook, the Gray Coughlin performed well because there were always a few drab insects on the water.

TYING STEPS

1. Tie in a tail of dun hackle fibers.

2. Tie in split, matched slips of duck quill.

3. Dub a body of Hare's Ear fur.

4. Wind two hackles, one brown and one grizzly.

Whip finish.

step 1

step 2

step 3

step 4

Hook:	10–22 (standard dry fly, TMC 100)
Tail:	medium dun hackle fibers
Body:	grayish-brown Hare's Ear dubbing (guard hairs untrimmed)
Wing:	matched sections of slate gray duck quill
Hackle:	brown and grizzly (mixed)

Even if the gray duck quill wings are solid when the fly is new they soon get frayed and separated. A messed up Gray Coughlin usually outfishes a fresh one. The practical tier can roll the wing sections in his fingers, creating a buzz of individual fibers, before tying them onto the hook.

Gray Coughlin

LOG ENTRY: AUGUST 12, 1990
NORTH FORK OF THE SUN RIVER

The North Fork and the South Fork of the Sun both come out of the Bob Marshall Wilderness Area, joining just above Gibson Reservoir. They are very productive fisheries, if the angler can ignore the scenery long enough to concentrate on presenting a fly. Like many backcountry waters, both forks receive more pressure each year, from outfitters and individuals, and by mid-summer the trout are no longer easy and eager. They get fussy and a little spooky.

Yesterday, a horse packer dropped us and our gear fifteen miles up the North Fork. Terry Dixon, Scott Fletcher, and I are going to backpack out five miles each day, camping and fishing down to the trailhead. The river is so low and clear, easily wadeable, and if the little bit of casting we squeezed in after pitching tents last night was a fair sample, the fishing is going to be great.

I'll qualify that "great." Terry and Scott are superb anglers, with skills honed on their Maryland trout waters, and they are using 6X, 12-foot leaders and size 18 and 20 flies. Already today we have met two groups of fishermen, all of them flogging away with size 10 and 12 attractors on 3X tippets, and complaining about the slow action. I have been using attractors, too, but they have been size 18 Aft Sparkles and Double Wings.

This river rewards good presentations. There are a lot of deep runs and pools, but the current is swift, and most of the surface area isn't very good for a small dry fly. The places for a size 18 fly are against the banks with slow edges and in midstream tangles of fallen trees (and even there the fly has to drift right down the gentler creases in the flow).

By 6:00 p.m., with an overcast building, the tiny attractors were no longer working as well. There were various insects flopping around, not too many of any one kind, and trout rose sporadically. The soft summer evening seemed right for a size 16 Gray Coughlin now that there were insects of that size on the water.

Why a Gray Coughlin? My usual drab searcher for mid-summer would be a cream or white fly, but with the gray clouds a darker fly apparently seems more natural to the trout. Other patterns might do as well as a Gray Coughlin—a Clear Wing Spinner, with bright, spent wings, or a Shroud, with its radically colored, soft red marabou tail—but these would be bold choices on an evening when trout would gladly accept the simple dry fly.

There was one notable fish among a good number of fat rainbows. He was rising in a crook of branches below a downed tree. The tree wasn't dead, and with its roots holding in the bank, the branches were still thick with leaves. Terry was casting to the trout, attempting to snake the fly through a maze, but on the fourth try he hooked up on a limb. He didn't want to break off the fly because pulling would shake the branch in the water and scare the fish. He laid his rod to the side and borrowed my rod. His first cast missed the rising trout, but when the fly drifted downstream he hooked a different rainbow, 16 inches, and landed that one and gave me back my rod for a shot at the original trout. My cast, blessed with luck, tucked through the opening, and the fly settled right above the trout's nose.

It was right at that moment that the choice of the Gray Coughlin proved so perfect. There was no doubt that the fly itself would not stop that fish from rising. In its simple drabness there was nothing wrong about the pattern. A strong attractor, designed to pull a fish, might have made the trout hesitate at the final instant. If the Gray Coughlin didn't drag, or if the trout didn't take a real insect just as the Gray Coughlin passed near, there would be a strike.

The rainbow sucked in the fly. He leapt, somehow missed tangling in the limbs, and ran free of the tree. He wasn't easy to net, even out in the open pool, but he never tried to reach cover. He kept jumping right until he was wrapped up, still green and ready to fight. He measured out at 16 inches, too, no bigger than other fish in easier places, just tougher to hook.

By 6:00 p.m., with an overcast building, the tiny attractors were no longer working as well. There were various insects flopping around, not too many of any one kind, and trout rose sporadically. The soft summer evening seemed right for a size 16 Gray Coughlin now that there were insects of that size on the water.

Lady Heather

The Lady Heather is a B.S. pattern (this has nothing to do with manure—it was developed "Before Scuba"). It may have been the fly that drove me to scuba. It was created with old-fashioned doggedness, with weeks of on-stream flogging. The frustration of this trial-and-error puzzle was trying to make sense of all the variables, all the unknown factors that muddled the results of day-to-day fishing.

I created the Lady Heather for overcast and rainy conditions. Every time the weather turned nasty it was my job to rush out fishing with various prototypes of the pattern, sometimes alone but usually with a friend.

Once, after a day of drenching cloudbursts, Bill Seeples and I walked into his kitchen and he said to his wife, pointing at me, "If it's raining and he calls again, tell him I'm out mowing the lawn."

We tested the fly on the Big Hole below Divide (browns and rainbows), the upper Clark Fork between Deer Lodge and Warm Springs (almost all browns), and the Little Blackfoot near Avon (almost all browns). These have been my home waters for over twenty years, and it is not surprising that the idiosyncrasies of these rivers shaped many of my early fly designs.

My first attempts at developing a good dry fly for gray days all suggested simplification. This was a difficult concept for me to accept—all of my patterns were supposed to be dazzling deviations from the norm, caricatures that attracted even as they imitated important food forms. But on dark days active trout showed a preference for basic, drab flies; and each new version of the Lady Heather evolved into a simpler pattern.

From the beginning the Lady Heather was meant to be a Trude variation. The differences were the mixed grizzly and gray hackles and a prominent egg sac. That egg sac ended up being the biggest problem with the fly. It was lime green or burnt orange on the first

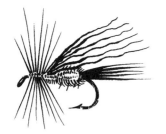

Lady Heather

test versions, logical choices considering the coloration of real insect eggs, but trout shied from those bright hues on gray days. We left the egg sac off on some test variations, but in the close comparison of head-to-head fishing a Lady Heather with a gray egg sac (that no one remembered tying) did better than the fly with the all-cream body. That gray ball at the rear of the pattern helped because it provided a contrast with the cream body and white wing without the brightness of the earlier egg-sac imitations.

The tests gave me my gray-day pattern—a downwing, easy to see, riffle-water dry fly. It broke one of the oldest axioms in fly fishing: Gray day, gray fly. It was drab, except the white wing, but it wasn't all gray. The Lady Heather did as well or better in tests against my other favorite patterns for cloudy days, the Gray Trude and Gray Wulff.

The Lady Heather has another interesting quirk. It caught more brown trout than other flies in overcast conditions; the all-gray flies did better on rainbows. Many anglers have noted that browns have an odd affinity for the color white. My experience with the Lady Heather bears that out. Brown trout come further to take a Lady Heather, especially under the darkest, most threatening skies.

Lady Heather

step 1

step 2

step 3

step 4

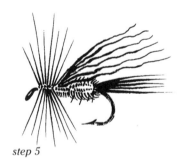

step 5

TYING STEPS

1. Tie down hackle fibers for a tail.

2. Dub a thick butt of gray muskrat fibers.

3. Dub or wrap a thin body of cream fur.

4. Bind down a wing of white calf tail.

5. Tie in a dun hackle and a grizzly hackle; wrap them together.

Whip finish.

Hook:	10–18 (standard dry fly, TMC 100)
Tail:	dark blue dun hackle fibers
Butt:	gray muskrat fur (dubbed)
Body:	cream fur (wrapped or dubbed; thinner than the butt)
Wing:	white calf tail
Hackle:	grizzly and dark blue dun (mixed)

LOG ENTRY: JUNE 21, 1990
BITTERROOT RIVER

Even through the worst years of drought the Bitterroot has fished well. The Montana Department of Fish, Wildlife and Parks has purchased water from Painted Rocks Reservoir and these releases keep the Bitterroot flowing well in mid-summer.

Ed Brown, Glen Tryan, and I floated the stretch above Hamilton and proved what everyone says, "The Root is a moody river."

Two weeks ago Green Drakes and Brown Drakes were all over the water. Browns and rainbows were in the prime lies and schools of whitefish were spread out over the flats. The rise went on all afternoon.

This morning the weather looked perfect, the same solid overcast, not dark but medium gray, that produced great dry fly fishing during the Drake hatches. There were no bugs of any kind on the water today, however, and only a few sporadic rises.

At first a Gray Wulff did as well as anything, pulling up fish as we drifted and cast to banks. Ed was in the back seat, throwing accurately, with enough slack to get good drifts right on the foam line, and he was catching a few trout (best a 17-inch brown). Glen wasn't doing as well, but his problems had nothing to do with the fly. Fishing from a boat was new to him, and he was casting too straight, his line devoid of slack on the water. He started changing patterns every ten minutes, looking for magic that didn't exist.

When we stopped to wade a long riffle, Glen fished beautifully, all of his confusion in the boat gone, but he was still switching flies. Even after catching a fish, he would snip off the successful pattern.

"What are you doing?" I asked.

"Playing around," he said.

Here was a man after my own heart. The least I could do was give him a few more patterns to play with on a slow fishing day. I handed him a few Lady Heathers with the batch of flies.

The storm was building, the clouds piling up thicker in the river valley. All this gloom apparently perked up the trout for dry flies, both Glen and Ed yelling with each hookup. I was working subsurface, dead drifting a Prince Nymph on the bottom, terrorizing the whitefish and occasionally catching a nice trout, but the fishing stayed the same for me.

Ed called me down to take a picture of a fat, 19-inch brown. The trout had a Lady Heather in her mouth and Ed pointed to it, "This has been taking fish for the last half hour."

"Have you been changing flies every time you catch something?"

"Heck, no. I got this from Glen and I'm not giving it back."

Once it started raining fly choice stopped being so important. After an hour the water even began to get stained, probably from the small stream coming in on the far bank. The fish still rose to dry flies, but they wanted large, bushy patterns and any color—black or yellow or green—seemed acceptable.

> This morning the weather looked perfect, the same solid overcast, not dark but medium gray, that produced great dry fly fishing during the Drake hatches. There were no bugs of any kind on the water today, however, and only a few sporadic rises.

Mess

The Mess, specifically designed to match large mayflies, is a wild imitation even for my warped reality. It features a forward-angled tangle of rooster hackle and mallard feather at the head to mimic the upright wings of the dun. It looks nothing like a mayfly to the human eye; and the fact that it works consistently on even the fussiest feeding trout isn't always enough for the skeptics.

So it was nice to hear from someone who believes in my sanity. William Ninke wrote to me about his work with computer imaging:

> . . . about the Mess. Let me tell you why you aren't as crazy as some may propose. After all, he who laughs last laughs best.
>
> I work professionally with computers and I did some experiments on how different styles of flies floating on the surface would look to a trout under water. The techniques are called "ray tracing." You see the application of these techniques all the time in fancy, animated logos and in commercials on television.
>
> I was able to model the different styles of flies, the reflection of light rays off these patterns, and the refraction of the light rays entering the water's surface (Snell's Law) and duplicate what ended up in the trout's eye. So, I got recordings of what's there for a trout to see.
>
> The major thing that I learned is that forward-angled, fan-shaped wings at the head of a fly produce an early and exaggerated 'flare' at the edge of the window before the body of the fly enters it. So, there is a good physical reason why flies such as your Mess are effective. Your creation has a strong basis in the physics of light refraction. Some may think that you're a bit loony, but I don't. In physics is truth.

William's work definitely belongs in a book or on a video. The first-time anglers would be able to see a fly

Mess

from the trout's (or the scuba diver's) perspective. This vision would give credence to even the strangest creations arising from our underwater research.

The Mess has other odd features in addition to the flared hackle at the head. The body of dubbed synthetic seal's fur doesn't match the color the natural insect—it matches the color of the female's eggs inside the body. There is a strip of overlapping, translucent foam tied over the back—it is colored with a felt tip marker to match the color of the mayfly's body.

Mess

step 1

step 2

step 3

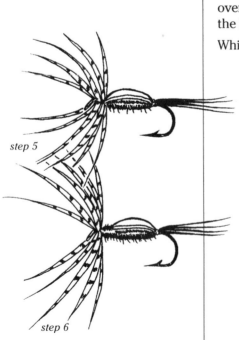

step 4

step 5

step 6

TYING STEPS

1. Tie in four hackle fibers for a tail; split them.

2. Tie in a strip of closed-cell foam; let it dangle for the moment.

3. Dub a body of synthetic seal's fur.

4. Pull the strip of foam forward and tie it down over the body.

5. Wrap a double hackle, with rooster at the rear and mallard at the front; force the hackle fibers forward by wrapping behind them with the tying thread.

6. Dub a little more body material over the wraps of thread behind the hackles.

Whip finish.

Hook: 6–12 (2X long shank and 1X fine wire, TMC 2312)

Tail: four hackle fibers (split two on each side)

Back: strip of foam (colored with a felt tip marker; the edges overlap the sides of the body)

Body: synthetic seal's fur (dubbed)

Hackle: rooster (rear) and mallard (front) feathers

The colors are altered to match various mayfly species. Important combinations include (the first color refers to the rooster hackle and the second color refers to the dubbed body): medium gray/lime, medium gray/orange, slate/olive, cream/lime, and cream/orange. I often color the foam to match the color of the insect right on the stream with a permanent marker.

LOG ENTRY: SEPTEMBER 5, 1991
LOWER YELLOWSTONE RIVER

The Yellowstone is a bit too far away from my home to be one of my regular fishing spots, but it has been such an important river in my research work that it will always be a special place for me. For four years, from a base in West Yellowstone, I guided both in Yellowstone National Park and on the Corwin Springs section in Montana. To compile an emergence chart for Caddisflies, *I collected at various points every three days, one of the sites far downriver at the Greycliff access. While preparing to do a River Rap audio tape with John Bailey, I fished the whole river hard during the summer of 1989.*

A long section of the Yellowstone, from Greycliff to Laurel, is a transition zone, the river changing from a cold-water to a warm-water fishery. There are large trout, great insect populations and very few fishermen (none of them fly fishermen in all my trips) in this section. When the Ghost Fly hatch (*Traverella albertana*), a size 10 white mayfly, explodes on the river, this is the last unknown fly fishing paradise in America.

Rob Dolven and Pat Truax put in with me this morning at Greycliff for a nine-mile float (the take-out is at a private access). On a slow-moving river like this the trip would take most of the day, but we planned to be on the water during the afternoon to hit the hatch, which can pop from 1:00 p.m. to 8:00 p.m., depending on the cloud cover.

Two years ago the three of us had the exact same plan, but we floated a stretch even farther downriver, not far from Laurel. The river was bigger, slower, and muddier, but when the hatch appeared fish started rising everywhere. We hooked fish all afternoon, landing more than sixty, but most of them were not trout. Included in our catch were carp, sauger, and catfish, all taken fair-and-square on dry flies. The rainbows we did fool included a few fat 18-inchers.

By late afternoon we were tired of slinging streamers. The rewards, a trout every 500 casts or so, were not all that great, either. Pat caught the biggest, a 19-inch brown, but in our dreams the trout were supposed to be much larger.

The problem with this hatch is that there is no one to call and ask, "Is the Ghost Fly going yet?" There are no fly shops this far downriver, and none of us have fly fishing friends living on the water. The hatch might be over, or maybe it hasn't started yet.

We were ready to give up on it and row on downriver, when duns started poking out on the surface. The river that looked featureless, and so intimidating to a fly fisherman, suddenly had feeding creases marked by working fish.

Mess Log

We made no attempt to test different imitations of the Ghost Fly. The issue was decided two years ago, during the float down "strange-water alley" (Pat's name for the lower river), when the fish, especially the carp, really liked a matching, Cream/Lime Mess. Those carp were much more critical than the saugers, not only about the fly but also about tippet size.

We had a rule: When one of us landed a fish, he took over the rowing. We just climbed over each other to switch positions, never stopping the boat. As the hatch built to a peak, large duns all over the river, we were changing seats so fast that the action looked like a tag-team wrestling match.

On this trip we found more trout than last time, rainbows and browns totaling at least 50 percent of the catch. The hookups came too fast for anyone to keep a total count of fish landed, but the largest trout was 23 inches, the largest carp was 21 inches (with bigger ones lost), and the largest sauger was 16 inches. No one caught a catfish. The rainbow trout were concentrated in the riffle sections. The carp were always along the slow edges or in backwaters (the same areas that produced the biggest brown trout).

Rob, unlike Pat and me, never broke off. He used the same Mess, right up until nightfall, and must have landed fifty fish on it. He shined his flashlight on the fly to take it off and said, "It still looks all right."

Pat said, "It really couldn't look any the worse for wear now, could it?"

Long ago, Pat and Rob decided that this was one new fly that would never become popular, and it doesn't matter how good it is at matching big mayflies. They believe that it is too strange to ever become acceptable to anyone who knows what a mayfly dun looks like on the water.

> We had a rule: When one of us landed a fish, he took over the rowing. We just climbed over each other to switch positions, never stopping the boat. As the hatch built to a peak, large duns all over the river, we were changing seats so fast that the action looked like a tag-team wrestling match.

Mohawk

Our early experiments with the Mohawk, which was created by my daughter Heather, focused on how this fly attracted trout. The Air Head uses brightness, the Double Wing uses color, and the Wiggler uses the movement of soft body parts to get the attention of fish searching the surface. The Mohawk relies on its relative bulk, a large portion of the fly pressed below the meniscus, to excite trout.

Part of the Mohawk's allure is visual. The way it is tied, the hair trimmed in a radical V-cut entirely on top of the hook shank, the fly sinks down into the water. This sunken portion comes into the trout's range of vision much sooner than other dry flies.

Another part of the Mohawk's allure may be auditory. The scuba divers observed that trout seem to hunt for the "sound" of the fly. The Mohawk, wobbling as it drifts, might create pressure waves that trout can pick up with their lateral lines.

A valuable aspect of the Mohawk series is that the strength of the attraction varies proportionately with the size of the fly. In the larger hook ranges it is powerful, often too powerful, getting frequent roll-under and jump-over refusals. In the smaller hook ranges it is subtle, adding a little bit of attraction to an otherwise beetle-like imitation.

Mohawk

Mohawk

TYING STEPS

1. Spin a rear section of colored deer hair from the bend of the hook (this section is two-thirds of the total deer hair).

2. Spin a front section of white deer hair (this section is one-third of the total deer hair).

3. Tie off the thread; take the fly out of the vise and trim the deer hair close on the bottom and in a radical V-shape above the hook shank (like a Mohawk hair cut).

4. Put the hook in the vise and wind an oversized white or cream hackle.

Whip finish.

Hook: 8–16 (standard dry fly, TMC 100)

Body: deer hair (white section in front and colored section in back; spun and clipped)

Hackle: cream or white rooster

Only the colored section of deer hair changes. My favorite patterns are orange, green, golden yellow, brown, and natural gray.

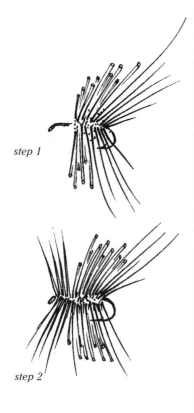

step 1

step 2

step 3

step 4

LOG ENTRY: JULY 11, 1991
LITTLE PRICKLY PEAR CREEK

This stream flows through a canyon of crumbling cliffs, hits the flood plain below the town of Wolf Creek, and enters the Missouri River near the Craig bridge. It is a wonderful early season alternative when the Missouri River is fishing poorly. There are lots of rainbows and browns in Little Prickly Pear, and the average size of these trout is surprisingly high for a small stream. But by mid-July the Prickly Pear typically gets low, leaving fish exposed and vulnerable and subject to undue stress from anglers.

Three of us were fishing together today, but it was easy enough to spread out on Little Prickly Pear. We drove two vehicles up the frontage road and dropped off fishermen at mile intervals. My section was the last one, at the parking area, just below where the stream comes out of the canyon.

I thought that I would be all alone, but someone else, not part of our group, came wading upstream as soon as I reached the bank. "The water is too high," he said. "Maybe I should have fished nymphs."

"What flies did you try?"

"A hopper did the best. It caught three fish."

"It has been a wet spring, and it's a little early for grasshoppers."

He lived in the area, and knew that the grasshoppers were late, but he added, "I figured that I needed something big enough for the trout to see."

Little Prickly Pear was running full, and the water was stained a little bit, but the air was so warm and still that the day felt perfect for a dry fly. If a straight imitation, such as a grasshopper, wasn't working very well, maybe an attractor might bring fish to the surface.

Out of habit I started with a size 16 Green Mohawk. I had a string of successful days with the fly on this stream last summer; and it only seemed fair to let it have the first dance. I waded up the middle of the creek and cast to all of the water, beginning against the right bank and in small slices moving across the stream to the left bank. The little Mohawk picked up two small rainbows in the slow current against the grass.

I tied on a size 12 Green Mohawk and this did better. The trout came towards the fly faster. Maybe they saw it easier, the increased bulk (with more of the bigger, heavier fly below the surface) providing a larger target. It still only caught fish near the banks, not out in the runs and riffles.

I should have been satisfied with the tally of the size 12 Mohawk. The fly was taking trout steadily, and there were a number of fat, 14- and 15-inch fish in the catch. I had to find out, though, what would happen with an even bigger one.

I had a single, size 8 Orange Mohawk in my box. I tied it on and methodically covered the stream slice by slice from one side to the other. The difference this time was that the process was interrupted a couple of times by trout rising to the fly.

The size 8 Mohawk unlocked all areas of the stream. The big fly, successful for me on occasion as a smallmouth bass bug but almost always too strong an attractor for trout, must have looked perfect to the fish in the high, stained water. The Mohawk vacuumed the stream, picking up everything, small, medium, and large trout, from everywhere, including a brown over 18 inches.

I still had my doubts about the big Mohawk. Maybe the fish had suddenly started feeding opportunistically, searching for food. Maybe any pattern, as long as it was big enough, would have done just as well.

I had to go back to the car and meet my friends. I didn't have time to try another large fly on this stretch of water. I was walking up to the parking lot and I met the stranger again. "How did you do?"

He shook his head, "I stuck with the hopper. It was the same all afternoon, a fish here and a fish there. Great fishing, not great catching."

"That's the way it is sometimes."

"It just wasn't a dry fly day."

My friends, Wayne Anderson and George Close, were already at the car. They had used nymphs and had had wonderful fishing (and I had used nymphs part of the day).

One evening Justin Baker was paddling around Beavertail Pond, near Missoula, in his float tube. He was casting a size 16 Mohawk, letting it sit dead on the water, catching sunfish and small trout (hatchery planters). Suddenly, a largemouth bass rose and rolled on the tiny fly—it weighed 3 pounds in the net.

The Mohawk does pull.

Occasion

The Occasion is a hanging style of dry fly. The hook on this pattern sinks below the surface film, suspended by the circle of hackle at the head. It is not unique in this vertical posture. Two old patterns, the English Mole Fly and the French Pont-Audemer, are proven standards in their own countries. Unlike those two patterns, the Occasion has two hackle tips that stand straight up as wings when the fly is positioned on the water.

Denny Peabody not only likes the Occasion as a searching fly, but, as he wrote in a letter, he likes "any fly that diminishes the importance of what you call primary and secondary characteristics. With most patterns you give the trout something to look at, but with hackle patterns, and this can mean a Bivisible or Skating Spider, not just the Occasion, the trout doesn't have anything solid to look at. He looks up and sees 'through' the stacked hackle fibers. My contention is that this type of fly looks more like a changeable, general image of an insect (it can be anything) than any pattern with prominent, solid (light blocking) parts. This is what makes the Occasion a great searching fly."

Occasion

TYING STEPS

1. Wrap a floss body, starting halfway up the shank.

2. Tie in two light hackles and one dark hackle.

3. Wrap the dark hackle, trim the excess.

4. Wrap the two light hackles; let the tips extend straight out over the eye of the hook.

Whip finish.

Hook: 12–16 (3X fine wire, TMC 5230)

Half Body: red floss

Hackle: one cree feather and two cream feathers

Wings: hackle tips of two regular cream hackles

The Tantrum, a color variation, uses green floss for the half-body and a dun feather and two grizzly feathers for the hackle and the wings.

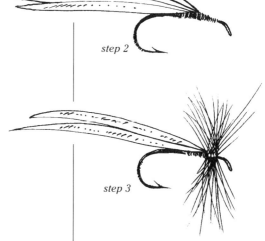

step 1

step 2

step 3

step 4

LOG ENTRY: AUGUST 14, 1990
NORTH FORK OF THE BLACKFOOT RIVER

The North Fork, a wilderness river, is protected from everything except overfishing. For years it produced mainly 10- to 12-inch cutthroats and rainbows, too many of which ended up on a stringer, but recently more restrictive regulations have increased the average size of the fish. The North Fork will never grow a lot of big trout, especially in the upper, tumbling water, but it already holds a lot of 12- to 16-inch fish.

By mid-summer the water on the North Fork is extremely clear, every one of the yellow and light gray rocks on the bottom visible. The fish, especially the cutthroats, are difficult to see in the river. Even when they rise, and the angler can watch them swim back to the stream bed, they disappear into the background.

I camped at the same site as last year. This was the stretch of water where Denny Peabody fished at least twelve hours a day. He'd get up early and start casting at the pool in front of the tent and wade up five miles of stream, stumbling back exhausted just before dark.

Occasion Log

Denny always used the Occasion (and its color variation, the Tantrum) in the evening. Around 5:00 p.m., when the shadows from the pine trees started criss-crossing the river, and the various insects started bouncing on the water, he'd put the fly on with a Uni Knot, leaving an open loop at the eye of the hook, and fish it with an upstream presentation. The Uni Knot allowed the fly to float hook down.

He sometimes gave the fly a little pull, which would make it jump up on the hackle edges for a moment. Usually he drifted it dead over feeding fish, more often than not getting a take. After landing a trout he had to slide open the loop in the Uni Knot again with his fingernail. He caught over thirty rainbows and cutthroats every evening on the Occasion.

I came back here this year to try to duplicate his successes with the Occasion. I didn't even tie the fly on until 5:00 p.m., fishing various terrestrial imitations before then. At 5 o'clock a number of different insects started emerging or egg-laying, creating a confusion of midges, stoneflies, mayflies, and caddisflies on the water. I began catching fish with the Occasion.

It was a fine evening with the dry fly, but surprisingly (at least it surprised me) I didn't do as well as Dennis had last year. Maybe it was my method of presentation, the down-and-across stream cast instead of the upstream cast; maybe it was all the time wasted fussing with the unfamiliar Uni Knot; or maybe my fishing pace was just more relaxed than Denny's frenzied attack. Nonetheless not a single trout tonight refused the Occasion after focusing on it and starting to rise to it—and that was a triumph for the hanging pattern.

Shroud

The simplest truth is that a trout looks up at the dry fly. The fish waits at his hold, searching through his window for objects on the surface. He responds not to the whole fly or the whole insect, but he keys in that fragmented world of refracted light on one prominent part of the item.

There is another truth, still pretty simple but not as recognized— if any portion of that floating fly hangs below the surface, the trout looks ahead, not just up, at the dangling part. This allows a fish to spot and react to an item a second or two quicker than with traditional flies.

The work for *The Dry Fly* included a series of experiments designed to create, piece by piece, an effective new attractor pattern. As many as eight alternative methods or materials were tested for each part of the fly. Sometimes, in these double-blind studies, one choice proved clearly superior, but typically the winning solution was only slightly better than the other attempts. For the tail of the new fly there were two very strong contenders—one maximized the color of the pattern (and eventually this was the tying technique chosen for the Double Wing) and the other let material dangle below the surface.

It seemed a shame to waste a ploy as effective as the hanging red tail. The challenge was to create the rest of a fly to accentuate the allure of soft marabou awash in and under the surface film. We found the best design to include neutral colors for contrast on the body and a heavy hackle for tilt at the head. The limp-tailed, red-and-gray fly was named the Shroud.

Shroud

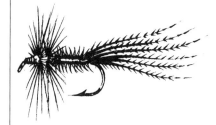

Shroud

step 1

step 2

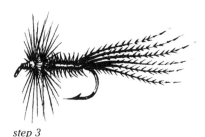

step 3

TYING STEPS

1. Tie in red marabou fibers for the tail (as long as the gap of the hook).

2. Dub a rough body of gray mink or muskrat fur.

3. Wrap three blue dun hackles together (dull side forward).

Whip finish.

Hook:	8–14 (3X fine wire, TMC 5230)
Tail:	red marabou
Body:	gray mink or muskrat fur (dubbed rough, with the guard hairs mixed in the blend)
Hackle:	medium blue dun

**LOG ENTRY: JULY 15, 1991
DEARBORN RIVER**

This tributary of the Missouri is one of Montana's small rivers. They are like private treasures. There is no heavy out-of-state use, and they are not even a destination spot for in-state fishermen. They don't get the crowds because these are not the places that produce big trout.

I have been looking for land along the Missouri River. There was a parcel offered on the Dearborn, a short way up from the mouth of that stream, and the price certainly seemed reasonable. I called the telephone number and the owner of the property described a small piece of paradise.

I asked him, "Do you fish?"

"No."

"So you don't know whether or not the Dearborn is any good right there?"

"It looks beautiful."

"Do you mind if I spend an afternoon fishing it when we go up to look at it?"

The land is a small piece of paradise, but it isn't the right spot for me. There was a three-mile drive up a private, dirt road, unplowed in the winter, and there was no electricity near the place. It is a wonderful setting for a summer cabin, not a permanent home. The river, however, runs in a series of gentle riffles and pools less than four hundred yards from the property.

The water was still high from the spring's heavy rain. A few miles upstream the river flows out of nearly twenty miles of canyon, but this close to the Missouri the banks, lined with cottonwoods, slope gently back from the water.

Nymph patterns worked well throughout the afternoon. If they were drifted on the inside curve of a bend, in the dissipating currents, they caught trout; on the outside curve, against a bank, the flow was too strong for a good, deep presentation. With the high, slightly stained water it looked like a subsurface day. The best flies were a Hare's Ear, Prince Nymph, and a small Natural Drift Stonefly Nymph.

Then, at dusk, the trout really slid into the shallows. No particular insect dominated my drift nettings, neither nymphs nor adults. The fish, searching the flow, ranged over a wide territory to feed on the smorgasbord. They took nymphs, emergents and adults as these stages presented themselves.

It shouldn't have been a surprise that these trout were easy to catch. At least, they were easy to catch on nymph and emerger patterns. Various dry flies, all except the Mohawk, failed badly on the shallow fish. The occasional success of the Mohawk, drifting partially below the surface, inspired me to try the Shroud.

The Shroud matched the excellent catch rates of nymphs and emergers. Numerous fish swirled around and took it after it had drifted past. Other fish moved forward aggressively to intercept the drift. There seemed to be an unusual abundance of large trout, with 15- to 22-inch browns and rainbows snatching the Shroud.

In England, as the result of articles in Trout & Salmon, the Shroud has gained some popularity over the past few years as a still-water dry fly. Anglers there use it as a general searcher on the reservoirs.

Slider

My contribution to the creation of the Slider was simply a suggestion. At a Phrozen Phantom Fly Tyers meeting on the Bitterroot one spring, John VanderHoof was putting goop on the flat faces of large steelhead dry flies with clear cement. "Has anyone ever tried a smaller version of that fly for trout?" I asked.

John tied a few for me in drab colors on size 12 hooks. The pattern, still unnamed, went into my box and stayed there until summer. It caught the occasional fish, but it didn't get extensively used until a week of scuba diving that August.

It was fun to compare it with a Hewitt Skating Spider. The classic Skating Spider hopped on the water, every wavelet bouncing it up into the air, and trout often jumped out of the water to take the fly. The new Slider cut across a river, not even leaving the surface on a riffle— it was truly a "slider." The fish saw the Slider more clearly than a Skater, often racing beside it instead of behind it, and on these occasions they took it with a sidewards roll. The ratio of solid hook ups to strikes was better with a Slider, too.

Slider

TYING STEPS

1. Wind a body of a stripped hackle quill; lacquer the quill.

2. Tie in a deer hair wing; do not trim the stubs— flare them, stand them straight up, and trim them into a semicircle.

Whip finish.

3. Soak the semicircle of deer hair with clear bonding cement.

Hook:	10–16 (3X fine wire, TMC 5230)
Body:	stripped quill from a brown hackle (lacquered)
Wing:	deer hair (downwing)
Face:	deer hair (cut to shape and glued flat)

step 1

step 2

step 3

LOG ENTRY: JUNE 7, 1990
MISSOURI RIVER

The stretch below Holter Dam, my favorite for floating, has such free-rising trout that it seems a sacrilege at times to fish for them with anything other than a dry fly.

So sometimes it takes me twenty years to figure out a problem. There is a giant backwater on the Missouri— the angler launches at the Craig access and after a mile float the eddy is below a high bench on the left. There are almost always pods of fish rising here, but over the years and quick casts back into it on every float trip, my tally has been pathetic. Even stopping and walking the shoreline (it's so deep that an angler cannot wade into it) hasn't been particularly productive.

The problem is the weed, mats of it, floating around and around the backwater. It either slides sideways, looping into long strings, or else it billows up from the depths, trapping any fly on the surface. All this time trout and whitefish rise to insects in the open patches, the pods shifting to avoid the grass. A perfect cast to a clear area only allows the fly a short drift, and on each pick-up grass drapes from the hook, every knot on the leader, and the line-leader junction.

Slider Log

This is my second float this year on this stretch of the river. My borrowed drift boat has an anchor, letting me stop right at the edge of the eddy and cast back into it. The fishing is with a Slider, which has nothing in common with the spot-casting, salad-picking frustration of dead-drift presentation here.

On my first trip with the Slider grass was hanging up on the leader knots and line-leader connection, but the fly itself skipped and hopped with the steady retrieve over every piece and clump of weed. Before this year my best day ever on this backwater had been two fish (one a whitefish), but the active fly took three trout.

The problem is the weed, mats of it, floating around and around the backwater. It either slides sideways, looping into long strings, or else it billows up from the depths, trapping any fly on the surface. All this time trout and whitefish rise to insects in the open patches, the pods shifting to avoid the grass.

I anchored the boat next to the eddy at 9:30 a.m., tied on a knotless leader, and epoxied the line-leader knot. By the time the epoxy hardened the fish were rising steadily to midge pupae, mayfly duns, and caddis pupae. All of these insects were drowned and bedraggled, funneling in from the main current. I never even tried casting to specific fish, instead popping the Slider out about sixty feet and letting the current make a belly in the line. Drag made the fly cut an arc, the smooth line interrupted only when the deer hair face of the Slider hit grass and kicked the hook up and over the floating vegetation.

The fishing was not furious, but about every fifteen minutes a trout grabbed the fly. This was not bad, considering how preoccupied the fish were with sipping drowned forms. The catch from this one backwater from 9:30 a.m. to 12:00 noon was eleven trout hooked—five rainbows landed (best of 17 inches) and two browns landed (best of 22 inches). A couple of monsters either tore or broke free.

What is it going to be like on a day when the trout are feeding more aggressively on larger mayflies, caddisflies, or damselflies? They should be a lot more willing to hammer a moving dry fly.

What surprised me most about this day was the response of the biggest fish. They took the fly the instant it came off a large mat of weeds. The Slider would bounce across one of these 3- to 5-foot slop mats, and a fish, who wasn't feeding on the surface with a pod, seemed to be waiting for it.

Snow Stone

The small, black stoneflies of winter, *Capnia* sp., never appear in huge numbers. But enough of them crawl around the snow banks along Rocky Mountain rivers in January and February to interest trout. They end up on the water during egg-laying and frequently by accident, blown in by breezes. They are important because they are often the only major insect active during the coldest months. There are days when even midges do not fly, but the little Winter Stones scurry alongside the stream.

The Snow Stone is an accurate downwing imitation of the adult. The bright olive egg sac and the white, front hackle are minor changes in other, older patterns. For the fisherman, that white hackle is a valuable addition, making the fly easier to see on gray winter days, when the light is coming in at such a low angle that an all-black pattern gets lost on the water.

Snow Stone

Snow Stone

step 1

step 2

step 3

step 4

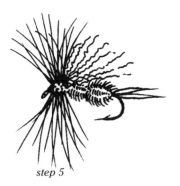

step 5

TYING STEPS

1. Tie in two slips of gray duck quill; split them.

2. Dub a ball of olive fur for the egg sac; make it thicker than the rest of the body.

3. Dub a dark brown body.

4. Tie in a downwing of black calf tail hair.

5. Wrap two hackles, black at the rear and white at the front.

Whip finish.

Hook:	16–20 (standard dry fly, TMC 100)
Tail:	two slips of gray duck quill
Egg Sac:	olive synthetic seal's fur (dubbed into a thick ball)
Body:	very dark brown mink fur
Wing:	black calf tail hair
Hackle:	one black and one white hackle

LOG ENTRY: FEBRUARY 2, 1991
CLARK FORK RIVER

In the sixties and seventies, during my years as a student at the University of Montana, I used to fish in the winter more than I do now. I'd walk down from the campus and hunt along the Clark Fork, looking for rising fish, or I'd drive up the Bitterroot or Blackfoot. On many days, not below freezing, the air temperatures in the high thirties or low forties, but overcast and gusting, the dry fly fishing to trout rising to little Winter Stones was at its best.

I was at the University today. The town, Missoula, was locked under clouds as usual and there was an occasional spit of sleet. Everything just felt right for dry fly fishing.

I took Chester and went upstream a half mile, an easy walk on the abandoned railroad bed. I stopped to watch the river, to make a decision about the fishing. My choices, as usual during the winter, were limited— either find rising trout and fish a dry fly or work the water blind with a deep nymph. Casting an attractor dry to drum up non-feeding trout wasn't, in my experience, a good cold-weather option.

I only searched the quieter currents on the inside curve of the bends, and even then there had to be a snow bank or a rim of ice right up to the river's edge. I saw fish feeding off one of these spots, a half dozen of them lined up in a string within inches of the overhanging snow.

On this first group of trout, all rainbows, I caught the first, missed the second, and hooked and landed the third, ruining the spot when this last fish splashed all over the shallows. I found another bunch of rising trout, in the same kind of water, and did no better on these, catching two of the five.

The Snow Stone worked fine. The double hackled dry fly floated well and it was easy to pick out on the water. The trout did seem a bit selective, feeding only on the Winter Stones and ignoring midges, but they never hesitated in taking the fly as long as it drifted close enough to them.

The cold weather got to me. I had on a coat and neoprene waders, but no gloves and no hat. I forgot how to dress for winter fishing. I was chilled, and poor Chester, after walking in the water to lick every fish landed, was shivering hard. There was a third line of feeding trout just upstream, but the air was getting colder and, since I wasn't fishing well anyway, I started back to the University.

My choices, as usual during the winter, were limited— either find rising trout and fish a dry fly or work the water blind with a deep nymph. Casting an attractor dry to drum up non-feeding trout wasn't, in my experience, a good cold-weather option.

Spruce Moth

The spruce moth is one of those cyclical terrestrials worth chasing around the trout regions. During years with heavy infestations, fish get spoiled by a daily dumping of insects, changing feeding times and habits to match the arrival of the moths. They grow progressively fussier about imitations over the four to six weeks of steady insect falls.

It should be easy enough to match the spruce moth. It is a chunky, tan-and-cream bug, equal to a size 12 or 14 hook, wings folded flat over the body. Any good downwing caddis pattern, such as an Elk Hair Caddis or a Dancing Caddis, looks at first glance suitably like the natural.

In actual fishing situations, however, the downwing dry fly fails badly. An upwing pattern, the Blonde Wulff, caught many more trout in careful, day-by-day comparisons. In certain seasons, years when the spruce moth populations peaked on Rock Creek and the Gallatin River, the Wulff caught more trout for me than any other dry fly.

The Blonde Wulff wasn't the perfect imitation. It still got refusals, especially late in the day. The trout preferred active moths, not the drowned, sodden ones, and apparently the upright wings of the Wulff gave some illusion of struggle, but other parts of the fly did not correspond to the shape of the insect.

The specific Spruce Moth imitation, tested over three seasons by a lot of trial-and-error fishing, features a bulkier body, roughly dubbed, bristling with the guard hairs of mink fur. It has an elk hair wing slanted up at a 45 degree angle, a compromise between the flat downwing and the split upwing. The elk hair is even fanned upwards, almost like the wing on some variations of the rough water Haystack. The head is spun and clipped elk hair.

Spruce Moth

240

TYING STEPS

1. Dub a body of cream or ginger mink fur; use a dubbing loop, leaving the guard hairs in the blend for a rough body.

2. Tie in a wing of light elk hair (slant it upwards at a 45 degree angle).

3. Spin a head of light elk hair (clipped round).

Whip finish.

step 1

step 2

step 3

Hook: 12–14 (standard dry fly, TMC 100)

Body: cream or ginger mink fur (the guard hairs chopped and mixed into the dubbing blend)

Wing: light elk hair (flared)

Head: light elk hair (spun and clipped)

Spruce Moth

LOG ENTRY: SEPTEMBER 3, 1990
ROCK CREEK

There must be plenty of trout streams with periodic infestations of spruce budworm moths. They must be tightly kept secrets, however— the only two in Montana that I know get strong spruce moth "hatches" are the Gallatin River and Rock Creek. Both rivers run through canyons, pine forests crowding their edges instead of the deciduous trees that take over on flat, bottomland streams. The moth populations build up slowly over three or four years, until the population explodes during a plague season.

It's easy enough to pinpoint the spruce moth on Rock Creek. The fisherman just drives up and down the dirt road until he sees the insects flying in that erratic, distinctive manner of all moths They are active on warm days, moving between 10:00 a.m. and 8:00 p.m. sometime during July and August.

I wonder often about the psychology of trout, but I only wonder about the thought processes of insects when the terrestrial spruce moths are at their suicidal best. The simplest creatures possess survival mechanisms. Grasshoppers, for example, know when they are over water; and they know that they don't belong there. With a head wind they try to return to the original bank, but with a tail wind grasshoppers try to fly all the way to the far shore. If possible they avoid the water. Spruce moths are strong fliers, and unlike those heavy, clumsy grasshoppers, would have no trouble staying off the stream, but by the thousands they settle gently and purposely onto the surface. They have no reason to be there. As soon as they touch the water they are trapped, their wings, covered with scales instead of the water-repellent hairs of caddisflies, soaked and useless. They struggle feebly for a short time as they drift along. Eventually they collapse and die.

The fall of spruce moths today was the heaviest since the madness of 1985. The greatest concentration was near the Harry's Flats Campground. The moths were on the water early with the warm weather.

It was as if the trout were waiting for them. There were no rises on the stream until the first smattering of insects hit the water. Every one of those early moths were taken with enthusiastic, rolling gulps that indicate an aggressively feeding fish. Soon there were so many insects that the trout could hold in regular feeding stations, rising to everything in a steady rhythm.

This was the early stage of the spruce moth fall. The browns and rainbows were so intent on capturing as many insects as possible that they took any reasonable match on the surface. For the first hour Jess Uehling fished right alongside me with a size 12 Light Elk Hair Caddis and caught just as many trout as I did with the specific spruce moth imitation.

The middle stage extended from 11:00 a.m. until almost 1:00 p.m. The fish kept rising, not hurrying at all. There was no way for a single trout to grab all the moths floating by a good lie. The dead insects piled up in backwaters and along quiet edges, ignored by the fish. The smaller trout virtually disappeared, very few under 12 inches feeding after the first hour. Maybe they were gorged on the chunky moths. The larger browns and rainbows started getting fussy about the food item and the matching fly, sucking down only live, struggling insects and preferring upwing imitations. The trout we caught on a size 12 Spruce Moth were the big bottom feeders, many up to 21 inches, that never rise to insects. Today, they were slurping with abandon.

The late stage, which might never happen during a sparse fall of spruce moths, began at 1:00 p.m. The fish kept feeding, but only sporadically. An individual trout might rise once every three minutes. The angler had to keep casting to that single fish, hoping the fly floated over him at the right moment. All of the trout turned very critical about imitations, refusing everything except the Spruce Moth and sometimes even snubbing that fly (they sometimes rejected real insects, too). Sometimes, the fly had to quiver for the fish to finally accept it.

There was a third angler with us today, Gary Icopini, but he was in Montana to help us with some nymph fishing experiments scheduled for the following week. He wanted to keep his nymph techniques sharp and, in an incredible display of discipline, he ignored the rising fish. He worked the bottom all day with Bead Heads, Hare's Ears and Pheasant Tails, but, amazingly for a nymph fisherman of his skill, he only caught a few sub-twelve-inch trout. He did land over forty whitefish.

Gary said that evening, "I never would have believed that every trout in the stream could be so focused on the surface."

Chuck Xue told me about catching a 20-inch brown during a spruce moth fall on the Gallatin. The fish was bleeding badly from an injured gill and Chuck kept it. He examined the stomach contents, the entire digestive track gorged and distended, and counted over 150 spruce moths in this one trout. The fish, from the time the hatch started until he was caught, couldn't have been feeding more than two hours.

Were Wulff

One of the more reliable mayfly hatches on the Big Hole is the Brown Drake (*E. simulans*). It comes out when the Green Drake emerges, but the big Green Drake is so spotty on the Big Hole, that most fly fishermen concentrate on the smaller Brown Drake.

My guiding on the Big Hole meant floating clients down the river in a raft or drift boat. These people often had problems seeing a dark fly (this was not their fault— the light on the Big Hole can be tricky). There was no easy-to-spot Brown Drake imitation available for these fishermen.

The Were Wulff is a simple variation on the Wulff theme. Bill Blackburn, a fellow guide out of the Complete Flyfisher, and I developed it to roughly match the Brown Drake. It is bulkier than the natural, and has white wings to make it more visible for our floating anglers.

Oddly enough, it quickly replaced more exact imitations as the favorite match for the Brown Drake on the Big Hole. Even fishermen wading the river adopted it. They liked the fly's visibility; and they weren't having any problems catching rising trout on broken water.

The Were Wulff stayed popular that season even after the Brown Drake hatch ended on the river. The guides had their clients use it as a searching fly on riffles and runs. The Were Wulff was bulky enough to make an impression on the surface, but with its simple, drab colors there was nothing alarming about it. It made a reputation more with day-to-day consistency than with spectacular catches.

Were Wulff

244

TYING STEPS

1. Tie in brown deer hair for a tail.

2. Tie in white calf tail fibers; divide and post them for a wing.

3. Dub a body of hare's ear fur.

4. Wrap two hackles, one brown and one grizzly, together.

Whip finish.

Hook:	8–16 (standard dry fly, TMC 100)
Tail:	brown bucktail hair
Body:	hare's ear (dubbed)
Wing:	white calf tail
Hackle:	brown and grizzly (mixed)

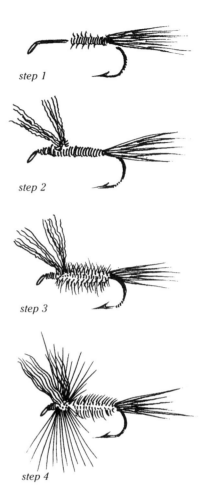

step 1

step 2

step 3

step 4

Were Wulff

LOG ENTRY: JUNE 4, 1990
ROSEBUD RIVER

This tributary of the Stillwater is one of my "stopping places." It may not be a stream that I'll travel to just to fish, but if I am going near it I'll usually spend a day on it.

Why the Rosebud? It's a small river, full of rainbows and browns ranging from 10 to 18 inches, with a few browns a lot bigger. It winds through bottomland for three miles. The deep undercuts and pools are always mysterious. The riffles are as consistent as the pools are mysterious, however, and the chunky little rainbows hop all over a dry fly. There is water on this river to match any mood that I happen to be in at the moment.

This was the last day of a three-day trip. After fishing East Rosebud Creek one day and West Rosebud Creek the next, catching a mix of brooks, browns, and rainbows in great quantities, it was time for a bit of tougher fishing, and maybe larger trout, on the main Rosebud.

I started today at 10:00 a.m., but nothing was rising to dry flies and I changed to nymphs and worked them through the darker, deeper water. This subsurface fishing caught trout (mostly on a weighted Hare's Ear), but none of them were over 12 inches. Then the first mayfly duns began popping out on the surface and browns and rainbows, some obviously big, were feeding all over the river.

I must be getting lazy in my old age— either that, or I'm getting more excitable. I didn't bother to take a minute or two to capture and look at the mayfly. More than likely it was the Brown Drake (that's what it appeared to be on the water). With the fish slopping up every insect drifting into the run in front of me the temptation was to cast first and wonder, if necessary, later.

What had me so excited was that there were no Green Drakes on the water at the same time to confuse the situation. There were thousands of the size 12, brownish duns and nothing else. The trout fed on these mayflies with a hurried greediness that made them easy to catch.

I alternated between a good Brown Drake imitation, a Mahogany Parachute, and a fair Brown Drake imitation, a Were Wulff, and at least on this day it made no difference to the fish. The trout stacked up below the riffles, taking any insect or artificial fly that drifted into his window.

I waded upstream about a mile during the hatch, changing from a Mahogany Parachute when it got waterlogged to a Were Wulff, or vice versa, and, unusual for me, never had the urge to put on something wildly inappropriate, such as a Royal Trude, to find out if it would catch fish, too. This was probably because it was still early in the season.

It was a fine hatch for fishing because there were very few Green Drakes on the water. The same would be true if it was the opposite situation— a Green Drake hatch with few or no Brown Drakes. When both insects appear on a stream individual trout often pick out one or the other and feed selectively. The angler has to choose the right fly for each particular fish.

The Green Drake in size 8 is a much larger insect than the Brown Drake in size 12, but a simple measurement of the two mayflies doesn't give a valid comparison. The Green Drake tends to lay its abdomen straight out onto the surface; the Brown Drake tends to curl its abdomen up at the back end, tapping it occasionally on the water. This behavioral difference makes the Green Drake seem much larger to the trout.

One very good imitation for the Green Drake is an extended body, Para Drake pattern. Maybe "good" should be qualified— the fish hit the fly. It's a lousy pattern on other counts. It is a poor hooking fly, trout often bumping their lips on the stiff, extended deer hair body poking out behind the hook and never actually taking the imitation inside their mouths (this fact discovered during underwater observation).

It's futile using a Green Drake Wulff, a fly sold commercially, to match the big insect. The only reason it catches anything when the Green Drake and the Brown Drake are both hatching is because fish take it for the Brown Drake. The Green Drake Wulff is a complete failure when there are only Green Drakes on the water.

So what is the angler supposed to do? One friend of mine, David Ruetz, suggests that fishermen study the microhabitat above a rising fish. Is the bottom rocky and riffly? Then more Brown Drakes will be hatching. Is the bottom slow and silty? Then more Green Drakes will be hatching. This can help the angler pick out the right fly much quicker in a mixed hatch of Green Drakes and Brown Drakes.

A Mess, in appropriate colors, is now my favorite imitation for the Green Drake. A Mahogany Parachute is the best fly for matching the Brown Drake if the trout are feeding fussily, but even with a white, kip-tail post it sits lower and is harder to see than a Were Wulff. The Were Wulff works well for what it was designed for— popping casts from a drifting boat.

So what is the angler supposed to do? One friend of mine, David Ruetz, suggests that fishermen study the microhabitat above a rising fish. Is the bottom rocky and riffly? Then more Brown Drakes will be hatching. Is the bottom slow and silty? Then more Green Drakes will be hatching. This can help the angler pick out the right fly much quicker in a mixed hatch of Green Drakes and Brown Drakes.

White Deer Hair Moth

White Deer Hair Moth

There are some heavy hatches at night and trout feed selectively on them, keying on the size and the shape of the insects. They also eat a lot of nymphs, taking them as they drift in the current. But otherwise fish forage very opportunistically in the dark. They react to the vibrations of anything in or on the water, moving towards objects instead of waiting for them.

My basic list of night flies would include a top-water swimmer (a slim deer hair bug or a Creature), a shallow-water, bulky streamer (a Muddler or a crawfish pattern), a deep-water streamer (a Woolly Bugger), a stonefly nymph (a Natural Drift Stone), a big mayfly pattern (a Mess), a big, skating caddisfly pattern (a Dancing Caddis) and a dry moth imitation.

The Deer Hair Moth has the attributes of a good night fly. It gets soggy, the head eventually wicking up moisture, and it lands on the surface with an attractive splat. The pattern is bulky, sitting flush, pushing water with every twitch and sending out vibrations. The wings, out at an angle, fold up and spring back out as the fly moves and stops.

This pattern was developed during a crazy summer, a solid seven-week stretch of night fishing. Bill Seeples and I usually slept during the days, but if we had to go outside we wore two pairs of sunglasses to protect our night vision. We traveled to all of the great rivers of the state, including the Madison, Beaverhead, Missouri, Smith, and Yellowstone. We fished hard every night of that period.

How did we do? We probably would have caught more trout during the same number of fishing hours in daylight, but the average size of the browns and rainbows was much larger, roughly 17 inches. We wondered where the fish under 14 inches stayed at night. They certainly didn't hit our flies. We caught nearly as many rainbows as browns. We found enough brutes, trout over 5 pounds, to keep us always alert to the possibility of trophy fish. Our biggest trout were an 8½-pound brown from the Missouri and a 9-pound brown from the Beaverhead.

By the third week of our spree the White Deer Hair Moth had evolved through trial and error to its finished form. It became the main fly for the 10:00 p.m. to 12:00 p.m. part of the night. Over the summer it caught more fish, if not bigger ones, than any other pattern.

White Deer Hair Moth

step 1

step 2

step 3

step 4

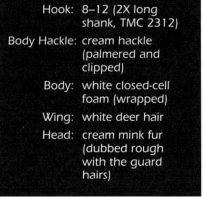

TYING STEPS

1. Tie down a strip of foam; let it dangle for the moment.

2. Tie in a cream hackle; let it dangle for the moment.

3. Pull the foam down over the hook shank; bind it down by ribbing it with the tying thread on the bobbin.

4. Palmer the cream hackle; clip the fibers short all the way around.

5. Tie in a heavy downwing of deer hair.

6. With a dubbing rope (created by twisting mink fur in a dubbing loop), figure-eight the wings (leaving the hair split in a 45 degree backwards angle); wrap enough fur in front of the wings to form a head.

Whip finish.

Hook:	8–12 (2X long shank, TMC 2312)
Body Hackle:	cream hackle (palmered and clipped)
Body:	white closed-cell foam (wrapped)
Wing:	white deer hair
Head:	cream mink fur (dubbed rough with the guard hairs)

step 5

step 6

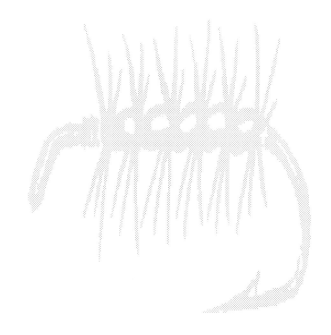

LOG ENTRY: JULY 29, 1990
HOUND CREEK

There are smaller fisheries in the state, like this tributary of the Smith River, that are good enough to drag me away from the famous waters. The last few miles of Hound Creek, winding through bottomlands before joining the Smith, are prime meadow water. It is a great stretch day or night for slapping terrestrial imitations. This is one of those streams where the fish become conditioned to meaty terrestrials on the surface and, more so than in other types of trout water, they watch for them.

Alan Hauwiller came with me to the Smith River to pick up friends who were floating the river. The group was scheduled to end a five-day trip this afternoon. Our job was to shuttle the trucks and trailers and bring the beer.

We didn't come with the idea of night fishing, but when the floaters didn't show up by 7:00 p.m., we knew that we were probably going to be here until morning. The mouth of Hound Creek was nearby and we went up to look for an evening hatch.

The fishing was so good (caddisflies, matched with a size 14 Brown and Yellow Emergent Sparkle Pupa) that we kept wading upstream and casting right into the dark. Alan was laughing and chattering, happy with his first day in Montana, and finally when everything slowed down said, "This is my first time at night fishing, too."

"You never fished at night in Pennsylvania?"

"Never."

"Well, this is not night. This is dusk. Let's fish until one or two in morning."

Alan, so skilled and assured during the day, stumbled into night like any other beginner. He moved too fast and too far, tripping on rocks and logs. Twice he fell into the stream, thrashing in panic. He cast too long a line, hooking every bush and tree along the bank. He fumbled with his tackle, dropping boxes in the water. He wasted too much time untangling his leader and tying knots in the blackness. He reminded me of myself on my first night fishing trip— except he caught some trout.

At 10:00 p.m. he wanted to quit because the fish were no longer rising. The stream was not quiet. All of those night birds and bats were swooping up and down the channel. There were bugs on the water, but the trout weren't taking dry flies, nymphs, or streamers.

This is the way it has always been on trout waters for me. After the final glimmer of dusk, with the onset of true night, there is a strange lull in the feeding. It only lasts about an hour, but this is when most anglers tromp off the stream and go home.

At 11:30 p.m. the fish of Hound Creek came out of hiding. Occasionally they slashed at something in the shallows. A few trout rose sporadically in the deeper pools. The fish, both browns and rainbows, were on a hunting spree.

White Deer Hair Moth Log

It is not a large creek, maybe ten to twenty feet across on average, and brushy enough to make casting in the dark difficult. The easiest way to fish it is to wade straight upstream, avoiding the deeper outside corners. The best areas to fish are the boundaries of a pool— the head, the tail, and both banks (anywhere except the deep center).

Alan caught trout on a Muddler, landing six of them in an hour, the best a 20-inch brown. He missed too many fish at first on an erratic, strip retrieve. He started hooking more of them on an across-stream cast and a simple, short-line swing, most of the strikes coming as the fly straightened out and hung below him.

My choice for a pattern was the old reliable, the White Deer Hair Moth, not only because it would catch trout but also because it would bring them to the surface hard. Up and across stream casts, thrown with a curve, hooked the Moth in against the deep banks. With a dry fly this slice of the stream was more productive than the tails of the pools and runs (where Alan picked up his fish on a Muddler).

At 11:30 p.m. the fish of Hound Creek came out of hiding. Occasionally they slashed at something in the shallows. A few trout rose sporadically in the deeper pools. The fish, both browns and rainbows, were on a hunting spree.

The best retrieve, at the end of the drift, was a quick upstream mend of the bellying line. This maneuver not only threw new slack for another drift but made the fly dash upstream in a smooth, one- to two-foot jot. The movement gave fish a new chance to notice the bulky imitation silhouetted against the sky.

Browns and rainbows took the fly, crashing the surface loud enough for me to know when to strike. The numbers of decent trout, all above 13 inches, in this stream was surprising, even to someone who had fished it a lot during the day. Four over 18 inches were landed. Some fish, of course, hit the Moth with huge swirls but were never hooked, and these, always the biggest in my mind, made the night special.

Wiggler

The roots of this pattern go back thirty-five years, to an old bluegill fly of mine called the Shimmy. The dressing for that attractor was a green foam body, a palmered grizzly body hackle, rubber legs, and a brown head hackle. It had rubber legs, so common on bluegill flies, but it used them in a different way. The legs were separated by winds of hackle. The feathers forced the rubber strands apart, kept them wiggling independently, and seemed to make the Shimmy more effective than regular rubber-leg flies.

In August 1990, a bunch of us were sitting around a table at a café after a day of fishing on the Missouri River. I mentioned, "I have an idea for a new attractor dry fly."

Skip Neiminen, not a regular part of our group, looked puzzled, "You have the Air Head, the Mohawk, and the Double Wing. What do you need another attractor for?"

Tom Poole responded, "You can't have too many attractors."

There is a basic rule of fly choice. Imitation is certain; attraction is uncertain. The angler doesn't need a lot of imitations for a particular situation. When caddisflies are emerging the members of our group use an Emergent Sparkle Pupa. They don't even carry any other imitations for this stage of the insect's life cycle. The same stubborn certainty applies to midges, mayflies, stoneflies, terrestrials, etc. Any angler knows where to start once he identifies the food item trout are eating.

With attractor dry flies there is no certainty. When trout are not actually feeding on the surface, a floating pattern must either look like an irresistible food item or an intriguing oddity. But no one knows at any given moment what might trigger a curiosity rise in a fish. It may be solid bulk (the Mohawk), translucence and brightness (the Air Head), or intense color (the Double Wing). The angler needs as many different aspects of attraction in his fly assortment as possible.

Wiggler

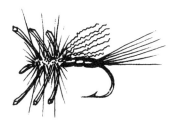

Wiggler

The Wiggler emphasizes movement. It has a foam body for buoyancy and a clear Antron wing for visibility, but it's those rubber legs, shaking with every push of current, that make the fly tantalizing to a trout. That motion might mimic a struggling, trapped insect; the Wiggler might represent an odd but easy meal that a fish is too greedy to let drift downstream.

I designed the Wiggler for the Jackson Hole One Fly Contest. This event, started by Jack Dennis to raise money for conservation, is not meant to be a big prize competition. The idea of limiting the anglers to one fly for a day of fishing elevates the element of luck.

The Wiggler is a good pattern for the One Fly because it is durable, buoyant, visible, and versatile. It can be fished wet or dry, or both wet and dry on the same presentation. It brings trout up from the bottom. It doesn't get a lot of last minute refusals. It's an attractor that is ideal for streams like the Snake where trout feed opportunistically.

TYING STEPS

1. Tie in the tail fibers.

2. Tie in a strip of foam; wrap the foam halfway up the shank as a body— color it with a marker.

3. Tie in a wing of clear Antron fibers.

4. Tie in two or three sets of rubber legs; trim to length.

5. Wind the thread back and tie in two hackle feathers; wind each carefully one turn through the rubber legs— trim a V into the bottom of the hackle.

Whip finish.

Hook: 8–16 (2X long shank, TMC 2302)

Tail: hackle fibers

Body: closed-cell foam (colored with a permanent marker)

Wing: clear Antron (fine fibers; sold by National Feathercraft as Hi-Viz)

Legs: yellow rubber (two sets on sizes 14 and 16; three sets on larger sizes)

Hackle: two rooster feathers (different colors mixed; the wraps of hackle separate the sets of rubber legs)

Good color combinations include:

- Green Wiggler—grizzly tail, chartreuse body, and grizzly and dyed-olive grizzly hackle,

- Orange Wiggler—cree tail, orange body, and grizzly and brown hackle,

- Gray Wiggler—gray tail, gray body, and grizzly and dark blue dun hackle,

- Pink Wiggler—red tail, pink body, and grizzly and cree hackle,

- White Wiggler—cream tail, white body, and grizzly and cream hackle.

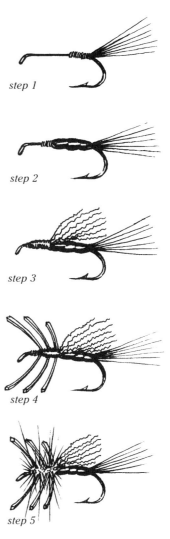

step 1

step 2

step 3

step 4

step 5

Wiggler

LOG ENTRY: AUGUST 29, 1991
WILLOW CREEK

There are miniature, tailwater fisheries flowing out below irrigation reservoirs all over the state. The lakes are smaller, but the way they spread out the water into an expanse of algae-producing surface area still creates a rich trout fishery below the dam. These creeks run clear when other waters are high; they run cold when other waters are warm.

My daughter Heather, Justin Baker and I drove down to West Yellowstone to meet up with Runnar Warhuus. Runnar, editor of *Vilmark Livs*, a Scandinavian fishing and hunting magazine, was my host during my visit to Norway last year. I had permission to fish a ranch on upper Willow Creek, and this was a chance to show him a special part of Montana.

We stayed the night at the Old Kirby Place, Walter Cannon's lodge on the Madison. The next morning all of us climbed into two vehicles. We didn't go straight to Willow Creek. We did something more important than any day of fishing. We stopped and visited A. J. McClane for an hour at his house. This was my first meeting with one of my heroes, and when we left he said to me at the door, "Let's go fishing sometime," but this was shortly before his death and the invitation remained just a promise.

This was the first trip to Willow for any of us. We followed directions intended to take us to the dam, but ended up in a pasture far from there. Downstream the creek twisted through a quarter mile of meadow before hitting a major irrigation diversion. Upstream it tumbled through a steep canyon. This wasn't the water we wanted— it wasn't the weedy flats below the dam where large trout sipped insects.

I put on a size 14 Irresistible for the rougher water in the canyon, but made the first casts right there in front of the car in the meadow. On the third drift a fat, 13-inch brown hit the fly. He wasn't a monster fish, but he was a good start.

Everyone spread out and began fishing. Walter went downstream. The rest of us moved up into the canyon. Runnar, Justin, and I hit any good-looking piece of holding water, but there were very few deeper, slower spots. Heather came up with us, too, taking photographs and looking everywhere for rattlesnakes (the stream has a reputation).

The day was disappointing, more because of inflated expectations than the actual fishing. My count of trout through the afternoon was more than twenty rainbows and browns, these fish averaging 11 inches. It was a fast day of riffle popping in a mountain creek. Normally, an experience like this would be one of the highlights, not the disappointment, of the season. The catch just didn't match accounts of two- and three-pound fish.

The fast-water pockets kept giving up small trout. I was roughly 1½ miles up the canyon, still prospecting, when I found the first deep runs. The stream meandered on a short plateau, and against the canyon wall there was a deep slot and back eddy.

One fish was rising, sipping a small mayfly, and he fell to a size 18 Duck Butt Dun, but he was only 9 inches. More casts with the imitation, blind drifts over every part of the deep run, didn't bring anything else to the surface.

This was a familiar situation. Here was great looking water, and there was no reason that it shouldn't hold the best fish in this stretch of the stream. Whatever was down in those depths wasn't going to rise to a small fly. That left two basic choices (more if nymphs and streamers were considered, but for the moment they weren't)— a grasshopper imitation, a prime chunk of food to tempt a trout, or an attractor, a strange floater to tease a trout.

Tempt or tease? The great majority of anglers would choose a grasshopper pattern, not a bad fly when there were so many naturals jumping in the weeds. A grasshopper would be the easy choice; and after a hot climb up this canyon easy seemed perfect to me.

I fished grasshopper imitations, four different patterns, for a half an hour over the runs and cuts of the plateau, but these flies only brought up a few more 10-inch rainbows. I felt at that moment that no dry fly, not even an attractor, was going to succeed on this water. It wasn't a pool. It was a deeper, churning run, with a braid of currents below the surface that made rising to a dry fly too much work for a larger trout. This was the kind of stream that drowned any real grasshoppers quickly. The big fish probably ate plenty of them near the bottom.

I tied on a size 8 Green Wiggler. I edged on my belly through the high weeds to the bank and cast downstream. Then, gently, I put the rod tip underwater, bending it against the bottom, and stripped the Wiggler at a depth of two feet back against the current. When I stopped retrieving, the fly popped up to the surface for a moment, like a dog shaking off water. I peeled out slack line and let the fly drift down the river. A 16-inch brown came up under the fly and jumped into the air with it. With the Green Wiggler, and this "pop-up" technique, I caught four more nice trout, in that 14- to 16-inch range, on the deeper water of the little plateau.

I hiked back down to join the others. Heather and Justin had just returned from a trip to town for lunch. They drove up to the field, the front of the car coated with dead grasshoppers roasting in the grill and on the radiator.

Walter came up from the meadow water. He grabbed me and kissed me on both cheeks (he's a good kisser). He had found some bigger fish in the lower meanders, catching two browns over 20 inches on a grasshopper pattern.

This lower section wasn't the stuff of my dreams, but it was a fine stream by any other measure. And there were better parts of it to search for on another trip.

> Tempt or tease? The great majority of anglers would choose a grasshopper pattern, not a bad fly when there were so many naturals jumping in the weeds. A grasshopper would be the easy choice; and after a hot climb up this canyon easy seemed perfect to me.